D0700146

TEAM COGNITION

TEAM COGNITION

UNDERSTANDING THE FACTORS THAT DRIVE
PROCESS AND PERFORMANCE

EDITED BY
Eduardo Salas and Stephen M. Fiore

AMERICAN PSYCHOLOGICAL ASSOCIATION
WASHINGTON, DC

Published by
American Psychological Association
750 First Street, NE
Washington, DC 20002
www.apa.org

To order
APA Order Department
P.O. Box 92984
Washington, DC 20090-2984
Tel: (800) 374-2721; Direct: (202) 336-5510
Fax: (202) 336-5502; TDD/TTY: (202) 336-6123
On-line: www.apa.org/books/
E-mail: order@apa.org

In the U.K., Europe, Africa, and the Middle East, copies may be ordered from
American Psychological Association
3 Henrietta Street
Covent Garden, London
WC2E 8LU England

Typeset in Goudy by Stephen McDougal, Mechanicsville, MD

Printer: Sheridan Books, Ann Arbor, MI
Cover Designer: Berg Design, Albany, NY
Technical/Production Editor: Casey Ann Reever

The opinions and statements published are the responsibility of the authors, and such opinions and statements do not necessarily represent the policies of the American Psychological Association.

Library of Congress Cataloging-in-Publication Data

Team cognition : understanding the factors that drive process and performance / edited by Eduardo Salas and Stephen M. Fiore.—1st ed.
    p. cm.
  Includes bibliographical references and indexes.
  ISBN 1-59147-103-6 (hardcover : alk. paper)
  1. Teams in the workplace. 2. Cognition. I. Salas, Eduardo. II. Fiore, Stephen M.

  HD66.T422 2004
  302.3'5—dc22   2003026064

British Library Cataloguing-in-Publication Data
A CIP record is available from the British Library.

Printed in the United States of America
First Edition

To Janis A. Cannon-Bowers, a colleague and a friend, whose thinking has shaped the foundation for the field of team cognition.

CONTENTS

CONTRIBUTORS

Brian Bell, PhD, Postdoctoral Assistant, Applied Psychology Program, Arizona State University East, Mesa

Hoon-Seok Choi, PhD, Assistant Professor, School of Management, University of Ottawa, Ontario, Canada

Nancy J. Cooke, PhD, Professor, Applied Psychology Program, Arizona State University East, Mesa

Elliot E. Entin, PhD, Senior Scientist, Aptima, Woburn, MA

J. Alberto Espinosa, PhD, Assistant Professor of Information Technology, Kogod School of Business, American University, Washington, DC

Stephen M. Fiore, PhD, Director, Consortium for Research in Adaptive Distributed Learning Environments, Department of Psychology and Institute for Simulation and Training, University of Central Florida, Orlando

Saul Greenberg, PhD, Professor, Department of Computer Science, University of Calgary, Alberta, Canada

Carl Gutwin, PhD, Associate Professor, Department of Computer Science, University of Saskatchewan, Saskatoon, Canada

Verlin B. Hinsz, PhD, Professor of Psychology, Psychology Department, North Dakota State University, Fargo

Preston A. Kiekel, PhD, Graduate Research Assistant, Department of Psychology, New Mexico State University, Las Cruces

Robert E. Kraut, PhD, Herbert E. Simon Chair Professor of Computer–Human Interaction, Human–Computer Interaction Institute, School of Computer Science, Carnegie Mellon University, Pittsburgh, PA

F. Javier Lerch, PhD, Director for Interactive Simulations, Graduate School of Industrial Administration, Carnegie Mellon University, Pittsburgh, PA

John M. Levine, PhD, Professor, Department of Psychology, University of Pittsburgh, Pittsburgh, PA

Michael Lewis, PhD, Associate Professor, Department of IS and Telecommunications, University of Pittsburgh, Pittsburgh, PA

Jean MacMillan, PhD, Chief Scientist, Aptima, Woburn, MA

Joan R. Rentsch, PhD, Professor, I/O Psychology Program, Department of Management, University of Tennessee, Knoxville

Eduardo Salas, PhD, Professor and Trustee Chair, Department of Psychology and Institute for Simulation and Training, University of Central Florida, Orlando

Jonathan W. Schooler, PhD, Professor of Psychology, University of Pittsburgh; Research Scientist, Learning Research and Development Center, Pittsburgh, PA

Daniel Serfaty, MS, MBA, President and CEO, Aptima, Woburn, MA

Katia Sycara, PhD, Research Professor, The Robotics Institute, Carnegie Mellon University, Pittsburgh, PA

David J. Woehr, PhD, Professor, I/O Psychology Program, Department of Management, University of Tennessee, Knoxville

ACKNOWLEDGMENTS

The creation of this volume was partially supported by Grant F49620-01-1-0214 from the Air Force Office of Scientific Research to Eduardo Salas, Stephen M. Fiore, and Clint A. Bowers. Many people contributed to this volume in differing ways. First and foremost, we thank the publishers at the American Psychological Association for supporting such a multidisciplinary edited volume. It was a challenge for us, and a risk for them, and we appreciate the opportunity they provided. Second, we acknowledge and thank our many colleagues who have contributed to the team cognition movement. Stephen M. Fiore thanks his many mentors who encouraged an appreciation of multidisciplinary approaches. He thanks Carmi Schooler and his colleagues at the National Institute of Mental Health Section on Socio-Environmental Studies who helped to develop an understanding of how social structure and culture interact in complex ways with human cognition to impact psychological function across the life span. The outstanding faculty at the University of Pittsburgh's Learning Research and Development Center similarly instilled an appreciation of diverse scientific knowledge. In particular, he thanks Jim Voss, who sparked an interest in team cognition during his graduate seminar on human problem solving. John Levine and Richard Moreland encouraged this interest during their enlightening special topics seminar on groups and teams. Last, Jonathan Schooler not only supported the pursuit of this area of study but also contributed substantially to cogitating on this topic via discussions that are too numerous to recall.

TEAM COGNITION

1

WHY *TEAM* COGNITION? AN OVERVIEW

EDUARDO SALAS AND STEPHEN M. FIORE

Organizations are increasingly relying on teams to address a variety of complex and difficult tasks. The rationale can be based on factors associated with pragmatics; that is, when decisions with severe consequences must be made or when safety is involved, the belief is that the added input of multiple individuals will either converge on superior decisions or result in safer performance. Alternatively, the rationale can be based on factors associated with organizational dynamics, for example, using interindividual motivation to promote collaboration. In short, the reasons behind the wide application of teams are varied, but the fact remains that teams continue to be viewed as an important organizational tool.

Because of this prevalence of teams in organizations today, many are formed without much forethought along with the expectation that only gains in productivity can result from teamwork. Although there are substantial benefits associated with teamwork (Cannon-Bowers & Salas, 1998), the reality is that there is little guarantee of success, as many teams fail for any

The views herein are those of the authors and do not necessarily reflect those of their affiliated organizations. Writing this chapter was partially funded by Grant No. F49620-01-1-0214 from the Air Force Office of Scientific Research to Eduardo Salas, Stephen M. Fiore, and Clint A. Bowers.

number of reasons (e.g., Hackman, 1998). Thus, given the increasing reliance on teams, it is critical that a full understanding of the factors affecting team effectiveness be delineated.

Teamwork, by its very definition, is achieved when members interact interdependently and work together toward shared and valued goals. Further, teamwork involves the adaptation of coordination strategies (e.g., backup behavior) through closed-loop communication and a sense of collective orientation so that they can reach these goals (Salas & Cannon-Bowers, 2000). As such, teamwork is more than work accomplished by a group of individuals, and we submit that teamwork can be viewed as the result of collective cognitive, behavioral, and attitudinal activity. The cognitive processes arising during this complex and dynamic interaction are the focus of this volume. We emphasize how it is that team process and performance are affected by interindividual and intraindividual factors. In particular, team members must have a requisite set of knowledge enabling them to perform their team tasks. This knowledge can manifest itself in the form of a *process* (e.g., how to engage in a team-related task) as well as a *product* (e.g., memory for teammate capabilities).

Cognitive science has substantially influenced this study of teams, and it has been over a decade since the original applications of constructs from cognitive psychology were used to foster the development of the team cognition movement (e.g., Cannon-Bowers, Salas, & Converse, 1993; Hutchins, 1991; Orasanu, 1990). Since then, much cross-disciplinary attention has focused on determining how team cognition contributes to effective team performance. What is invariant across these disciplines is the notion that shared information processing among group members has both inter- and intraindividual outcomes (e.g., Levine, Resnick, & Higgins, 1993), whereby constructs such as encoding, storage, and retrieval of information are thought to be equally applicable to both individuals and groups (e.g., Hinsz, Tindale, & Vollrath, 1997; Larson & Christensen, 1993; Tindale & Kameda, 2000).

We suggest that, as the science of teams and team training matures (Salas & Cannon-Bowers, 2000), we must broaden our understanding of the dynamic factors driving team performance. As our understanding of the team cognition construct similarly matures (e.g., Cannon-Bowers & Salas, 2001; Thompson, Levine, & Messick, 1999), we can now pursue the development of theoretically driven and empirically based guidelines for designing, managing, and developing teams. With this developing body of knowledge we can now begin to document what influences the complex cognitive factors driving the behavioral phenomena associated with teams. Only in this way can we hope to help the variety of military, industry, and academic needs surrounding the complexities and dynamics of teamwork and team functioning.

Although the issues surrounding the application of cognition to teams are far from resolved, this movement has made substantial strides in generating testable hypotheses that articulate causal factors in group performance (cf. Cannon-Bowers & Salas, 2001; Hinsz et al., 1997; Tindale & Kameda, 2000). Additionally, an increasing number of journals, from disciplines as diverse as industrial engineering to medical science to organizational psychology, are publishing work that directly or indirectly bears on team cognition. Because of this tremendously diverse field of research, oftentimes, important findings in one area are left unknown to researchers in differing fields. Indeed, to be properly exposed to the findings, one would have to be a true renaissance person to stay on top of issues surrounding team cognition.

This volume was conceived to address a perceived need in the team cognition literature. In particular, the purpose of this volume is to provide an avenue with which researchers from a diverse array of fields can present their theories, thoughts, methodologies, and findings on team cognition in one volume. As such, chapters have been written by recognized leaders within their own discipline so that they are able to discuss their research in the context of a broad-based approach. In this way researchers from differing disciplines can be exposed to a variety of the theoretical and methodological issues surrounding team cognition. Our overall goal with this volume is to illuminate team cognition through discussion of the many approaches that have been used to converge on a better understanding of this relatively elusive concept.

STRUCTURE OF THE BOOK

We take a three-pronged approach to tackling the issues surrounding team cognition and the progress that has been made in the last decade. In general, in this volume we provide a variety of approaches to understanding team cognition with chapters discussing theory and methods used to define and measure the construct along with experimentation conducted to explore operationalizations of the construct. In the first section we present some of the theoretical developments in team cognition. We follow this with a set of chapters discussing the methodological issues surrounding the team cognition construct. Last, we present a set of chapters describing a variety of applications of the team cognition construct.

Part I: Theoretical Issues Surrounding Team Cognition

In the opening section we present a representative sample of the theoretical developments in team cognition by bringing together researchers with organizational, social, and cognitive approaches. These authors discuss how constructs from the cognitive sciences have been used as an organizing framework to guide their own research.

First is the chapter by Rentsch and Woehr (chap. 2), who approach team cognition from the team schema literature. By integrating models from social psychology, they begin to quantify components of team member schema similarity. More specifically, by incorporating the notion of awareness of team-mates' knowledge into their approach, in addition to overlap in teammate knowledge, they present an added perspective on the factors contributing to shared cognition. They adopt a *social relations model* to team cognition and demonstrate how person perception and *team schemas* can be quantified to help us understand team cognition. Next is a chapter by Hinsz (chap. 3), who continues with his unique application of constructs from cognitive psychology to the team cognition literature by describing how metacognitive processes in teams are related to mental models and performance. By focusing on *metamemory* and incorporating theories of mental models, Hinsz develops a *belief association matrix* to help overcome theoretical issues associated with team metacognition.

Part II: Methodological Issues Surrounding Team Cognition

In this section, we present a sample of the research that has attempted to address the varied methodological issues surrounding the complex process of measuring and defining team cognition. Given the tremendously diverse array of disciplines studying this issue, our goal was to illustrate varying approaches to tackling the team cognition construct. In this way, researchers can assess the practicality of applying the differing approaches to their own idiosyncratic needs.

First is the chapter by MacMillan, Entin, and Serfaty (chap. 4), who present an empirically derived framework uniting structural factors associated with teams and the differing impact on team communication such structures have. Their chapter presents an overview of the innovative methodologies they have used to define and measure team process and performance. They argue that understanding how team factors impact team communication is foundational to team cognition. Specifically, they argue that team communication, both verbal and nonverbal, presents a form of workload (i.e., *communication overhead*) that can attenuate team cognition. Second is the chapter by Cooke, Salas, Kiekel, and Bell (chap. 5), who address the complex methodological issues associated with measuring team cognition. They argue that one cannot understand team performance without understanding how team cognition contributes to effective team functioning. Under the rubric of *holistic measurement*, they present a set of validated methods and newly developing techniques for measuring team cognition to show how a systematic and theoretically based approach can illustrate the complex relation between team cognition and team performance. Third is the chapter by Espinosa, Lerch, and Kraut (chap. 6), who discuss how task factors can alter both explicit and implicit coordination and the subsequent impact on team cognition. By focusing on *task dependencies*, they show how coordination mechanisms vary, not only in their application but also depending on the level of team cognition arising from team experience. They do this within the context of distributed teams to begin to address how one's understanding of team cognition can be effectively applied to this burgeoning field of study.

Part III: Applications of the Team Cognition Construct

In the final section we offer a sample of the applications of this approach through presentation of empirical investigations of team cognition. In this section researchers discuss experimentation as well as interventions and provide an integrative view of their research.

First is a chapter by Fiore and Schooler (chap. 7), who discuss *team problem models* within the larger area of *team problem solving*. They suggest that the reification of team cognition in the context of problem solving can only occur by means of external mechanisms to scaffold problem identification. Second, Levine and Choi (chap. 8) illustrate how altering the composition of teams through *personnel turnover* can alter team performance and team cognition. Using empirical examination of the impact of membership changes, they show how this affects social processes and individual and group cognition. Specifically, they examine how factors associated with the team members (e.g., status) can interact with personnel change and show the differential effects of team member ability and team member status. Third, Gutwin and Greenberg (chap. 9) discuss how technology developed out of an understanding of the complex social and cognitive factors affecting teamwork can facilitate awareness of team member actions. Their construct of *workspace awareness* was devised to drive efficient and effective computer-supported collaborative work. Workspace awareness describes a product of distributed teamwork resulting from knowledge of not only team and task artifacts but also the coordination of these situated factors during distributed interaction. Fourth is a chapter by Sycara and Lewis (chap. 10), who incorporate theories and findings from the team training and performance literature into intelligent agent technology. They describe the instantiation of advances in computer science and robotics that are allowing the introduction of *artificial intelligence into teamwork*. Their research addresses how artificial team members can provide assistance for rudimentary cognitive activity and what type of role they may play in providing this assistance. By using models of teamwork, they integrate agent technology into complex and dynamic team environments.

CLOSING REMARKS

We believe that progress toward understanding what comprises effective team functioning continues. This volume and others that have been published in recent years offer, we think, more and better concepts, information, data, methods, and findings about team cognition. We sincerely hope that the contents of this volume further encourage research in this important area. It is clear that we need more theoretically driven and empirically validated principles of team functioning to help researchers, practitioners, teachers, and students better understand, compose, manage, and develop teams in many settings. This volume is just a small step in getting us there. Only time will tell.

REFERENCES

Cannon-Bowers, J., & Salas, E. (1998). *Making decisions under stress: Implications for individual and team training.* Washington, DC: American Psychological Association.

Cannon-Bowers, J. A., & Salas, E. (2001). Reflections on shared cognition. *Journal of Organizational Behavior, 22,* 195–202.

Cannon-Bowers, J. A., Salas, E., & Converse, S. A. (1993). Shared mental models in expert team decision making. In N. J. Castellan Jr. (Ed.), *Individual and group decision making: Current issues* (pp. 221–246). Hillsdale, NJ: Erlbaum.

Hackman, J. R. (1998). Why teams don't work. In R. S. Tindale (Ed.), *Theory and research on small groups: Vol. 4. Social psychological applications to social issues* (pp. 245–267). New York: Plenum Press.

Hinsz, V. B., Tindale, R. S., & Vollrath, D. A. (1997). The emerging conceptualization of groups as information processors. *Psychological Bulletin, 121,* 43–64.

Hutchins, E. (1991). The social organization of distributed cognition. In L. B. Resnick & J. M. Levine (Eds.), *Perspectives on socially shared cognition* (pp. 283–307). Washington, DC: American Psychological Association.

Larson, J. R., & Christensen, C. (1993). Groups as problem-solving units: Toward a new meaning of social cognition. *British Journal of Social Psychology, 32,* 5–30.

Levine, J. L., Resnick, L. B., & Higgins, E. T. (1993). Social foundations of cognition. *Annual Review of Psychology, 44,* 585–612.

Newell, A., & Simon, H. A. (1972). *Human problem solving.* Englewood Cliffs, NJ: Prentice Hall.

Orasanu, J. (1990). *Shared mental models and crew performance* (Cognitive Science Laboratory Report No. 46). Princeton, NJ: Princeton University Press.

Salas, E., & Cannon-Bowers, J. A. (2000). The anatomy of team training. In S. Tobias & J. D. Fletcher (Eds.), *Training and retraining: A handbook for business, industry, government, and the military* (pp. 312–335). New York: Macmillan Reference.

Thompson, L. L., Levine, J. M., & Messick, D. M. (1999). *Shared cognition in organizations: The management of knowledge.* Mahwah, NJ: Erlbaum.

Tindale, R. S., & Kameda, T. (2000). "Social sharedness" as a unifying theme for information processing in groups. *Group Processes and Intergroup Relations, 3,* 123–140.

I

THEORETICAL ISSUES SURROUNDING TEAM COGNITION

2

QUANTIFYING CONGRUENCE IN COGNITION: SOCIAL RELATIONS MODELING AND TEAM MEMBER SCHEMA SIMILARITY

JOAN R. RENTSCH AND DAVID J. WOEHR

Researchers who study cognition in teams have approached the topic from a variety of perspectives (e.g., Cannon-Bowers, Salas, & Converse, 1993; Klimoski & Mohammed, 1994; Mitchell, 1986; Moreland, Argote, & Krishnan, 1996; Rentsch & Hall, 1994). Consistent across these perspectives is the fundamental hypothesis that common cognitions among team members will be associated with team effectiveness. Recent evidence supports this assertion by reliably revealing both direct and indirect relationships between team effectiveness and various operationalizations of common cognitions among team members (e.g., Marks, Sabella, Burke, & Zaccaro, 2002; Mathieu, Heffner, Goodwin, Salas, & Cannon-Bowers, 2000; Rentsch, Burnett, McNeese, & Pape, 1999; Rentsch & Klimoski, 2001; Walsh, Henderson, & Deighton, 1988). Research on this topic has also linked cognition in teams to effective team training (e.g., Marks et al., 2002), particularly to training military teams (e.g., Smith-Jentsch, Campbell, Milanovich, & Reynolds, 2001).

In recent years, the theoretical and empirical research on cognition in teams has progressed rapidly. Researchers in this area have accomplished the "feasibility" work, so to speak. The accumulating evidence indicates that cognition in teams is a rich area for investigation with implications for research questions basic to many areas of psychology and organizational behavior. In addition, this research is likely to have much to offer with respect to improving team functioning in actual organizations. At this point, we suggest that conceptual and empirical work should be directed at broadening how cognition in teams is conceptualized and operationalized.

The purpose of this chapter is to describe how identifying new forms of cognition in teams may enlarge the research domain. We begin by describing how researchers have operationalized cognition in teams in past research. Next, we describe one current conceptualization of cognition in teams: team member schema similarity. Then, we explore how cognition in teams may be elaborated by the study of person perception within teams and, specifically, by the application of the social relations model (SRM; Kenny, 1994; Kenny & LaVoie, 1984). In doing so, we provide an overview of the SRM, and then we describe a new perspective on cognition in teams inspired by the SRM.

COGNITION IN TEAMS

The recognition of common cognitions among team and organizational members as being an important precursor of high performance is long-standing (e.g., Bettenhausen, 1991). These strands of thought and research began taking a coherent form with respect to team research within industrial and organizational (I/O) psychology in the early 1990s. Cannon-Bowers and Salas (1990) and Cannon-Bowers et al. (1993) offered an influential introduction to the notion of cognition in teams, which they referred to as *team mental models*. They suggested that to the extent that mental models are shared (i.e., commonly held) by team members, improved team performance should result. They also noted that multiple mental models might exist in teams (e.g., equipment model, task model). Their work had grounding in engineering and human factors psychology. Klimoski and Mohammed (1994) and Rentsch and Hall (1994) independently examined cognition in teams. Klimoski and Mohammed (1994) reviewed "team mental model-like concepts" (p. 426) that were being used in the team performance, strategic decision-making, and training literatures. They presented a model in which they hypothesized that team cognition was related to team performance indirectly. Rentsch and Hall (1994) came to the topic of cognition in teams through their research on meanings in organizations. They elected to refer to the cognitions as schemas and specified the origination of cognition as existing within individuals. They referred to the overlapping of cognitions among team members as *team member schema similarity*, which they hypothesized to be related to team effectiveness. They also introduced the notion of schema accuracy (i.e., the relationship between a team member's schema and a target).

Within I/O psychology, subsequent conceptual work has continued (e.g., Hinsz, Tindale, & Vollrath, 1997; Kraiger & Wenzel, 1997; Mohammed & Dumville, 2001). Specifically, these researchers have attempted to develop theoretical models describing possible antecedents of cognitions in teams and how these cognitions relate to team performance. This work has stimulated empirical research designed to test the proposed hypotheses (e.g., Levesque, Wilson, & Wholey, 2001; Marks et al., 2002; Mathieu et al., 2000; Rentsch & Klimoski, 2001; Smith-Jentsch et al., 2001). However, empirical work on the topic has lagged behind the conceptual work. One reason for this lag is that researchers attempting to study cognition in teams are faced with the challenge of operationalizing the key variables. Indeed, it has been concluded that much confusion exists with respect to measuring cognition in teams (Kraiger & Wenzel, 1997; Mohammed, Klimoski, & Rentsch, 2000).

Along these lines, researchers have applied many methods to the study of cognition, including repertory grids, verbal protocols, and card sorting. Mohammed et al. (2000) identified pathfinder analysis, multidimensional scaling analysis, interactively elicited cognitive mapping, and text-based cognitive mapping as four promising techniques for assessing cognition in teams. Recent studies have used multidimensional scaling analysis (Rentsch & Klimoski, 2001), card sorting (Smith-Jentsch et al., 2001), concept mapping (Marks et al., 2002), and network analysis (Mathieu et al., 2000). All of these techniques have been applied and evaluated as methods for examining the degree to which team members have *common* mental representations of team-related information.

Indeed, to date, most researchers have focused their attention on an aspect of cognition in teams referred to as the degree of common understanding, overlap, agreement, congruence, or sharedness of cognitions. One perspective on this form of cognition in teams is based on the fundamental assumption that each team member possesses cognitions (e.g., thoughts, understandings, interpretations, beliefs, schemas, mental models) regarding some aspect of the team's work, such as the interpersonal teamwork processes or the team's task strategy. The degree of common understanding, overlap, agreement, congruence, or sharedness of cognitions is assessed by examining the degree to which matches exist among team members' cognitions. The aggregation of the degree of the matches that exists represents the degree of common understandings within a given team.

There is evidence that this type of cognition in teams can be measured meaningfully and that it is consistently related to theory-based team outcomes. This evidence has been obtained in studies in which the content of the cognitions assessed was related to teamwork or task work (although Cannon-Bowers et al., 1993, indicated that the content of team cognition may form with respect to a wide variety of team-related issues). For example,

Mathieu et al. (2000) assessed *task mental models* using eight critical task attributes identified on the basis of a task analysis. Examples of these items are banking or turning, selecting and shooting weapons, and reading and interpreting radar. They assessed what they referred to as a team mental model using seven such attributes as amount of information, roles, liking, and team spirit. Participants completed pair comparisons within each set of attributes. These ratings were subjected to network analysis, which produced a team-level value used to assess the degree of overlapping cognitions within the team. Marks et al. (2002) used a similar methodology to examine what they referred to as team interaction mental models. In their study, participants rated the relatedness of items such as select target, fire weapons, and adjust speed. These ratings were subjected to pathfinder analyses to assess overlap among team members' cognitions. Rentsch and Klimoski (2001) also used a paired-comparison method, but they assessed teamwork schemas. Their participants rated items such as "Personal preferences are compromised to meet team goals" and "Members are concerned with working for their own personal benefits." These ratings were analyzed using multidimensional scaling analysis. In all of these studies, the cognition variable, which was operationalized as a form of cognitive congruence, was related, as predicted, to team outcomes.

We suggest that a next step in this line of research is to broaden the conceptualizations of the variables of interest. Specifically, we suggest that new and varied forms and contents of team cognition be delineated. Below, we begin this discussion by describing one current conceptualization of team cognition.

TEAM MEMBER SCHEMA SIMILARITY

Team member schema similarity (TMSS; Rentsch & Hall, 1994) is a term describing cognition in teams. Although the term itself may be somewhat cumbersome, we elect to highlight it because each component communicates information and the term specifies most clearly the aspects of cognition in teams that we are most interested in studying. The reference to *team member* conveys that cognition in teams does not originate at the team level, rather it originates within each individual team member. Terms such as *team cognition* and *team mental model* do not specify the point of origination of the cognition. *Schema* specifies the nature of the cognition to be organized— structured knowledge that enables individuals to understand, interpret, and give meaning to stimuli (Brewer, 1987; Lord & Maher, 1991; Rumelhart, 1980; Schank & Abelson, 1977). Schemas may contain information related to a specific domain, be interrelated, represent knowledge at all levels of abstraction, and influence perception and memory (Brewer, 1987; Rumelhart, 1980). Each team member's schemas are expected to have some degree of similarity with other team members' schemas. *Similarity* articulates that team members' schemas will not be identical (as is implied by the word *shared*). Thus, TMSS refers to the degree to which team members have similar or compatible knowledge structures for organizing and understanding team-related phenomena.

Team member schema similarity consists of at least two components: team member schema congruence[1] and team member schema accuracy. The degree of team member schema *congruence* that exists is indicated by the degree of match between team members' schemas in content, structure, or both. Thus, the notion of congruence corresponds to the type of team member cognitions typically studied as was described above. When team member schema congruence exists among team members and the schema content is functional, they are likely to engage in smooth interpersonal interactions and constructive task behaviors. For example, a team member who intends to collaborate constructively may exhibit such behaviors as pointing out the weaknesses of arguments (Tjosvold, 1991) and offering dissenting opinions (Amason & Sapienza, 1997). Those teammates who interpret these behaviors similarly (i.e., as being constructive) are likely to engage in constructive conflict, thereby improving the team's performance. However, those teammates who interpret these behaviors differently, perhaps interpreting them as personal attacks, may begin to engage in nonproductive conflict, thereby hindering team performance (Rentsch & Zelno, 2003). Although congruence on functional schemas is expected to be strongly related to team effectiveness and to team processes, research evidence has shown that the degree of congruence without controlling for functionality is associated with positive team outcomes.

Team member schema *accuracy* refers to the degree to which a team member's schema is similar to a prespecified target value or "true score." For example, training effectiveness may be evaluated by examining the degree to which trainees' schemas match the instructor's schema (i.e., the target value) at the conclusion of training (Smith-Jentsch et al., 2001). Schema accuracy also exists to the degree that a team member's schema of a target matches the target's actual schema. For example, team members may form perceptions of their teammates' schemas of teamwork. By way of illustration, let us assume that Mitch's schema of teamwork contains "getting along," "speaking one's mind," "encouraging others," and "doing one's part." Donna's perception of Mitch's schema of teamwork is inaccurate because she does not realize that "doing one's part" and "encouraging others" are parts of Mitch's schema. In addition, her perception of Mitch's schema is inaccurate, because she thinks that for Mitch "relying heavily on others" is a component of teamwork, but Mitch's schema does not contain this component. Because Donna's schema

---

[1]We use the term *schema congruence* to refer to what Rentsch and Hall (1994) referred to as *schema agreement*.

of Mitch is inaccurate, when she observes Mitch agreeing with and encouraging another teammate, she interprets this behavior as Mitch's attempt to rely on others rather than Mitch's effort to contribute unique ideas to the team. Mitch, on the other hand, believes that he is making an effort to do his part by speaking his mind (i.e., indicating that he agrees with the teammate) and by encouraging his teammate. Because Donna's schema of Mitch's schema is inaccurate, her reaction to his behavior may be counterproductive and may cause Mitch to counterreact negatively. Ultimately, Donna's low schema accuracy will decrease the team's performance level. The degree to which team members form accurate schemas of their teammates' schemas of teamwork has been shown to be related to team effectiveness (Rentsch et al., 1999). The primary difference between team member schema congruence and team member schema accuracy is that schema congruence reflects the degree of match in cases in which there is no target or "correct" value, whereas schema accuracy reflects the degree of match in cases in which a "true score" or target value exists.

In summary, research to date has primarily examined team member cognitions about task-related characteristics or general team process characteristics. Furthermore, as noted earlier, schemas might be examined from the perspective of an individual team member's schema or from the perspective of a team member's perception of other team members' schemas (e.g., "How do I think about the task?" vs. "How do I think he/she thinks about the task?"). Largely unexamined in this research are team member schemas about other members of the team. We suggest, however, that cognitions regarding the nature of teammates are a potentially important determinant of team functioning and team performance. Specifically, the schemas that team members have about each other and themselves may provide insight into team functioning. Researchers studying person perception have examined the congruence and accuracy of these types of interpersonal cognitions.

AN INTERPERSONAL PERCEPTION APPROACH TO TEAM MEMBER SCHEMA SIMILARITY

A team is typically defined as a group of individuals working interdependently toward a common goal (Ilgen, 1999). Team members may be interdependent in terms of their roles, goals, and outcomes (Sundstrom, 1999), and, typically, the interdependence required to achieve the team objective involves each member of the team interacting directly or indirectly with each of the other team members. Through their direct or indirect interactions with each other, each team member is likely to form impressions of the other team members. For example, team members might develop impressions of their teammates in terms of such personal characteristics as competence, cooperativeness, reliability, communicativeness, and so on. These characteristics may relate to the team's task (e.g., task-related knowledge, task-related constraints), teamwork (e.g., beliefs about goal interdependence), or general personality characteristics (e.g., openness). It is likely that these interpersonal perceptions among team members will affect the nature of team members' interactions and of team functioning. In other words, how a team member views and is viewed by other team members may be an important determinant of team effectiveness.

The basic premise that the set of perceptions team members have about one another is a potential determinant of team functioning and hence team effectiveness leads to two key questions: (a) What are the perceived team member characteristics that are most relevant to team functioning and performance? (b) How do we best examine the nature of team members' perceptions of these characteristics? To address the first question, we draw primarily on work done on team member schema similarity and intrateam conflict. Then, we elaborate the social relations model and posit that it provides an approach especially suited for addressing the second question.

Components of Interpersonal Schemas

Team members may form impressions of each other and of themselves, and these impressions constitute schemas, self-schemas, and schemas corresponding to each teammate. These schemas might contain information related to perceptions regarding any type of personal and interpersonal characteristic. Here we focus on perceptions of personal and interpersonal characteristics related to the team's task (e.g., task-related expertise, task-related constraints), teamwork (e.g., beliefs about goal interdependence), or general personality characteristics (e.g., openness), because these appear most likely to be related to team functioning.

To illustrate the possible effects of these types of schemas on team functioning, we focus on intrateam conflict as one aspect of team functioning. For example, the accuracy of a team member's perceptions about a teammate's team-specific, task-related characteristics might affect team functioning, particularly as team functioning relates to intrateam conflict. More specifically, team member schema accuracy is hypothesized to be negatively related to socioemotional conflict, because team members who have accurate schemas of each other will be able to interpret each other's behaviors nonemotionally (Rentsch & Zelno, 2003). If team members perceive the behavior exhibited by another member as undesirable and they have an accurate schema of the "offending" person, then they may be able to correctly attribute the behavior to forces such as the individual's personal constraints rather than to personality. If team members do not have accurate schemas of teammates' characteristics, then they may find it difficult to interpret evocative behaviors exhibited by teammates in such as way as to avoid emotional conflict. Indeed, they are likely to attribute the offending behavior to the hostile intentions of the individual (i.e., the hostile attribution bias) rather than looking for an alternative explanation for the behavior. Having the knowledge to make another type of attribution will assuage the possibility of creating emotional conflict (Baron, 1997). In addition, members in teams characterized by highly accurate schemas for teammate's characteristics will likely justify their own perspectives to their teammates. Therefore, team members' perceptions of their teammates' task-related expertise and task-related constraints (e.g., pressure from one's superior, professional ethics) may be useful in creating a smooth teamwork process devoid of intrateam conflict (Rentsch & Zelno, 2003), thereby facilitating team effectiveness.

Team member perceptions of characteristics related to teamwork in general (e.g., beliefs about goal interdependence) are also likely to influence interactions associated with intrateam conflict, specifically with constructive task conflict. Team members' perceptions about teammates' beliefs about goal interdependence may be particularly relevant. The belief that there is a positive relationship between the attainment of one's own goals and the attainment of others' goals is referred to as *cooperative goal interdependence*. When team members hold such beliefs, they are likely to engage in behaviors related to constructive task conflict (rather than avoiding or misinterpreting these behaviors; Rentsch & Zelno, 2003). These behaviors include actively participating in discussions, attending to others, being influenced by teammates, encouraging and assisting teammates, correcting errors, pooling information, integrating perspectives, and feeling personally secure (Tjosvold, 1984).

Team members' perceptions of the degree and type of goal interdependence existing within the team are based, in part, on their interpretations of behaviors occurring within the team (Tjosvold, 1984). When team members perceive their teammates' potentially personally offensive behaviors (e.g., correcting errors) as consistent with cooperative goal interdependence, they are likely to engage in behaviors supportive of task conflict (Alper, Tjosvold, & Law, 1998). Alternatively, if team members perceive their teammates hold different beliefs about goal interdependence (e.g., win–lose), then they may not engage in constructive task conflict, and thereby inhibit team effectiveness.

The perceptions that team members form about each other's personality are also likely to affect team functioning. For example, team members' perceptions of one another's degree of openness might affect the manner in which team members engage in constructive conflict. Openness behaviors, such as sharing information, expressing opinions, raising doubts, airing objections, challenging ideas, and evaluating ideas of others, have been shown to be related to task conflict (Amason & Sapienza, 1997). Many openness behaviors, although conducive to task conflict, may cause team members discomfort if they do not interpret them as well intended. To avoid or minimize uncomfortable or anxiety-arousing situations within the team, members of newly formed teams are not likely to develop behavioral patterns that support task conflict (Cosier & Schwenk, 1990; Hackman & Morris, 1975). However, behavioral patterns that support openness result in high quality, innovative solutions, and consensual agreements (Tjosvold, 1991) and are positively related to reported levels of task conflict (Amason & Sapienza, 1997).

When team members perceive each other to have openness as a personality characteristic, then they are likely to accept and interpret these members' behaviors such as expressing opinions, raising doubts, airing objections, challenging ideas, and evaluating ideas of others as constructive. Therefore, the team may be more likely to engage in constructive task conflict without the detrimental effects of emotional conflict.

Schemas about other types of personality variables and variables related to person perception are likely to have significant effects on team functioning and team outcomes. For example, the degree to which team members perceive one another to be trustworthy may be related to constructive teamwork behaviors (Fiore, Salas, & Cannon-Bowers, 2001; Jones & George, 1998; Pape & Rentsch, 1998). Not only might the study of interpersonal content of schemas be an avenue for expanding the conceptualization of team member schemas, but perhaps the congruence and accuracy forms of schemas within teams may be elaborated. We suggest that the social relations model may supplement the work on cognitions in teams.

The Social Relations Model

The social relations model (SRM)[2] is a model for the study of perceptions, metaperceptions, and meta-accuracy in social interactions. The SRM provides a conceptual and statistical basis for modeling group interactions (Kenny, 1994). From a conceptual perspective, the SRM is predicated on examining individuals' behavior or perceptions within the context of dyadic interactions. Within the SRM framework, three major types of effects are posited: actor, partner, and relationship. The actor effect represents an individual's average level of a given behavior with respect to a variety of partners. The partner effect represents the average level of a response that a person elicits from a variety of partners. The relationship effect reflects an individual's behavior toward another specific individual, over and above any actor and partner effects. Here it is important to note that *actor* and *partner* are generic terms that are most appropriate in the context of behavioral data. Within the context of interpersonal perception, actor and partner effects might be appropriately labeled *perceiver* and *target* effects, respectively.

---

[2]For additional information regarding the SRM, see Kenny, D. A. (1994). *Interpersonal perception: A social relations model.* New York: Guilford. Also see Dr. Kenny's website at http://users.rcn.com/ dakenny/kenny.htm.

Statistically, the SRM is a special case of generalizability theory (Cronbach, Gleser, Nanda, & Rajaratnam, 1972), with the basic model consisting of a two-way, random-effects analysis of variance with actor as one variable and partner as another variable, and relationship as the interaction of the two. Thus, the model is designed to decompose variance in behavior or perceptions with respect to a particular construct into three components. Here it is important to note that the SRM does not focus on estimating the different effects for specific individuals or dyads. Rather the focus is on estimating variance due to general effects across individuals. So one might appropriately use the SRM to examine how members of high- (or low-) performing teams tend to interact or to perceive each other. The most common SRM design is the round-robin design in which each person interacts with or rates every other individual in the group and data are collected from both members of each dyad.

Within the context of interpersonal perception, the SRM allows for an examination of perception and metaperception. Metaperception is an individual's perception of another individual's perception of someone. In contrast to metacognition, which is considered to be a characteristic of adaptive expertise and involves the awareness of and ability to monitor and regulate one's own cognitive activities (Ford & Kraiger, 1995), metaperception involves one's ability or inclination to examine individuals' behavior and reactions to these behaviors (including one's own behavior) and to draw conclusions regarding other people's perceptions of the individual. Metaperception may be decomposed in terms of three effects analogous to the perceiver, target, and relationship effects in direct perception. Here perceiver effects are characterized as how the perceiver thinks others generally see him or her. Target effects reflect how individuals thinks a target generally sees others. Finally, relationship effects reflect how a perceiver thinks a target uniquely views the perceiver.

Nine Basic Components in Person Perception

Using the SRM framework and focusing on both perception and metaperception, Kenny (1994) summarized nine aspects of person perception. We further organize these nine components into three general categories: primary interpersonal perception components, perceptual congruence components, and perceptual accuracy components. Below, we briefly describe each of the nine components of person perception.

The first general category of interpersonal perception components contains the three primary effect types (see Table 2.1). *Assimilation* reflects the extent to which perceivers rate targets in the same way (i.e., variance associated with perceiver effects). The general question here is "Does the perceiver differentiate among targets?" For assimilation to occur, different perceivers

TABLE 2.1
Social Relations Model Primary Interpersonal Perception Components and Application to Teams

Component	General question	Team question	New form of TMSS
Assimilation	Does Mitch see others as alike?	Do team members see their teammates as similar?	*Team assimilation:* the extent to which team members view other members as similar to each other
Consensus	Is Donna seen the same way by others?	Is each team member seen the same by their teammates?	*Team consensus:* the extent to which all team members view each other member similarly[a]
Uniqueness	Does Mitch see Donna idiosyncratically (i.e., does Mitch perceive Donna differently than he views everyone else and differently than others view Donna)?	Does each team member perceive each teammate differently than he/she perceives other team members?	*Team uniqueness:* the extent to which team members view particular members as being different from other team members

Note. TMSS = team member schema similarity.
[a]Analogous to team member schema congruence.

must perceive differences across targets, but individual perceivers must view all targets similarly. *Consensus* is the extent to which multiple perceivers view a target in the same way (i.e., variance associated with target effects). Consensus requires not that all targets are viewed as the same but rather that all perceivers view each specific target in the same way. In essence, consensus reflects the level of interrater agreement across perceivers with respect to a given target so the question here is "Do perceivers agree in their perceptions of various targets?" Consensus is a fundamental concern in social science. It is also important to note that consensus is a necessary condition that must be met before many other questions in interpersonal perception can be addressed. Other components of person perception (elaborated below) such as self–other agreement, target accuracy, and meta-accuracy require consensus. *Uniqueness* reflects the degree to which perceivers view targets differently from how the perceivers see others and differently from how others see the targets (i.e., the variance associated with the perceiver by target interaction). The general question addressed here is "Do perceivers have unique perceptions of different targets?" Within the SRM framework, to separate error from relationship (i.e., uniqueness) variance, measures must be repeated across items or times.

TABLE 2.2
Social Relations Model Perceptual Congruence Components and New
Forms of Team Member Schema Similarity (TMSS)

Component	General question	Team question	New form of TMSS
Reciprocity	Do Mitch and Donna view each other similarly?	Do team members perceive each other similarly?	*Team reciprocity:* the extent to which team members tend to view each other similarly
Assumed reciprocity	Does Mitch think others perceive him as he perceives them?	Does each team member think his/her teammates perceive him/her as he/she perceives them?	*Team assumed reciprocity:* the extent to which team members believe that their teammates perceive them as they perceive their teammates
Assumed similarity	Does Mitch perceive others as he perceives himself?	Does each team member perceive his/her teammates as he/she perceives him/herself?	*Team assumed similarity:* the extent to which team members perceive their teammates as they (members) perceive themselves

Note. TMSS = team member schema similarity.

The second general category of interpersonal perception components focuses on the degree of congruence in perceptions (see Table 2.2). *Reciprocity* reflects the extent to which perceivers and targets view each other similarly (e.g., Mitch sees Donna as cooperative and Donna sees Mitch as cooperative). Reciprocity may be either generalized (i.e., perceivers and targets have similar perceptions of each other across dyads) or dyadic (i.e., perceivers and targets have similar perceptions of each other within dyads). *Assumed reciprocity* refers to the extent to which the perceiver believes the target sees the perceiver the same way the perceiver sees the target (e.g., Mitch thinks others see him in the same way he sees them). Assumed reciprocity may also be either generalized or dyadic. Generalized and dyadic reciprocity are typically assessed by the correlation between perceiver and target effects and the correlation between relationship effects, respectively. Assumed reciprocity is similarly assessed using metaperceptions. *Assumed similarity* refers to perceivers seeing others as the perceivers see themselves (e.g., Mitch perceives others as he perceives himself). Assumed similarity is typically assessed by the correlation between self-perception and perceiver effects.

The third general category of interpersonal perception components focuses on the accuracy of perceptions (see Table 2.3). *Target accuracy* is the extent to which the perceiver sees others as they really are (e.g., Mitch's view of Donna is correct). Kenny (1994) identified three types of target accuracy.

TABLE 2.3
Social Relations Model Perceptual Accuracy Components and New Forms of Team Member Schema Similarity (TMSS)

Component	General question	Team question	New form of TMSS
Target accuracy	Is Mitch's view of Donna correct?	Are team members' perceptions of each other correct?	*Team target accuracy:* the extent to which team members understand each other correctly
Self–other agreement	Do others see Mitch as he sees himself?	Do team members perceive each other as the others perceive themselves?	*Team self–other agreement:* the extent to which team members perceive their teammates as their teammates perceive themselves[a]
Meta-accuracy	Does Mitch know how he is seen?	Do team members know how their teammates perceive them?	*Team meta-accuracy:* the extent to which team members are accurate in understanding how their teammates view them

Note. TMSS = team member schema similarity.
[a] Analogous to team member schema accuracy.

Perceiver accuracy is the correspondence between how a perceiver sees others in general and how the others actually behave with the perceiver. Generalized accuracy is the correspondence between how an individual actually behaves and how he or she is seen by others. Dyadic accuracy is the correspondence between how the perceiver uniquely sees others and how others uniquely behave with the perceiver. It is important to note that all of the types of target accuracy described require a "true score." That is, to assess target accuracy, one must have some measure of the target's actual standing on the construct of interest that serves as the comparison standard. If self-ratings are the comparison standard, then target accuracy becomes *self–other agreement*. Analogous to target accuracy, three types of self–other agreement have been posited (i.e., perceiver, generalized, and dyadic). Finally, *meta-accuracy* indicates the degree to which individuals know how they are perceived by others. Again, Kenny differentiated perceiver, generalized, and dyadic meta-accuracy.

INTEGRATING THE SOCIAL RELATIONS MODEL AND TEAM MEMBER SCHEMA SIMILARITY

The application of the SRM may be useful in elaborating the notion of cognition in teams in terms of content, form, and methodology.

Content

In terms of content, both approaches are amenable to any team-related content. Schema congruence and schema accuracy may be assessed with respect to any type of schema content. As mentioned earlier, within the realm of team cognition, researchers have tended to focus on task and team-related contents. Cognitions regarding other team members have been proposed as legitimate cognitive contents for research, although this is an area in which there is a dearth of research. The SRM was founded on the basis of person perception, therefore; the typical content examined and the theory on which it is based is perceptions of individual difference characteristics. The explicit, theoretically based inclusion of these types of cognitions within the study of team member schemas can broaden our understanding of the role of cognition in teams. Targets in SRM are other people, and therefore, they could be teammates. However, it may be reasonable to consider the team's task, process, equipment, leader, and so on to be targets.

Form

Within the TMSS approach, two general forms of cognition are postulated: schema congruence and schema accuracy. Similarly, within the SRM, we can identify perceptual congruence and perceptual accuracy as major categories of person perception components. The notions of schema congruence and schema accuracy within the TMSS approach are somewhat simplistic, whereas the SRM offers elaborated notions of congruence and accuracy. Recall that, within the TMSS perspective, we defined schema congruence as the degree of match in cases in which there is no target or "correct" value. Thus, the SRM component most closely analogous to team member schema congruence is consensus (Do perceivers agree in their perceptions of various targets?). However, the notion of schema congruence becomes more intricate with consideration of other SRM components. Specifically, reciprocity is another component aligned closely with schema congruence. Assumed reciprocity and assumed similarity are additional, although somewhat remote from the original notion, forms of schema congruence.

SRM also offers elaborated forms of schema accuracy. We defined schema accuracy as reflecting the degree of match in cases in which a "true score" or target value exists. The SRM self–other agreement component corresponds most closely to schema accuracy. SRM also offers for consideration target accuracy and meta-accuracy as additional forms of schema accuracy.

Kenny (1994) summarized the nine components of person perception described above in a set of general questions about the nature of interpersonal perception. We propose that these general questions may be reframed with respect to the team-related perceptions among team members. We have modified these questions and presented an example set of them in Tables

2.1, 2.2, and 2.3 to illustrate how team cognition, in general, and team member schema similarity, in particular, may be elaborated by integrating these notions with components from the social relations model.

Methodology

The SRM components may be calculated for each team and analyzed as team-level variables in relation to other team-level variables. One advantage of the new forms of team member schemas is that within the SRM approach researchers can generate cognition variables, which originate as individual-level perceptions and are therefore theoretically consistent with the TMSS approach but that are orthogonal within each team. In other words, this approach enables the evaluations of the unique contributions of schema accuracy and schema congruence unhindered by multicollinearity problems. Therefore, the combined effects of the various forms of schema accuracy (e.g., team accuracy, team meta-accuracy, team self–other agreement) and of schema congruence (e.g., team reciprocity, team assumed reciprocity, and team assumed similarity) on team processes and outcomes may be tested meaningfully. Next, we focus on the new forms of TMSS and explore some possible questions that might be empirically examined using these new forms. Our intention is not to develop a model but rather to stimulate thinking about how this new approach might extend the research on cognition in teams.

NEW FORMS OF TEAM MEMBER SCHEMA SIMILARITY

Recall that one purpose of this chapter is to expand the nature of the questions being asked about cognition in teams. The application of the SRM to elaborate forms of TMSS reveals the potential complexity of team cognition in understanding team processes and performance, and it highlights the variety of research questions that can be posed to link cognition in teams to team functioning and to team performance. Next, we speculate as to how the new forms of team member schema accuracy and team member schema congruence may be related to team processes and outcomes.

Team Member Schema Accuracy

The application of the SRM in elaboration of team member schema accuracy results in several new forms that are likely to be related to team functioning and to team performance in ways that are consistent with past theorizing about team cognition. Team self–other agreement, which is analogous to team member schema accuracy, team accuracy, which is the extent to which team members understand each other accurately, and team meta-accuracy, which is the extent to which team members are accurate in understanding how their teammates view them, are likely to be related positively to team functioning and team effectiveness.

For example, Donna perceives that Mitch believes he is an engineering expert and Mitch does hold that belief (self–other agreement). Donna also perceives that Mitch is not the engineering expert he thinks he is but that he is a creative designer and her perceptions accurately reflect Mitch's true engineering expertise and creativity in design (target accuracy). In addition, Donna is accurate in her perception that Mitch believes that she knows nothing about engineering (meta-accuracy) although she is in fact very knowledgeable about engineering. Thus, when the team discusses constructing a bridge and Mitch presents the engineering requirements for his design idea, Donna focuses on Mitch's creative design idea. She also tolerates his inept assessment of the engineering problems. However, she addresses the engineering problems with the other team members in such a way as to avoid offending Mitch. Behaving as she does, one way in which she contributes to the team's effective functioning is by avoiding initiating negative conflict within the team. If, however, she did not have an accurate understanding of Mitch's perceptions and abilities, she could have reacted by taking offense at Mitch treating her as an incompetent engineer and responded to him in such a way as to make his engineering inadequacies painfully obvious to other members of the team. This type of response would result in escalating negative conflict within the team by causing Mitch and the other team members to experience negative feelings.

Team Member Schema Congruence

The complexity of cognitions in teams becomes apparent when considering the application of SRM components to elaborating team member schema congruence. Consensus, which is analogous to team member schema congruence, at an optimal level is hypothesized to be associated with team performance when the cognitive content is functional.

Assuming functional content, team member schema congruence in the forms of team reciprocity, team assumed reciprocity, and team assumed similarity may be related to team functioning. For example, if Mitch views Donna as cooperative and Donna views Mitch as cooperative, then they may develop a positive self-fulfilling spiral wherein each treats the other in a manner to promote cooperativeness and influences the other to behave cooperatively. If team assumed reciprocity exists within the team, then team members believe that their teammates perceive them as they perceive their teammates. For example, if team members believe that their teammates are conscientious and, therefore, they believe that their teammates expect them to be conscientious, perhaps they will behave conscientiously. They may also tend to be more accepting when a teammate makes an error, attributing it to external causes, or at least accepting it as well intentioned. Team assumed similarity will exist to the extent that members perceive their teammates as they perceive themselves. For example, team members who believe themselves to be open and who perceive their teammates to be similarly open may interpret their teammates' behaviors such as disagreeing and pointing out weaknesses as acts of openness intended to improve the team's performance rather than interpreting these behaviors as ego-driven or as personal attacks.

IMPLICATIONS FOR FUTURE RESEARCH

The primary purpose of this chapter was to describe how identifying new forms of cognition in teams, specifically new forms of team member schema similarity, may expand the nature of the research questions being investigated. Much of the literature on cognition in teams to date has neglected the idea that team effectiveness may be a function not only of the overlap of team members' cognitions but also of other forms of cognitive similarity, such as teammates' awareness of their teammates' schemas. Thus, the SRM provides a valuable analytic/methodological approach to the study of cognition in teams. More importantly, however, it also highlights a substantive area that has not received a great deal of attention to date. Specifically, it suggests an elaborated scheme for examining cognitions regarding personal and interpersonal schemas as they relate to team functioning.

The integration of TMSS and SRM highlights several potential avenues for future research. First, although we have not addressed it explicitly to this point, SRM has been traditionally applied as a descriptive tool in the study of person perception. It is clear that by applying it to the team context, the nature of the interpersonal issues explored expands. Also, within the team context, SRM may be used to test theoretically based hypotheses in addition to being used in its descriptive capacity.

Second, SRM highlights the study of new forms of TMSS and the study of additional schema contents. We suggest that researchers consider these new forms of TMSS with respect to various types of schema content (e.g., task-related issues, team member characteristics, team leadership). For example, team reciprocity, the extent to which team members tend to view each other similarly, may be related positively to team effectiveness to the extent that the perceptions reflect qualities related positively to functional team processes (e.g., cooperativeness). However, the nature of the relationship may differ depending on the characteristic being rated. For example, if Mitch views Donna as unreliable and Donna views Mitch as unreliable, then they may develop a negative situation in which each member experiences negative affect and behaves poorly.

Third, various forms of schema accuracy and schema congruence may operate in conjunction, forming complex profiles that predict team outcomes.

To refer back to the example above, what if Mitch and Donna perceive each other to be cooperative but they are not cooperative? Perhaps team reciprocity must be considered in conjunction with team accuracy to predict productive and smooth team member interaction processes. Perhaps, some form of schema accuracy is always important. For example, high levels of team consensus and team accuracy may be associated with the utilization of each team member's potential capacity; however, high team consensus and low team accuracy may result in imbalances of power and influence.

Finally, we suggest that researchers consider the nature of the schema content with respect to various criterion variables, for example, team effectiveness (member growth, team viability), team performance (objective outcomes, degree of consensus in decision making), and team processes (conflict, communication). Future research should be directed toward developing the nomological net around various aspects of team member schemas and team outcomes. Specifically, team member schemas may be elaborated both in terms of content and type of overlap (i.e., assimilation, consensus, accuracy, etc.), and this elaboration will suggest differential relations with various team-based outcomes. We believe that this approach will enrich theory and future research on team cognition and possibly the research on person perception.

REFERENCES

Alper, S., Tjosvold, D., & Law, K. S. (1998). Interdependence and controversy in group decision making: Antecedents to effective self-managing teams. *Organizational Behavior and Human Decision Processes, 74*(1), 33–52.

Amason, A. C., & Sapienza, H. J. (1997). The effects of top management team size and interaction norms on cognitive and affective conflict. *Journal of Management, 23*, 495–516.

Baron, R. A. (1997). Positive effects of conflict: Insights from social cognition. In C. K. W. De Dreu & E. Van de Vliert (Eds.), *Using conflict in organizations* (pp. 177–191). London: Sage.

Bettenhausen, K. L. (1991). Five years of groups research: What we have learned and what needs to be addressed. *Journal of Management, 17*, 345–381.

Brewer, W. F. (1987). Schemas versus mental models in human memory. In P. Morris (Ed.), *Modeling cognition* (pp. 187–197). New York: Wiley .

Cannon-Bowers, J., & Salas, E. (1990, April). *Cognitive psychology and team training: Shared mental models in complex systems*. Paper presented at the annual meeting of the Society for Industrial/Organizational Psychology, Miami Beach, FL.

Cannon-Bowers, J. A., Salas, E., & Converse, S. (1993). Shared mental models in expert team decision making. In N. J. Castellan (Ed.), *Individual and group decision making* (pp. 221–246). Hillsdale, NJ: Erlbaum.

Cosier, R. A., & Schwenk, C. R. (1990). Agreement and thinking alike: Ingredients for poor decisions. *Academy of Management Executive, 4*(1), 69–74.

Cronbach, L. J., Gleser, G. C., Nanda, H., & Rajaratnam, N. (1972). *The dependability of behavioral measurements: Theory of generalizability of scores and profiles.* New York: Wiley.

Fiore, S. M., Salas, E., & Cannon-Bowers, J. A. (2001). Group dynamics and shared mental model development. In M. London (Ed.), *How people evaluate others in organizations* (pp. 309–336). Mahwah, NJ: Erlbaum.

Ford, J. K., & Kraiger, K. (1995). The application of cognitive constructs and principles to the instructional systems model of training: Implications for needs assessment, design, and transfer. In C. L. Cooper & I. T. Robertson (Eds.), *International review of industrial and organizational psychology* (pp. 1–48). New York: Wiley.

Hackman, J. R., & Morris, C. G. (1975). Group tasks, group interaction process, and group performance effectiveness: A review and proposed integration. In L. Berkowitz (Ed.), *Advances in experimental social psychology* (pp. 45–99). New York: Academic Press.

Hinsz, V. B., Tindale, R. S., & Vollrath, D. A. (1997). The emerging conceptualization of groups as information processors. *Psychological Bulletin, 121,* 43–64.

Ilgen, D. (1999). Teams embedded in organizations: Some implications. *American Psychologist, 54,* 129–139.

Jones, G., & George, J. M. (1998). The experience and evolution of trust: Implications for cooperation and teamwork. *Academy of Management Review, 23,* 531–546.

Kenny, D. A. (1994). *Interpersonal perception: A social relations model.* New York: Guilford.

Kenny, D. A. (2001). *D. A. Kenny's homepage.* Retrieved April 3, 2001 from http://users.rcn.com/dakenny

Kenny, D. A., & La Voie, (1984). The social relations model. In L. Berkowitz (Ed.), *Advances in experimental social psychology* (pp. 141–182). Orlando, FL: Academic Press.

Klimoski, R., & Mohammed, S. (1994). Team mental model: Construct or metaphor? *Journal of Management, 20,* 403–437.

Kraiger, K., & Wenzel, L. H. (1997). Conceptual development and empirical evaluation of measures of shared mental models as indicators of team effectiveness. In M. T. Brannick, E. Salas, & C. Prince (Eds.), *Team performance assessment and measurement: Theory, methods, and applications* (pp. 63–84). Mahwah, NJ: Erlbaum.

Levesque, L. L., Wilson, J. M., & Wholey, D. R. (2001). Cognitive divergence and shared mental models in software development project teams. *Journal of Organizational Behavior, 22,* 135–144.

Lord, R. G., & Maher, K. J. (1991). Cognitive theory in industrial and organizational psychology. In M. D. Dunnette & L. M. Hough (Eds.), *Handbook of industrial and organizational psychology* (Vol. 2, pp. 1–62). Palo Alto, CA: Consulting Psychologists Press.

Marks, M. A., Sabella, M. J., Burke, C. S., & Zaccaro, S. J. (2002). The impact of cross-training on team effectiveness. *Journal of Applied Psychology, 87,* 3–13.

Mathieu, J. E., Heffner, T. S., Goodwin, G. F., Salas, E., & Cannon-Bowers, J. A. (2000). The influence of shared mental models on team process and performance. *Journal of Applied Psychology, 85,* 273–282.

Mitchell, R. (1986). Team building by disclosure of internal frames of reference. *Journal of Applied Behavioral Science, 22,* 15–28.

Mohammed, S., & Dumville, B. C. (2001). Team mental models in a team knowledge framework: Expanding theory and measurement across disciplinary boundaries. *Journal of Organizational Behavior, 22,* 89–106.

Mohammed, S., Klimoski, R. J., & Rentsch, J. R. (2000). The measurement of team mental models: We have no shared schema. *Organizational Research Methods, 3,* 123–165.

Moreland, R. L., Argote, L., & Krishnan, R. (1996). Socially shared cognition at work: Transactive memory and group performance. In J. L. Nye & A. M. Brower (Eds.), *What's social about social cognition? Research on socially shared cognition in small groups* (pp. 57–84). Thousand Oaks, CA: Sage.

Pape, L. J., & Rentsch, J. R. (April, 1998). The effects of trust and perspective-taking on team member schema similarity. In K. Smith-Jentsch (Chair), *To be a team is to think like a team.* Symposium conducted at the 13th Annual Conference of the Society for Industrial and Organizational Psychology, Dallas, TX.

Rentsch, J. R., Burnett, D. D., McNeese, M. D., & Pape, L. J. (1999, April–May). *Team member interactions, personalities, schemas, and team performance: Where's the connection?* Paper presented at the 14th Annual Conference of the Society of Industrial and Organizational Psychology, Atlanta, GA.

Rentsch, J. R., & Hall, R. J. (1994). Members of great teams think alike: A model of team effectiveness and schema similarity among team members. In M. M. Beyerlein & D. A. Johnson (Eds.), *Advances in interdisciplinary studies of work teams: Vol. 1. Series on self-managed work teams* (pp. 223–262). Greenwich, CT: JAI Press.

Rentsch, J. R., & Klimoski, R. J. (2001). Why do "great minds" think alike? Antecedents of team member schema agreement. *Journal of Organizational Behavior, 22,* 107–120.

Rentsch, J. R., & Zelno, J. (2003). The role of cognition in managing conflict to maximize team effectiveness: A team member schema similarity approach. In M. A. West, K. Smith, & D. Tjosvold (Eds.), *International handbook of organization and cooperative teamworking* (pp. 131–150). West Sussex, England: Wiley.

Rumelhart, D. E. (1980). Schemata: The building blocks of cognition. In R. J. Spiro, B. Bruce, & W. F. Brewer (Eds.), *Theoretical issues in reading and comprehension* (pp. 33–58). Hillsdale, NJ: Erlbaum.

Schank, R. C., & Abelson, R. (1977). *Scripts, plans, goals, and understanding.* Hillsdale, NJ: Erlbaum.

Smith-Jentsch, K. A., Campbell, G. E., Milanovich, D. M., & Reynolds, A. M. (2001). Measuring teamwork mental models to support training needs assessment, development, and evaluation: Two empirical studies. *Journal of Organizational Behavior, 22*, 179–194.

Sundstrom, E. (1999). *Supporting work team effectiveness: Best management practices for fostering high performance.* San Francisco: Jossey-Bass.

Tjosvold, D. (1984). Cooperation theory and organizations. *Human Relations, 37*, 743–767.

Tjosvold, D. (1991). Rights and responsibilities of dissent: Cooperative conflict. *Employee Responsibilities and Rights Journal, 4*, 13–23.

Walsh, J. P., Henderson, C. M., & Deighton, J. (1988). Negotiated belief structures and decision performance: An empirical investigation. *Organizational Behavior and Human Decision Processes, 42*, 194–216.

3

METACOGNITION AND MENTAL MODELS IN GROUPS: AN ILLUSTRATION WITH METAMEMORY OF GROUP RECOGNITION MEMORY

VERLIN B. HINSZ

The cognitive aspects of team interaction and performance have received considerable attention in the past decade. This attention reflects the influences of a number of trends. One trend is a heightened consideration of teams and groups in the social and organizational psychology literature (Cohen & Bailey, 1997; Guzzo & Salas, 1995; Ilgen, 1999; Levine & Moreland, 1998; Moreland, Hogg, & Hains, 1994; Sanna & Parks, 1997). An additional trend has been the evolving view of the social processing of information in groups

Portions of this research were presented in October 1996 at the Fourth Annual Society for Experimental Social Psychology Preconference on Small Groups, Sturbridge Village, Massachusetts. The study was conducted with the assistance of William Whiteman, Leissa Nelson, Chris Kozak, and Heidi Anderson. Preparation of this chapter was facilitated by grants from the National Science Foundation (BCS-9905397) and National Institute of Mental Health (1 R15-MH63734). This chapter benefited from a National Research Council Senior Research Associateship Award the author held at the Air Force Research Laboratory, Human Effectiveness Directorate, Brooks Air Force Base. I would like to thank Scott Tindale, Joan Rentsch, Nancy Cooke, John Levine, Steve Fiore, Glenn Littlepage, and Dennis Stewart for comments on earlier versions of this chapter.

and teams for reviews (see Hinsz, Tindale, & Vollrath, 1997; Levine, Resnick, & Higgins, 1993; for additional perspectives, see Larson & Christensen, 1993; Klimoski & Mohammed, 1994; Nye & Brower, 1996; Resnick, Levine, & Teasley, 1991). There has also been an increase in attention to shared cognitive processes in organizations (Cannon-Bowers & Salas, 2001; Thompson, Levine, & Messick, 1999). Similarly, another influence has been the application of selected constructs from cognitive psychology to help understand the cognitive processes of groups and teams (Hinsz et al., 1997). The goal of this chapter is to examine how metacognition as one of these constructs can enhance a person's understanding of the cognitive processes of groups and teams.

A metacognitive perspective for the ways information is processed in groups and teams is not new to the understanding of group interaction and performance, but it generally has not been the focal point of conceptualization and theorizing. I illustrate the use of this metacognitive perspective, and a number of features of metacognition in groups, by focusing on metamemory. In addition, I address important questions regarding metacognition in groups by incorporating the mental model construct from cognitive and engineering psychology (e.g., Gentner & Stevens, 1983; Rouse & Morris, 1986). The particular questions I address are the following: (a) What is metacognition and how is it applicable to groups and teams? (b) How can metamemory illustrate important topics to consider in the metacognition of groups? (c) How does one assess the accuracy of the metacognitive beliefs group members have regarding metamemory? (d) How can mental models aid one's representation of metacognition, in particular metamemory in groups? (e) How can shared mental models help one understand how metacognitive beliefs can be shared or unshared in interacting teams and groups? My approach to these questions is illustrated with previously unreported data from an experiment I conducted on recognition memory performance of groups (Hinsz, 1990). I hope this empirical demonstration of the metacognitive perspective with metamemory responses will aid the understanding and conceptualization of some of the cognitive processes that are important in the interaction and performance of groups and teams.

METACOGNITION IN GROUPS

Metacognition concerns the ways people think about their cognitive processes (Metcalfe & Shimamura, 1994; Nelson, 1992, 1996). There are many perspectives one might take when considering metacognition in teams and groups. The view I take is from social–organizational psychology rather than the more established approach of cognitive psychology, although cognitive psychology research has fostered my thinking. I consider metacognition as what people know about the way they process information.

Metacognition is useful for understanding small group processes and performance on cognitive tasks (Hinsz et al., 1997; Tindale, Kameda, & Hinsz, 2003). Given the definition provided above, metacognition in groups can be considered "what group members know about the way groups process information" (Hinsz et al., 1997, p. 58). If group members have mental representations about the way that groups operate and function, then these mental representations can illustrate how group members think about the way groups process information and perform cognitive tasks (e.g., solve a problem, make a decision, integrate information, remember and learn material, frame situations). The mental representations group members have about the way groups process information and perform cognitive tasks are examples of metacognition about groups.

Metacognition has implications for groups and teams on a variety of cognitive tasks they perform. This chapter focuses on metacognition regarding recognition memory processes in groups (i.e., metamemory). Metacognition could also be considered for the way group members think about how groups make decisions (metacognition for decision making in groups; Tindale et al., 2003). Another aspect of metacognition that has received attention in the cognitive psychology literature has been problem solving (Davidson, Deuser, & Steinberg, 1994). There can also be metacognition for problem solving in groups (Artzt & Armour-Thomas, 1997). Metacognition would also be relevant for areas of group judgment such as the use of member expertise (Littlepage & Reddington, 1997). All these types of cognitive tasks might involve different features of metacognition. Consequently, it is important to note that metacognition in groups is task specific.

Metacognition has surfaced as an important topic in elements of group and team research. Orasanu (1993) considered metacognition in flight teams. Hinsz (1995) discussed the impact of mental models for jury decision making. Morgan and Bowers (1995) considered metacognition as it relates to teamwork stress and team decision making. Endsley (1995) examined metacognition in the context of situation awareness. Researchers have generally been aware of the impact of metacognitive notions in the work they have published. However, oftentimes it has not been labeled in terms of the metacognition described in the cognitive psychology literature. One aim of this chapter is to make researchers aware that they are studying and discussing metacognition in groups. I also hope that this will allow researchers and students of group and team processes to rely on the metacognition literature to aid their explorations of cognitive processes in teams and groups.

There is much in group contexts that falls in the realm of metacognition of groups. However, previous work has not systematically investigated these issues with the guidance of individual-level metacognition research and the insights that this research provides. Given the potential of metacognition-related notions to aid the understanding of the cognitive processes of groups and teams, I briefly review a few of the issues and insights gleaned from metacognition research that are relevant to metacognition in groups, and metamemory of group members in particular.

METACOGNITION AND METAMEMORY

One area of research in metacognition concerns *metamemory*, which is what people know about the way they remember (Nelson, 1992). Metamemory is relevant to group memory and remembering in groups (for reviews, see Clark & Stephenson, 1989; Hinsz et al., 1997). Metamemory in groups relates to what group members know about how they remember in groups. A number of researchers (Clark & Stephenson, 1989; Hinsz, 1990; Stephenson, Clark, & Wade, 1986; Stewart & Stasser, 1995; Vollrath, Sheppard, Hinsz, & Davis, 1989; Wegner, 1987; Wegner, Erber, & Raymond, 1991) have argued that memory processes in groups have implications for a variety of group and interactive situations (e.g., decision-making groups, families, juries). Metamemory is also important in group contexts because what people know about how groups remember may affect group memory performance. That is, the metamemory of group members may influence how the members act with regard to remembering in their groups, which may influence how remembering operates in the groups and thus has an impact on the outcomes of group remembering.

ACCURACY OF METACOGNITION

One critical question in metacognition research is the accuracy of a person's metacognition. That is, does the person's understanding of the cognitive processes reflect an accurate representation of how those processes operate? Accuracy of metamemory concerns the accuracy of people's knowledge of how memory functions relative to how memory actually functions. With regard to groups, the question of accuracy of metamemory differs slightly: How accurate is group members' knowledge of how memory functions in groups relative to how memory in groups actually operates?

Nelson (1996) argued that one of the problems confronted when conceptualizing metacognition is finding a way to represent a person's metacognitive knowledge and experiences (Flavell, 1979). The problem of representation is particularly important for testing the accuracy of the person's metacognition. In general, metacognition research requires sufficient knowledge of cognitive processes to describe ways in which the cognitive processes vary in some domain. Using this knowledge of cognition, a researcher can test to see if the person's metacognition appears to reflect knowledge of the way situations influence cognitive processes. Similarly, for an assessment of metamemory, it is important to know how memory processes change as a function of changes in situations (e.g., a forgetting curve over time). If actual memory processes change as a function of changes in the situation, then an accurate metamemory should change in corresponding ways.

The investigation of the accuracy of metamemory in groups raises two issues related to the research from individual metacognition. First, it is apparent that a solid foundation of knowledge about memory processes in groups for some domain is important for comparisons with metamemory about groups. Another issue is constructing a way to represent group memory processes so they can be compared with member metacognitive beliefs and expectations. I use a model of a mental model to address the second issue; however, the first issue still requires some attention for specification. A domain of group memory needs to be sufficiently understood so that it can serve as a basis for examining member metamemory. I chose group recognition memory performance because it provides a basis for addressing both of the preceding questions.

Two factors make large contributions to group recognition memory performance: consensus and correctness (Hinsz, 1990). The consensus factor indicates that as the number of group members favoring an alternative (i.e., true or false) increases, a group is more likely to choose that alternative as the group's response. Moreover, the consensus function is nonlinear with a discontinuity when half of the members favor the correct alternative. Correctness represents the finding that actually correct alternatives are more likely to be chosen as the group response. The correctness factor in group recognition memory performance is consistent with other research on group problem solving and judgments on intellective tasks that shows that correct responses are more likely to be the group judgments than responses that are in error (Laughlin, 1980).

The consensus and correctness factors predict the vast majority of the variance in group recognition memory responses (approximately 85% in Hinsz, 1990). Consequently, correctness and consensus can serve as two important aspects of group memory to which a person should be sensitive if he or she has an accurate metamemory for group recognition memory. Other features of group remembering may also play a role in group memory performance (Hinsz, 1990), but those aspects may not be as important as consensus and correctness and may be too subtle for group members to believe they have an impact on group memory performance. Consequently, for the research discussed in this chapter, accuracy of the metamemory focuses on the capability of group members to recognize and respond indicating an appreciation of the impact of consensus and correctness on group recognition memory performance.

People may or may not have accurate metamemory for group memory performance. Herrmann (1982) suggested that individuals are moderately accurate in predicting their own memory performance. The metamemory literature suggests that at a gross level, individuals do have accurate metamemory for their own memory performance (Nelson & Narens, 1990). However, individuals often exaggerate the impact of specific influences, underestimate the influence of other factors, and may not be attuned to the influence of subtle variables on memory performance (Nelson, 1996). Therefore, the metamemory group members have about their group recognition memory performance might accurately reflect the actual group recognition memory performance. Alternatively, group members may have a weak understanding of group memory processes (Nisbett & Wilson, 1977) and may be unable to make adequate descriptions of the process (Brehmer, 1984).

REPRESENTATION OF GROUP RECOGNITION MEMORY

To be able to test the accuracy of metamemory in groups and to address other issues, one needs a way of representing group recognition memory performance. A conceptual formulation that can represent the consensus and correctness processes in group recognition memory should be developed. A representation of a person's metamemory can then be compared with this conceptual formulation to examine the accuracy and structure of people's metamemory of group recognition performance. Fortunately, earlier research provides such a formulation in terms of a matrix with probability entries (Hinsz, 1990).

Group recognition memory performance can be represented in terms of a matrix called a *social decision scheme* (see Table 3.1; Davis, 1973; Hinsz, 1990). The responses to the recognition items in Hinsz (1990) have two possible outcomes: correct or incorrect. Within the six-person groups studied, there are seven possible distributions of group members initially taking the correct and incorrect positions (6–0, 5–1, 4–2, 3–3, 2–4, 1–5, and 0–6). These seven distributions of group members' initial responses are arrayed in the left-most column of Table 3.1. The two middle columns represent the conditional probabilities that groups having specific distributions of initial responses (e.g., four members favoring the correct and two favoring the incorrect response) will choose a specific alternative (e.g., correct) as the group response. The right-most matrix column indicates the number of specific distributions of the group members observed in the sample. Table 3.1 illustrates observed probabilities and frequencies for data gathered on group recognition performance (Hinsz, 1990).

The impact of the consensus and correctness factors for group recognition memory performance can be seen in Table 3.1. As the number of group members initially favoring the correct (or incorrect) response increased (consensus), the likelihood of a group choosing that response increased as well. Note that the impact of the number of group members favoring a response is not proportional. Distributions such as 4–2 lead to a correct response (.88) at

TABLE 3.1
Observed Distribution of Group Recognition Responses Across All Items

Member responses	Group response		
(Correct–Incorrect)	Correct	Incorrect	*n*
6–0	.98	.02	544
5–1	.94	.06	728
4–2	.88	.12	724
3–3	.77	.23	524
2–4	.61	.39	300
1–5	.41	.59	165
0–6	.33	.67	40
Group Distribution	2,514	511	3,025

Note. From "Cognitive and Consensus Processes in Group Recognition Memory Performance," by V. Hinsz, 1990, *Journal of Personality and Social Psychology, 92*, p. 712. Copyright © 1990 by the American Psychological Association. Reprinted with permission.

a rate greater than the proportion of group members favoring the correct response (.67). Moreover, the entries in the matrix are asymmetrical with regard to correct and incorrect responses, illustrating the influence of the correctness of the response. Group members who are correct in their initial judgments have a greater influence on the group judgment than group members who are incorrect. For example, although in the 3–3 distribution there are equal numbers of initially correct and incorrect group members, groups were more likely to choose the correct response (.77) than the incorrect response (.23).

The matrix presented in Table 3.1 provides a clear way of representing the two factors of consensus and correctness for group recognition member performance. Consequently, it also provides a basis to judge the accuracy of the metamemory for group recognition memory. The matrix conceptualization provided in the table also provides a basis for assessing the metamemory for group recognition performance. This method for assessment rests in part on the conceptualization of mental models of group functioning (Hinsz, 1995).

A MENTAL MODEL REPRESENTATION OF METAMEMORY IN GROUPS

I described metacognition in groups as the beliefs and expectations people have about the ways groups process information and perform cognitive tasks. Metacognition in this case can be seen as mental representations of cognitive processes in groups. As such, metacognition is similar to a number of cognitive representations. Consequently, methods of conceptualizing and assessing mental representations may be useful for representing and assessing metacognition in groups. Previous research on group performance (Hinsz, 1995) and of the conceptualization of groups as information processors suggests that mental models are useful cognitive representations for the cognitive processes in groups and teams (Hinsz et al., 1997; Klimoski & Mohammed, 1994).

There are rich literatures considering mental models in the human factors (e.g., Norman, 1983; Rouse & Morris, 1986) and cognitive psychology (e.g., Gentner & Stevens, 1983; Johnson-Laird, 1983) domains. Although many definitions of mental models exist, and mental models have been related to a number of other cognitive representations (Wilson & Rutherford, 1989), I base my consideration of mental models on a definition I constructed to make it relevant to group functioning. Because I see mental models as cognitive representations that help people understand the operation and functioning of some system, such as a group (Hinsz, 1995), I use beliefs and expectations as the core concepts to describe mental models. "A mental model is an individual's mental representation and beliefs about a system, and the individual's interaction with the system, with particular focus on how the individual's interactions with the system leads to the outcomes of interest" (Hinsz, 1995, p. 202).

This definition places mental models within traditional approaches to social psychology (beliefs, attitudes, stereotypes, and social cognition; Eagly & Chaiken, 1993; Fiske & Taylor, 1991). It also places mental models in the context of the assumption that mental representations of group members influence their actions. Moreover, if groups are conceived of as systems (Ancona, 1990; Arrow, McGrath, & Berdahl, 2000; Hinsz, 1995), this definition allows one to consider mental models of groups. If *group* is substituted for *system* in the preceding definition, a definition for mental models of groups results: A mental model of a group is an individual's mental representation and beliefs about a group and the individual's interaction with the group, with particular focus on how the individual's interaction with the group leads to the group- and member-related outcomes of interest. Mental models for groups can be seen as the mental representations group members have for how they see groups operate. Likewise, the mental models of groups can be viewed as the beliefs and expectations group members have about the manner by which groups function.

The mental representations group members have about their own group have a number of implications. The mental model construct provides a basis for considering shared mental representations. Do members of a group share aspects of their mental representations of some group processes, or are there elements of the mental models that differ among the members (Hinsz et al., 1997)? Moreover, the mental model construct provides a foundation for developing a method for assessing the metamemory of group members for group recognition performance.

ASSESSMENT OF METAMEMORY IN GROUPS

Mental models can illustrate metacognition because they incorporate the beliefs and expectations people have about how cognitive processes operate and function. Consequently, mental models can illustrate the beliefs and expectations group members have about how cognitive processes such as recognition memory operate and function in groups. A method for assessing these mental models and metacognition is critical for achieving this understanding (Hinsz, 1995). Fortunately, because mental models are predicated on the beliefs that individuals hold, the methods of belief assessment can be used to measure mental models (for descriptions of some of these procedures, see Hinsz, 1995; Langan-Fox, Code, & Langfield-Smith, 2000).

Beliefs can be defined as the degree of association (subjective probability) between some object and an outcome (Fishbein & Ajzen, 1975). Recognizing that beliefs can be specified as subjective probabilities allows us to refer back to the matrix in Table 3.1. If the cell entries in Table 3.1 were group members' *subjective* probabilities that groups with specific distributions would choose particular responses, the matrix in the table would be a *model* of a mental model for that particular group task. The cell entries in the table would reflect the beliefs that group members have about the way groups perform a recognition memory task. I have described this matrix that represents a model of the mental model as a *belief association matrix* (Hinsz, 1995).

The belief association matrix provides a method of assessing group members' expectations about the way their group might function with regard to a recognition memory task. If a group member were asked to predict how likely a group of six individuals would respond correctly or incorrectly on a recognition test, that prediction would be a subjective probability. Moreover, if the group member were told that the group was composed of four members favoring the correct response and two members favoring the incorrect alternative, the member's response would represent a belief corresponding to the conditional probability in the belief association matrix. In addition, if subjective probability judgments were made for all possible distributions of group member preferences (the left most column in Table 3.1) and the different possible group responses (e.g., correct and incorrect), then these beliefs would represent a *model* of a mental model. This mental model would reflect the way groups are expected to reach consensus on the group recognition memory task. Consequently, the belief association matrix provides a conceptual basis on which to assess metamemory of group recognition performance.

The belief association matrix provides a means for addressing additional issues related to metamemory in groups. If people have accurate metamemory, then changes in the number of advocates that favor the correct and incorrect responses should be reflected in their probability judgments. A comparison between the observed group recognition performance illustrated by Table 3.1 and the metamemory assessed in the belief association matrix can be compared directly. Moreover, the belief association matrix provides a basis for considering how much members of a group share their beliefs regarding the way their group functions while performing a memory task.

SHAREDNESS OF MENTAL MODELS AND METAMEMORY

An intriguing question is the degree to which the cognitive representations group members have for a task or situation are shared (Hinsz et al., 1997; Tindale, Smith, Thomas, Filkins, & Sheffey, 1996). Also of interest is the degree to which the beliefs and expectations that make up a group's metacognition regarding a cognitive task are shared. Are the mental representations that members have about the task and their interaction with it similar or different? This point relates to a traditional question in groups about the members of a group seeing the issue from the same or different perspectives (Hinsz et al., 1997; Levine, Higgins, & Choi, 2000). The question of shared representations also relates directly to the literature concerning shared mental models (e.g., Cannon-Bowers, Salas, & Converse, 1993; Hinsz, 1995; Klimoski & Mohammed, 1994) and shared situation awareness (Endsley, 1995).

Shared mental models are claimed to be important for team training, efficient interaction, competent performance, and team effectiveness (Cannon-Bowers et al., 1993; Klimoski & Mohammed, 1994; Kraiger & Wenzel, 1997; Mathieu, Heffner, Goodwin, Salas, & Cannon-Bowers, 2000; Peterson, Mitchell, Thompson, & Burr, 2000; Rasker, Post, & Schraagen, 2000; Rentsch & Hall, 1994; Rouse, Cannon-Bowers, & Salas, 1992; Salas, Prince, Baker, & Shrestha, 1995). Shared mental models are also considered to be important for the team situation awareness that is critical for groups performing tasks in rapidly changing environments (Endsley, 1995; Endsley & Jones, 1997; Stout, Cannon-Bowers, & Salas, 1996), such as cockpit crews (Orasanu, 1993) and emergency response teams (Young & McNeese, 1995). The speculation is that if members of a group have similar representations of the situation they face, the group members will interact more efficiently, agree on appropriate courses of action, have less conflict that would disrupt performance, and be more effective. Consequently, groups having shared representations should achieve higher levels of performance. Likewise, group members with unshared and dissimilar representations are expected to disagree on the nature of the situation or problem, disagree about approaches to resolving the situation, spend unnecessary time resolving conflicts, be misguided in their actions, take separate and uncoordinated actions, and achieve suboptimal levels of performance and effectiveness.

The potential of shared mental models is also relevant for shared metamemory in groups. If group members share similar mental models of how to remember material in a group, they will be more efficient, spending more time on performance and less on organizing their actions. If group members have similar representations of metamemory in groups, then they should focus on similar processes by which they could improve their group memory performance. Note that the expected benefits of shared metamemory in a group are predicated on an assumption that the group member metamemory is an accurate representation of group memory processes. If the group members' metamemory is very error-prone, then the sharedness of the member metamemory will likely diminish the quality of the group memory performance (Hinsz, 1995; Hinsz et al., 1997). Nevertheless, agreement among members about how the group should operate while performing the memory task should enhance the quality of interactions among the group members and improve the group members' satisfaction with their interactions in the group. Although these points have been made here with regard to metamemory, they should apply to other types of metacognition as well.

By conceiving of metamemory in groups as a set of beliefs about specific forms of group interaction in pursuit of consensus, then comparisons can be made between the assessed belief association matrices among the members of a group. In particular, the degree of consistency of group members' judgments regarding the different distributions of member preferences (as illustrated in Table 3.1) can be assessed with an intraclass correlation (Shrout & Fleiss, 1979). Alternatively, the specific level of direct agreement among the group members for each of the cell entries for the belief association matrix can be calculated by a different intraclass correlation. Moreover, the degree that members of one group are similar to members of other groups can be assessed with an entirely different intraclass correlation. These intraclass correlations are used in this study to investigate the sharedness of metamemory in groups.

OVERVIEW OF THE RESEARCH AND THE STUDY

This chapter introduces and explores metacognition in groups. To illustrate a number of issues, I discuss group member metamemory for group performance on a recognition task. The following study investigates these issues with regard to metamemory judgments of participants who had experience with a group recognition memory task. The participants' judgments are used to construct a belief association matrix, which serves as a model of participants' metamemory of group memory. By comparing group performance on a recognition memory task and metamemory judgments about this recognition memory performance, the accuracy of the group members' metamemory can be assessed. Moreover, the similarity of metamemory judgments of group members can be compared to uncover the degree metamemory is shared in the groups. Although these issues are addressed with data gathered from this study, its major objective is to demonstrate and illustrate how these issues can be examined in the context of an empirical investigation of metacognition in groups.

METHOD

The participants in this research were student volunteers who served as members of 55 six-person groups described in Hinsz (1990). Participants were greeted in a large room and were asked to sit around a large table. The students were given some introductory instructions and then were asked to watch a recording of a job interview on a video monitor. The participants were instructed that they would be tested on their memory of the content of the video recording. Once the video had finished, the students were randomly assigned to rooms, with six participants in each room. Once in the room, each student received an individual recognition memory test and a response form.

The recognition tests consisted of 60 items varying in difficulty based on statements and observations from the videotape. The students responded to the recognition items on computer-readable forms indicating whether they thought the item was true or false. The students were given extensive written and oral instructions for making their true/false judgments. After completing the individual recognition test, the students received a very similar second test. The participants responded to the second recognition test as a group. The group members were told to read each of the items together and to discuss the item among themselves to come to a group judgment regarding whether the item was true or false.

After completing the second recognition test, participants completed another questionnaire that assessed metamemory. The students were told that, on the basis of their experiences in this study and with other groups, we wanted their perceptions about how they thought groups similar to their own would respond to recognition memory items. The group members were asked to estimate the percentage of groups that would respond true or false to an item, given the number of members of the group who favored true and favored false. The students were also informed that either the true response or the false response was actually correct, which allowed an assessment of group responses for the possible distributions of responses as well as the asymmetry that occurs in memory-type tasks. In a random order, all possible combinations of true and false advocates were presented (i.e., 6–0, 5–1, 4–2, 3–3, 2–4, 1–5, 0–6) for true being correct and for false being correct. An example of 1 of the 14 items is, "What do you think would be the percentage of true and false group responses if *two* members of the group *favored* a *true* response and *four* members of the group *favored* a *false* response, when in reality *false* was the *correct* response?" There were 14 different questions because questions were asked for both true and false being correct. This differs from the observed matrix in Table 3.1, but it reduces demand by not focusing on the responses being correct or incorrect, although this information could be inferred in the question.

RESULTS

The actual distributions of group recognition responses are presented in Table 3.1 and are arrayed according to the group members' responses during the individual test. Given the distributions of recognition responses for a group are known, the group's recognition responses are entered into a matrix indicating whether the group response is correct or incorrect. Table 3.1 presents the relative frequency across items for groups having each of the distributions of responses favoring the correct or incorrect responses in their group recognition choices. The consensus and correctness factors are demonstrated in the matrix provided in Table 3.1, as well as some more subtle aspects of group recognition memory performance (see Hinsz, 1990).

Accuracy of Metamemory

The metamemory questionnaire asked the group members to indicate the likelihood they felt that groups would choose the true or false responses under all possible distributions of member responses. The mean and median metamemory judgments under these conditions are presented in Table 3.2. Comparisons between the observed proportion of correct group recognition responses and the mean and median metamemory judgments of group recognition performance (see Tables 3.1 and 3.2) indicate a good degree of similarity. The correlation between the observed responses and the metamemory judgments (correct responses only) was relatively high for the mean and median metamemory values collapsed across the true and false items ($r = .98$ for both). However, correlations in this analysis can be high for a variety of reasons (see Birnbaum, 1973).

To examine the nature of the metamemory of group members, I conducted a 2 (true or false being correct) × 7 (distribution of responses in the group) analysis of variance on the group members' probability metamemory judgments (see Table 3.2 for mean and median values). Because the likelihood of a group getting an item incorrect is the inverse of the likelihood of the group getting the item correct, analyses were conducted only on the metamemory judgments for a group responding correctly. A main effect for distribution of responses was observed, $F(6, 1974) = 1,368.33$, $p < .0001$, partial $\eta^2 = .81$, with group members expecting groups to choose an alternative that had more advocates among the members of the group. This finding suggests that group members believe the distribution of responses among group members (consensus) does have a strong impact on expected group memory processes. A main effect of true or false being correct was also observed, $F(1, 329) = 114.35$, $p < .0001$, partial $\eta^2 = .26$, indicating that group members expected groups to be more likely to get an item correct if it is a true response than if it was a false response. Both of these main effects were conditioned by the distribution of responses by true or false being correct two-way interaction, $F(6, 1974) = 20.56$, $p < .0001$, partial $\eta^2 = .06$. This interaction indicates that the impact of the item being correct for a true or false response was different for the different distributions of member responses.

TABLE 3.2
Mean and Median Belief Association Matrices of Metamemory for Group Recognition Memory Performance

	Collapsed across all items			True correct items			False correct items		
Proposed responses (C–I)	Proposed responses (C–I)	Estimated group response		Proposed responses (C–I)	Estimated group response		Proposed responses (C–I)	Estimated group response	
		Correct	Incorrect		Correct	Incorrect		Correct	Incorrect
Mean Belief Association Matrices									
6–0	6–0	.92	.08	6–0	.97	.03	6–0	.87	.13
5–1	5–1	.82	.18	5–1	.90	.10	5–1	.75	.25
4–2	4–2	.67	.33	4–2	.75	.25	4–2	.60	.40
3–3	3–3	.51	.49	3–3	.56	.44	3–3	.47	.53
2–4	2–4	.41	.59	2–4	.39	.61	2–4	.43	.57
1–5	1–5	.21	.79	1–5	.24	.76	1–5	.18	.82
0–6	0–6	.10	.90	0–6	.11	.89	0–6	.09	.91
Median Belief Association Matrices									
6–0	6–0	1.00	.00	6–0	1.00	.00	6–0	1.00	.00
5–1	5–1	.90	.10	5–1	.90	.10	5–1	.80	.20
4–2	4–2	.70	.30	4–2	.75	.25	4–2	.60	.40
3–3	3–3	.50	.50	3–3	.50	.50	3–3	.50	.50
2–4	2–4	.40	.60	2–4	.40	.60	2–4	.34	.66
1–5	1–5	.10	.90	1–5	.20	.80	1–5	.10	.90
0–6	0–6	.00	1.00	0–6	.00	1.00	0–6	.00	1.00

Note. C = correct, I = incorrect.

An analysis was also conducted to test for sensitivity to the correctness of the response. The estimates of the different distributions of groups when the group response would be correct were compared with those when the group would be incorrect. This analysis indicated that the participants were somewhat sensitive to the influence of correctness, with correct group responses being perceived as significantly more likely (M = 53.8%) than incorrect responses (M = 46.2%), $F(1, 329) = 113.31$, $p < .0001$, partial $\eta^2 = .26$. These responses are different from the 50%–50% that would be expected if the participants did not believe correctness had an influence on group recognition responses.

The responses to the judgments of group metamemory indicate that the group members believed groups were more likely to respond correctly to an item if "true" was the correct response. Because this aspect of group recognition memory performance was not identified in the original analyses of the group recognition memory data set (Hinsz, 1990), an analysis was conducted to determine whether this belief was accurate. The pattern of results observed in the original data set did not confirm the group metamemory judgments. Groups were about equally likely to respond correctly to a recognition item if the false response was correct (83.73%) than if the true response was correct (82.22%), with this difference being nonsignificant, $\chi^2(1, N = 3,025) = 1.15$, $p > .28$. This result suggests that the group members had inaccurate beliefs that whether a recognition item had true or false as a correct response is a variable that influences group recognition memory performance.

The issue of the accuracy of the group member metamemory can be addressed by determining if the metamemory judgments vary with changes in the distribution of group members and other characteristics. Note that the mean responses varied with different distributions of member responses indicating group members were responsive to situations that also influence group recognition memory performance. If the group members thought that chance processes were involved in group recognition memory responses, then 50%–50% responses should be expected for each distribution of member responses. This was not the case, indicating that the students had some metamemory that some factors influenced groups responding correctly or incorrectly. The metamemory judgments did suggest that the group members were influenced by changes in the way the recognition memory situation was described. There was some accuracy in the members' metamemory in that group members responded differently to changes in the distributions of member responses and the correctness of the response, but inaccuracy in the views of the influence of items being stated with true or false as the correct response.

Sharedness of Mental Models

The next question addressed is the degree to which group members might share the same mental model of group recognition memory. The more similar the mental models, the more group members are believed to be approaching the same situation with beliefs and expectations that are shared. If the mental models were different or unshared, then the members' beliefs and expectations would appear not to mesh.

Given the mental model structure used to represent the members' metamemory, the intraclass correlation is used as an index of sharedness. An intraclass correlation was calculated to determine the degree of consistency among the group members for the responses to the 14 metamemory items used to assess the mental model of group recognition memory. The intraclass correlation was relatively high for these groups (.68) and was clearly significantly different from zero, $F(13, 4277) = 695.65$, $p < .001$. This intraclass correlation indicates the overall level of reliability of the group member responses to the 14 items, but it may mask a variety of potential differences in the level of consistency for the various groups. Therefore, an additional analysis was conducted that examined the intraclass correlation for the 14 judgments by the group members of each of the 55 groups. The intraclass correlation by group varied from .28 to .93 ($M = .68$, $SD = .15$). This analysis suggests that groups were relatively homogeneous with regard to the degree of consistency in the responses of the group members to the 14 judgments. These results also suggest that there is at least a moderate level of sharedness of the metamemory among the group members.

Although the preceding intraclass correlation results suggest that members of the groups share metamemory as assessed with the judgments, these results might occur for a different reason. The intraclass correlation could be relatively high because the group members might all respond in a similar fashion to the 14 judgments regardless of the group of which they are members. If this were the case, then the intraclass correlation for the participants to the 14 items would be about the same value as the intraclass correlation for the responses when membership in a group is considered. Analyses did reflect this later pattern, with the intraclass correlation among group member judgments disregarding group membership (.68) being virtually identical to the intraclass correlation when group membership was considered (.68).

Another way the question of the sharedness of the metamemories can be addressed is to examine if members of one group respond differently from members of different groups. If participating in a group leads the group members to respond more alike, then this suggests the groups would tend to homogenize the responses of its members. An intraclass correlation can be calculated to determine the degree to which members of one group are more alike in their responses than they resemble members of other groups (Kenny & LaVoie, 1985). The observed intraclass correlation that addresses this question is −.01, suggesting that members of a group did *not* respond more like each other than they responded like members of other groups. This leads to the conclusion that although members of a group did respond in a similar fashion to the 14 items assessing metamemory, they are not similar because they are members of that group. Rather, all members of all groups responded in a similar fashion, regardless of the group of which they were members.

DISCUSSION

This study addresses a number of issues regarding metacognition in groups. In particular, this chapter examines metamemory of group members for the way they consider how their groups perform a group recognition memory task. Metamemory is used to illustrate the way that group members think that their groups perform cognitive tasks (i.e., metacognition). The mental model concept was described to help address a number of the questions raised in this chapter. One formulation of mental models, the belief association matrix, was used to demonstrate ways of solving conceptual problems that arise when metacognition in groups is considered. The results of the study answer some of the questions raised as well as illustrate the methods of conceptualization and analysis used to address the questions. The remainder of this chapter considers the issues initially outlined and how this conceptualization and study enhance one's understanding of these issues.

Accuracy of Member Metamemory

Group member metamemory was partially accurate and somewhat inaccurate. It is clear that the group members were aware of the impact of consensus on group recognition memory performance. The group members did expect that the distribution of group member responses (e.g., four correct and two incorrect) would influence the likelihood the group would get the recognition item correct. However, the group members underestimated the influence of majorities and overestimated the influence of minorities, particularly minorities that were incorrect (see Table 3.2). The group members' metamemory did not fully account for the impact of group members accurately recognizing the correct response (i.e., correctness). Thus, the metamemory of the group members was accurate to a degree in terms of sensitivity to factors that influence group recognition memory performance, but the group members did not have complete understanding of group recognition memory processes. This result is similar to that found for metamemory of individuals in that they have imperfect knowledge about their own cognitions (Nelson, 1996).

A surprising result observed from this data set was the impact of the correct response being a true or false response. Because metamemory judgments were assessed in this experiment with true or false responses indicated as the correct response, the participants could demonstrate some metamemory that was not anticipated. The participants in this experiment believed that groups would respond more correctly to "true" responses. Analysis of the original group recognition responses (Hinsz, 1990) did not reveal this pattern. Groups were equally likely to get a group response correct if the correct response was false than if it were true. The group members' metamemory judgments indicated an error of commission in that they believed some processes occurred (i.e., true more likely to be correct) when they did not. In group memory research, errors of commission are also reported in which groups report remembering material that was not initially presented (Clark & Stephenson, 1989; Hinsz, 1990). This metamemory of true responses being judged as more likely to be correct is inaccurate for the group recognition responses the group members made. Therefore, in addition to concluding that the group members had somewhat accurate metamemory, it is also necessary to say that the group members had inaccurate metamemory. As more is learned about the memory processes of interacting groups, it will be possible to better determine the degree of accuracy of group members' metamemory.

Representing Group Memory Processes

The matrix conceptualization of group recognition memory performance illustrated in Table 3.1 provided a means to consider the influence of both consensus and correctness on group responses. As a simple structure, the matrix in Table 3.1 elegantly summarized much of the knowledge about group recognition memory performance. Moreover, it provided cell entries indicating the probability that specific distributions of group member responses would lead groups to select the correct or incorrect response. This matrix provides a framework and template on which to consider the metamemory of group members. This led to the adoption of the mental model concept as a means of representing metamemory in groups.

The participants in this study were asked to make judgments about the ways they expected groups to respond to recognition memory items under a number of conditions. These judgments reflected the group members' metamemory and also the group members' beliefs and expectations about how a group would operate and function when confronting a recognition memory task. Because these metamemory judgments correspond to particular aspects of the belief association matrix, the members' responses illustrate a structure for their metamemory that can be considered a model of the members' mental model of the group's recognition memory. The analysis of these metamemory judgments suggests that the participants were quite capable of making these judgments. Moreover, the group members' judgments had substantial internal consistency. As an initial attempt at assessing metamemory, it appears that the belief association matrix approach was successful in measuring the intended aspects of the metamemory of group members.

Mental Models

This chapter used the mental model concept as a way of representing the structure of the group members' beliefs and expectations about the ways groups remember. A mental model might reflect group members' schemas regarding how the group interaction on a recognition task leads to group memory performance outcomes. Mental models are particularly useful in this context because they help specify the beliefs of interest and their relation to group memory outcomes. Mental models have been implicated in a number of group performance and group interaction situations (Cannon-Bowers et al., 1993; Hinsz, 1995; Klimoski & Mohammed, 1994; Rentsch & Hall, 1994; Stout et al., 1996); however, the great difficulty with the application of mental models in groups has been their assessment (Hinsz, 1995; Langan-Fox et al., 2000).

In this chapter, the mental model concept was linked to the social-psychological notions of beliefs and expectations to provide a basis for a *model* of mental models termed the belief association matrix. The belief association matrix related important states of groups facing a recognition memory task (distributions of member responses) and the potential group recognition outcomes (correct or incorrect responses). The belief association matrix, as a model of the mental models members may have for group recognition memory performance, provides a way to consider a variety of issues regarding metamemory and metacognition in groups. Consequently, the belief association matrix contributes to the capability to use the mental model concept when considering metacognition in groups. The belief association matrix is merely one approach to considering mental models of groups (Hinsz, 1995). Other approaches might also contribute to one's understanding of metacognition in groups, but the utility of the belief association matrix is apparent as one awaits the potential advances provided by other approaches.

Shared Mental Models

The analyses of sharedness of metamemory judgments suggest an interesting pattern. Overall, group members were relatively similar (.68) in their metamemory judgments. That is, it appears that group members shared much of their mental models of group recognition memory performance as assessed here. However, on closer inspection, this similarity is common to all members of all the groups and was not specific to members of particular groups. That is, the group members were similar to each other in their metamemory judgments but did not have distinctive metamemory or mental models for the particular group of which they were members. All group members were as similar to each other as they were to members of their own specific group. Although this analysis does not reflect the potential of shared mental models, it does illustrate one way the sharedness of mental models can be assessed. The approach used to assess the sharedness of mental models appears to be useful even if the results were not as intriguing as hoped.

The metamemory judgments indicated that the group members believed that recognition items that had "true" as the correct responses were more likely to be responded to correctly by the group than if the correct response was "false." This belief was inconsistent with the actual relationship observed in the group recognition responses. Although there are limitations to this finding, it provides a basis for discussing potential pitfalls in the use of shared mental models. A shared mental model that is inaccurate and applied by the group members as if it is appropriate could lead to very biased actions on the part of the group members and to destructive outcomes (e.g., shared stereotypes of outgroups and shared illusion of invulnerability as contributing factors to the fiascos associated with groupthink; Janis, 1982). It is important to recognize both the promise and pitfalls of shared mental models for the processes and performance of small groups.

One reason for the interest in mental models is their potential to contribute to one's understanding of how task groups and teams function (Salas, Dickinson, Converse, & Tannenbaum, 1992). If people share mental representations of how groups act and members interact, they should function more effectively and efficiently. Although there has been much discussion about the importance shared mental models for effective group functioning, research has been much less successful in finding ways to accurately measure mental models, and even less able to assess the sharedness of mental models. The belief association matrix as a model of mental models provides a basis on which to assess the sharedness of metamemory in a group and the degree of similarity of the assessed mental models of group functioning.

Mental Model Representations

This chapter postulates that groups and group members have specific mental representations that help in the understanding of metacognition in groups. Mental models were selected for use with metamemory because they appear to provide the best structure for the memory processes of groups. A variety of other cognitive structures could be implicated for memory processes, but perhaps none of these are accurate representations of the cognitive processes of groups. Group members' actual mental representations probably differ in important ways from the mental representations described in this chapter. Research examining mental representations of groups is still in its infancy, and it is difficult to foresee how it might develop. Further explorations of the mental representations of group members and the use of mental representations in groups may better illuminate the actual features of the mental representations that are used in groups.

This discussion of mental representations in groups does lead to an important question that needs to be resolved: Can anything of value be gained by postulating a mental representation at the group level? Is it reasonable to speak of a group mental model or a similar group-level mental representation (team mental models; Klimoski & Mohammed, 1994)? An important question is how similar and shared are the cognitive representations of group members (e.g., shared stereotypes). Although much may be gained by considering the mental representations of group members, it may be premature to speak of a group-level mental representation (Hutchins, 1991). Mental representations occur at the level of the individual and in the minds of individuals. These individuals may be members of groups, but a group-level mental representation harks back to the debate about a group mind (Allport, 1924; see Wegner, 1987, 1995, for a different perspective). Consequently, I refrain from referring to group-level mental representations (e.g., group mental models) but rather describe group member mental representations or the implications of mental representations in groups (e.g., metacognition in groups).

Some Strengths and Limitations of This Study

The data collected in this study provide a strong basis to examine the various issues considered. The study included judgments from members of 55 different six-person groups. The groups responded to 60 recognition items, and the 330 group members made 14 metamemory judgments that reflected the important metamemory characteristics of consensus and correctness. Consequently, a sufficient sample was used in this experiment. Of course, generalization is hampered because this study focused on one recognition test performed with university students who were asked to remember one set of rich social material (i.e., a job interview).

One important limitation of this study is that the groups may not have interacted sufficiently to develop distinct representations about how particular groups operated and functioned. If the groups had a longer and richer history, they may have had mental models that were shared among the members of a group and yet distinct from members of other groups (Hinsz, 1995). Moreover, the metacognitive judgments of the group members could have been based on more experience and may have reflected stronger beliefs that were predictive of their group's actual performance of a cognitive task. These limitations of this study provide clear direction that future research can explore.

Metacognition in Groups and Teams

Metacognition has only recently emerged as a topic of consideration in social psychology (Metcalfe, 1998) and small group research (Hinsz et al., 1997). Metacognition of groups is the way group members understand how groups process information and perform cognitive tasks. The aim of this chapter is to begin to describe the way that metacognition can lead to new explorations and explanations of the ways groups process information and perform cognitive tasks. Metacognition represents a way in which group member beliefs and expectations influence member actions in the group, which in turn may affect group operations and functioning, and perhaps the eventual outcomes of group interaction. In this chapter, metacognition in groups is explored with regard to a number of issues regarding how information is processed in groups, in particular group remembering. The study reported involved group members making metamemory judgments that assessed their beliefs about the ways groups would respond to recognition test items. The metamemory of group members was found to be partially accurate and somewhat inaccurate. The results of the analysis of the sharedness of mental models of group performance were not as anticipated, but were intriguing.

Metacognition has been considered an important element in the teamwork strategies that appear to be critical to a number of dynamic task environments (Hinsz, 1998; Morgan & Bowers, 1995). In these situations, the members of the team need to have a shared understanding of the problem (i.e., shared mental model) and who will do what, when, and how (Hinsz, 1998). Moreover, effective teams will have developed strategies for coming to the aid of other team members in times of need (Harris & Barnes-Farrell, 1997). When team members understand and anticipate the actions of other team members, they can act and react in a more efficient fashion. In these situations, one can see that metacognitive strategies are used to help the group members interact in a more efficient fashion and to process information more effectively. Wherever groups are found, the beliefs and expectations that group members have about how their groups operate and function might influence the way that they act in the group, and ultimately impact the outcomes of the group and the members' relationships with the group. Consequently, this attempt to examine the impact of metacognition in groups demonstrates new ways of thinking about the processes involved in groups and has the potential to greatly influence one's understanding of group and team performance and processes.

REFERENCES

Allport, F. H. (1924). *Social psychology*. Boston: Houghton Mifflin.

Ancona, D. G. (1990). Outward bound: Strategies for team survival in an organization. *Academy of Management Journal, 33*, 334–365.

Arrow, H., McGrath, J. E., & Berdahl, J. L. (2000). *Small groups as complex systems: Formation, coordination, development, and adaptation*. Thousand Oaks, CA: Sage.

Artzt, A. F., & Amour-Thomas, E. (1997). Mathematical problem solving in small groups: Exploring the interplay of students' metacognitive behaviors, perceptions, and ability levels. *Journal of Mathematical Behavior, 16*, 63–74.

Birnbaum, M. H. (1973). The devil rides again: Correlation as an index of fit. *Psychological Bulletin, 79*, 239–242.

Brehmer, B. (1984). The role of judgment in small-group conflict and decision making. In G. M. Stephenson & J. H. Davis (Eds.), *Progress in applied social psychology* (Vol. 2., pp. 163–183). New York: Wiley.

Cannon-Bowers, J. A., & Salas, E. (2001). Reflections on shared cognition. *Journal of Organizational Behavior, 22,* 195–202.

Cannon-Bowers, J. A., Salas, E., & Converse, S. A. (1993). Shared mental models in team decision making. In N. J. Castellan Jr. (Ed.), *Individual and group decision making* (pp. 221–246). Hillsdale, NJ: Erlbaum.

Clark, N. K., & Stephenson, G. M. (1989). Group remembering. In P. Paulus (Ed.), *Psychology of group influence* (2nd ed., pp. 357–391). Hillsdale, NJ: Erlbaum.

Cohen, S. G., & Bailey, D. E. (1997). What makes teams work: Group effectiveness research from the shop floor to the executive suite. *Journal of Management, 23,* 239–290.

Davidson, J. E., Deuser, R., & Steinberg, R. J. (1994). The role of metacognition in problem solving. In J. Metcalfe & A. P. Shimamura (Eds.), *Metacognition* (pp. 207–226). Cambridge, MA: MIT Press.

Davis, J. H. (1973). Group decision and social interaction: A theory of social decision schemes. *Psychological Review, 80,* 97–125.

Eagly, A. H., & Chaikin, S. (1993). *The psychology of attitudes.* Fort Worth, TX: Harcourt Brace Jovanovich.

Endsley, M. R. (1995). Toward a theory of situation awareness in dynamic systems. *Human Factors, 37,* 65–84.

Endsley, M. R., & Jones, W. M. (1997). *Situation awareness information dominance and information warfare* (Tech. Rep.). Wright-Patterson AFB, OH: United States Air Force Armstrong Laboratory.

Fishbein, M., & Ajzen, I. (1975). *Belief, attitude, intention, and behavior: An introduction to theory and research.* Reading, MA: Addison-Wesley.

Fiske, S. T., & Taylor, S. E. (1991). *Social cognition* (2nd ed.). New York: McGraw-Hill.

Flavell, J. H. (1979). Metacognition and cognitive monitoring: A new area of cognitive–developmental inquiry. *American Psychologist, 34,* 906–911.

Gentner, D., & Stevens, A. L. (1983). *Mental models.* Hillsdale, NJ: Erlbaum.

Guzzo, R. A., & Salas, E. (Eds.). (1995). *Team effectiveness and decision making in organizations.* San Francisco: Jossey-Bass.

Harris, T. C., & Barnes-Farrell, J. L. (1997). Components of teamwork: Impact on evaluations of contributions to work team effectiveness. *Journal of Applied Social Psychology, 27,* 1694–1715.

Herrmann, D. J. (1982). Know thy memory: The use of questionnaires to assess and study memory. *Psychological Bulletin, 92,* 434–452.

Hinsz, V. B. (1990). Cognitive and consensus processes in group recognition memory performance. *Journal of Personality and Social Psychology, 59,* 705–718.

Hinsz, V. B. (1995). Mental models of groups as social systems: Considerations of specification and assessment. *Small Group Research, 26,* 200–233.

Hinsz, V. B. (1998). *Conceptualizing crew performance in dynamic task environments: A hierarchy of embedded action-control models* (Final Report to the AFOSR Summer

Faculty Research Program). Wright-Patterson AFB, OH: Air Force Research Laboratory.

Hinsz, V. B., Tindale, R. S., & Vollrath, D. A. (1997). The emerging conceptualization of groups as information processors. *Psychological Bulletin, 121,* 43–64.

Hutchins, E. (1991). The social organization of distributed cognition. In L. B. Resnick, J. M. Levine, & S. D. Teasley (Eds.), *Perspectives on socially shared cognition* (pp. 283–307). Washington, DC: American Psychological Association.

Ilgen, D. (1999). Teams embedded in organizations: Some implications. *American Psychologist, 54,* 129–139.

Janis, I. (1982). *Groupthink* (2nd ed.). Boston: Houghton-Mifflin.

Johnson-Laird, P. N. (1983). *Mental models.* Cambridge, MA: Harvard University Press.

Kenny, D. A., & LaVoie, L. (1985). Separating individual and group effects. *Journal of Personality and Social Psychology, 48,* 339–348.

Klimoski, R., & Mohammed, S. (1994). Team mental model: Construct or metaphor? *Journal of Management, 20,* 403–437.

Kraiger, K., & Wenzel, L. H. (1997). Conceptual development and empirical evaluation of measures of shared mental models as indicators of team effectiveness. In M. T. Brannick, E. Salas, & C. Prince (Eds.), *Team performance assessment and measurement: Theory methods, and applications* (pp. 63–84). Mahwah, NJ: Erlbaum.

Langan-Fox, J., Code, S., & Langfield-Smith, K. (2000). Team mental models: Techniques, methods, and analytic approaches. *Human Factors, 42,* 242–271.

Larson, J. R., & Christensen, C. (1993). Groups as problem solving units: Toward a new meaning of social cognition. *British Journal of Social Psychology, 32,* 5–30.

Laughlin, P. R. (1980). Social combination processes in cooperative problem-solving groups on verbal intellective tasks. In M. Fishbein (Ed.), *Progress in social psychology* (pp. 127–155). Hillsdale, NJ: Erlbaum.

Levine, J. M., Higgins, E. T., & Choi, H. S. (2000). Development of strategic norms in groups. *Organizational Behavior and Human Decision Processes, 82,* 88–101.

Levine, J. M., & Moreland, R. L. (1998). Small groups. In D. T. Gilbert, S. T. Fiske, & G. Lindzey (Eds.), *Handbook of social psychology* (4th ed., Vol. 2; pp. 415–469). Boston: McGraw-Hill.

Levine, J. M., Resnick, L. B., & Higgins, E. T. (1993). Social foundations of cognition. *Annual Review of Psychology, 44,* 585–612.

Littlepage, G., Robison, W., & Reddington, K. (1997). Effects of task experience and group experience on group performance, member ability, and recognition of expertise. *Organizational Behavior and Human Decision Processes, 69,* 133–147.

Mathieu, J. E., Heffner, T. S., Goodwin, G. F., Salas, E., & Cannon-Bowers, J. A. (2000). The influence of shared mental models on team process and performance. *Journal of Applied Psychology, 85,* 273–282.

Metcalfe, J. (Ed.). (1998). Metacognition [Special issue]. *Personality and Social Psychology Review, 2.*

Metcalfe, J., & Shimamura, A. P. (1994). *Metacognition: Knowing about knowing.* Cambridge, MA: MIT Press.

Moreland, R. L., Hogg, M. A., & Hains, S. C. (1994). Back to the future: Social psychological research on groups. *Journal of Experimental Social Psychology, 30,* 527–555.

Morgan, B. B., & Bowers, C. A. (1995). Teamwork stress: Implications for team decision making. In R. A. Guzzo & E. Salas (Eds.), *Team effectiveness and decision making in organizations* (pp. 262–290). San Francisco: Jossey-Bass.

Nelson, T. O. (1992). *Metacognition: Core readings.* Boston: Allyn & Bacon.

Nelson, T. O. (1996). Consciousness and metacognition. *American Psychologist, 51,* 102–116.

Nelson, T. O., & Narens, L. (1990). Metamemory: A theoretical framework and new findings. *Psychology of Learning and Motivation, 26,* 125–171.

Nisbett, R. E., & Wilson, T. D. (1977). Telling more than we can know: Verbal reports on mental processes. *Psychological Review, 84,* 231–259.

Norman, D. A. (1983). Some observations on mental models. In D. Gentner & A. L. Stevens (Eds.), *Mental models* (pp. 7–14). Hillsdale, NJ: Erlbaum.

Nye, J. L., & Brower, A. M. (1996). *What's social about social cognition? Research on socially shared cognition in small groups.* Thousand Oaks, CA: Sage.

Orasanu, J. M. (1993). Decision-making in the cockpit. In E. L. Wiener, B. G. Kanki, & R. L. Helmreich (Eds.), *Cockpit resource management* (pp. 137–172). San Diego, CA: Academic Press.

Peterson, E., Mitchell, T. R., Thompson, L., & Burr, R. (2000). Collective efficacy and aspects of shared mental models as predictors of performance over time in work groups. *Group Processes and Intergroup Relations, 3,* 296–316.

Rasker, P. C., Post, W. M., & Schraagen, J. M. C. (2000). Effects of two types of intra-team feedback on developing a shared mental model in Command & Control teams. *Ergonomics, 43,* 1167–1189.

Rentsch, J. R., & Hall, R. J. (1994). Members of great teams think alike: A model of team effectiveness and schema similarity among team members. *Advances in Interdisciplinary Studies of Work Teams, 1,* 223–261.

Resnick, L. B., Levine, J. M., & Teasley, S. D. (Eds.). (1991). *Perspectives on socially shared cognition.* Washington, DC: American Psychological Association.

Rouse, W. B., Cannon-Bowers, J. A., & Salas, E. (1992). The role of mental models in team performance in complex systems. *IEEE Transactions on Systems, Man, & Cybernetics, 22,* 1296–1308.

Rouse, W. B., & Morris, N. M. (1986). On looking into the black box: Prospects and limits in the search for mental models. *Psychological Bulletin, 100,* 349–363.

Salas, E., Dickinson, T. L., Converse, S. A., & Tannenbaum, S. I. (1992). Toward an understanding of team performance and training. In R. W. Swezey & E. Salas (Eds.), *Teams: Their training and performance* (pp. 3–29). Norwood, NJ: Ablex.

Salas, E., Prince, C., Baker, D. P., & Shrestha, L. (1995). Situation awareness in team performance: Implications for measurement and training. *Human Factors, 37,* 123–136.

Sanna, L. J., & Parks, C. D. (1997). Group research trends in social and organizational psychology: Whatever happened to intragroup research? *Psychological Science, 8,* 261–267.

Shrout, P. E., & Fleiss, J. L. (1979). Intraclass correlations: Uses in assessing rater reliability. *Psychological Bulletin, 86,* 420–428.

Stephenson, G. M., Clark, N. K., & Wade, G. S. (1986). Meetings make evidence? An experimental study of collaborative and individual recall of a simulated police interrogation. *Journal of Personality and Social Psychology, 50,* 1113–1122.

Stewart, D. D., & Stasser, G. (1995). Expert role assignment and information sampling during collective recall and decision making. *Journal of Personality and Social Psychology, 69,* 619–628.

Stout, R., Cannon-Bowers, J. A., & Salas, E. (1996). The role of shared mental models in developing team situation awareness: Implications for training. *Training Research Journal, 2,* 85–116.

Thompson, L. L., Levine, J. M., & Messick, D. M. (1999). *Shared cognition in organizations.* Hillsdale, NJ: Erlbaum.

Tindale, R. S., Kameda, T., & Hinsz, V. B. (2003). Group decision making. In M. A. Hogg & J. T. Cooper (Eds.), *Sage handbook of social psychology* (pp. 381–403). Thousand Oaks, CA: Sage.

Tindale, R. S., Smith, C. M., Thomas, L. S., Filkins, J., & Sheffey, S. (1996). Shared representations and asymmetric social influence processes in small groups. In J. H. Davis & E. Witte (Eds.), *Understanding group behavior: Consensual action by small groups* (Vol. 1, pp. 81–104). Hillsdale, NJ: Erlbaum.

Vollrath, D. A., Sheppard, B. H., Hinsz, V. B., & Davis, J. H. (1989). Memory performance by decision-making groups and individuals. *Organizational Behavior and Human Decision Processes, 43,* 289–300.

Wegner, D. M. (1987). Transactive memory: A contemporary analysis of the group mind. In B. Mullen & G. R. Goethals (Eds.), *Theories of group behavior* (pp. 185–208). New York: Springer-Verlag.

Wegner, D. M. (1995). A computer network model of human transactive memory. *Social Cognition, 13,* 319–339.

Wegner, D. M., Erber, R., & Raymond, P. (1991). Transactive memory in close relationships. *Journal of Personality and Social Psychology, 61,* 923–929.

Wilson, J. R., & Rutherford, A. (1989). Mental models: Theory and application in human factors. *Human Factors, 31,* 617–634.

Young, M. F., & McNeese, M. D. (1995). A situated cognition approach to problem solving. In P. Hancock, J. Flach, J. Caird, & K. Vincente (Eds.), *Local applications to the ecological approach to human-machine systems* (pp. 359–391). Hillsdale, NJ: Erlbaum.

II

METHODOLOGICAL ISSUES SURROUNDING TEAM COGNITION

4

COMMUNICATION OVERHEAD: THE HIDDEN COST OF TEAM COGNITION

JEAN MACMILLAN, ELLIOT E. ENTIN, AND DANIEL SERFATY

To function effectively, a team must act as an information-processing unit, maintaining an awareness of the situation or context in which it is functioning and acquiring and using information to act in that situation. This *team cognition* differs from individual cognition, of course, because each team member acts as an individual information processor. For a team to act in concert to achieve common goals, the team must have shared information about both the situation and the other team members. Team cognition thus requires communication—a process that has no direct analog in individual cognition—in order for the team to build and maintain a shared mental model of the situation. Because communication is essential to team performance, effective team cognition has a communication "overhead" associated with the exchange of information among team members. Communication requires both time and cognitive resources, and, to the extent that communication can be made less necessary or more efficient, team performance can benefit as a result.

The team experiment efforts reported here were sponsored by the Office of Naval Research (ONR) and the Air Force Research Laboratory (AFRL). We would like to express our appreciation for the support and review of Willard Vaughan and Gerald Malecki at ONR and Sam Schiflett and Linda Elliott at AFRL.

61

In this chapter we present a theoretical framework that describes the relationship between team communication behaviors and team performance. Specifically, we look at how the *structure* of the team, as defined by both the nature of the team's tasks and the allocation of task responsibilities to individuals on the team, affects the coordination requirements for the team, and how those coordination requirements generate the need for communication among team members. Given a need for coordination and communication to accomplish the team's tasks, we examine how other factors such as the ability to preplan team actions affects the need to communicate to achieve effective performance. The intent is to show a linked pattern of relationships that flow from the nature of the team's tasks and the structure of the team through a series of intermediate variables such as the need for coordination, the need for mutual awareness among team members, the need for communication, and the efficiency of that communication, to affect the team's performance.

The theoretical framework that is presented has been developed over a number of years through an iterative process of top-down development of theory and bottom-up examination of empirical results. Theories can guide measure development by suggesting what it is important to measure. In contrast, process measures that have been empirically shown to be associated with team performance can shape theory by identifying patterns that the theories must explain. Theoretical explanations for observed relationships among phenomena can be used to extend empirical findings to predict outcomes in situations other than the ones that have been observed.

The framework is based on empirical patterns found in two team experiments. The first experiment focused on the design of an optimal team structure for a Joint Task Force team, and the other examined the value of electronic collaborative planning tools in facilitating the performance of a team performing a humanitarian assistance airlift mission. Although the experiments had different purposes and were driven by somewhat different theoretical constructs, there is enough similarity in the constructs and the data to support the construction of a metaframework that links the two empirical patterns into an overall "story" about how team structure affects the communication behaviors that underlie effective team performance.

The framework draws both on previous theories about the nature of team coordination and communication and on previous measures of communication behavior. We begin by briefly reviewing both theory and measures, pointing out how our work builds on and extends prior studies. Next we present results for two different team experiments and develop two partially overlapping theoretical frameworks. Finally, we combine the two frameworks into a single framework that is based on both sets of experimental results and discuss how this framework will help guide our future research.

THEORETICAL CONSTRUCTS AND MEASURES FOR TEAM COORDINATION AND COMMUNICATION

Coordinated action lies at the heart of effective team performance (Kleinman & Serfaty, 1989; Orasanu & Salas, 1993), and a variety of approaches have been taken to understand the nature of that coordination and the role that communication plays in coordination. A theoretical construct that has proved useful in understanding the nature of coordinated behavior is the distinction between *implicit* and *explicit coordination* (see, e.g., E. E. Entin & Serfaty, 1999; Stout, Cannon-Bowers, Salas, & Milanovich, 1999). Explicit coordination requires that team members communicate to articulate their plans, actions, and responsibilities, whereas implicit coordination describes the ability of team members to act in concert without the need for overt communication. For implicit coordination to be successful, team members must have a shared understanding of the situation and an accurate understanding of each other's tasks and responsibilities. The term *shared mental model* is often used to describe this shared team awareness (Cannon-Bowers, Salas, & Converse, 1993; Fiore, Salas, & Cannon-Bowers, 2001; McIntyre & Salas, 1995; Orasanu, 1990).

It is well understood that the advantages and disadvantages of implicit and explicit coordination (and, hence, the need for a shared mental model among team members) depend on the nature of the task and the task environment (Fiore et al., 2001). In aviation environments, for example, the failure to communicate explicitly has been linked to failures and accidents (Foushee, 1984). On the other hand, we have suggested in prior work (Serfaty, Entin, & Johnston, 1998) that the ability to coordinate implicitly can provide an advantage to teams during periods of intense task load by reducing the communication overhead needed for coordinated action. Implicit coordination is associated with effective performance if, and only if, team members have an *accurate* understanding of each other's needs, responsibilities, and expected actions; and communication may be necessary to build that understanding. In studies of the relationship between aircrew communication patterns and effective performance, Orasanu (1990, 1993; Orasanu & Fischer, 1992) found that effective aircrews alternated between implicit and explicit coordination, using communication during periods of relatively low task load to prepare and plan so that they could coordinate implicitly, based on an accurate shared understanding, during high-demand periods.

Coordination and Communication Measures

Because of the critical role that communication plays in a team's ability to achieve coordinated action, the measurement and analysis of communication behaviors have been an ongoing focus of team research. One useful approach has been the development and validation of rating scales for assessing the quality of communication behaviors in the team (Johnson, Smith-Jentsch, & Cannon-Bowers, 1997; Smith-Jentsch, Zeisig, Acton, & McPherson, 1998) and the development of behaviorally anchored rating scales for communication behaviors that are tied to specific scenario events (Dwyer, Fowlkes, Oser, Salas, & Lane, 1997; Fowlkes, Lane, Salas, Franz, & Oser, 1994). Other methods have categorized communications by type, based either on post hoc analysis of video, audio, or text records (e.g., Orasanu, 1990) or on real-time categorization performed during experiments or exercises (e.g., Serfaty et al., 1998) to analyze the relationship between the number of communications of different types and team performance. Some recent approaches have focused on sequential analysis of communication using statistical sequential analysis techniques (Sanderson & Fisher, 1994) to identify communication patterns such as feedback loops (Bowers, Jentsch, Salas, & Braun, 1998). Automated text processing technology such as latent semantic analysis (Landauer, Foltz, & Laham, 1998) has been used to identify sequential communication patterns without the need for extensive hand coding of communications data (Kiekel, Cooke, Foltz, & Shope, 2000).

Over the past decade, we have developed and used several measures, described below, that explicitly link the team's knowledge about each other and about their shared tasks (their team cognition) with the frequency and type of their communications. These measures are based on the theory that shared awareness among the team members (i.e., a shared mental model) results in the ability to coordinate implicitly, resulting in more efficient communication (i.e., a lower communication overhead for team cognition).

Anticipation Ratio

The anticipation ratio is a measure of communication efficiency that has proved to be associated with effective team performance for a variety of different types of teams (E. B. Entin & Entin, 2000; E. B. Entin, Entin, & Serfaty, 2000; E. E. Entin, 1999; E. E. Entin & Serfaty, 1999; E. E. Entin, Serfaty, & Deckert, 1994; E. E. Entin, Serfaty, & Kerrigan, 1998; Serfaty et al., 1998). The anticipation ratio measure calculates the ratio of the number of communications transferring information to the number of communications requesting information. Values greater than one indicate that team members "pushed" (sent) information more frequently than they "pulled" (requested) information, and that they anticipated each other's needs for information without being asked.

Mutual Organizational Awareness

We have also developed and used measures of *mutual organizational awareness* within the team (E. B. Entin & Entin, 2000) that we expect to be associated with higher levels of team performance. These measures assess the extent to which each team member had an accurate understanding, at selected points in time, of the tasks being performed by the other team members and can be viewed as indicators of the extent to which the team had a shared mental model of each other's activities. Our mutual awareness measures typically focus specifically on awareness of the activities of each of the team members at selected points in the scenario, in contrast to team situation awareness measures that typically have a broader focus, including a shared awareness of external scenario events and a shared understanding of the team's mission or goals (e.g., Bolstad & Endsley, 1999, 2000). Note that we use the term *organizational* here to describe mutual understanding within the context of the team and their task environment rather than within the broader scope of an entire organization.

Our theoretical explanation for the expected association of the anticipation ratio and the mutual awareness measures with team performance, and with each other, is based on the theory and findings concerning shared mental models and implicit coordination discussed earlier. Teams that have a more accurate awareness of each other's roles and actions can communicate more efficiently—more frequently transferring appropriate information without being asked. The ability to effectively push information reduces the communication overhead for the team because only one message, rather than two, is needed for information transfer. This communication efficiency reduces workload and can result in better performance. The reduction in the time and resources required for communication is especially important when the team is experiencing periods of heavy task loading (Serfaty et al., 1998; Urban, Weaver, Bowers, & Rhodenizer, 1996).

THE ROLE OF TEAM STRUCTURE IN TEAM PERFORMANCE

We have been involved for the past 6 years in a research program, sponsored by the Office of Naval Research, examining innovative team structures and organizational architectures and their relationship to team performance. A major contribution of this Adaptive Architectures for Command and Control (A2C2) program (Serfaty, 1996) has been the development of methods for designing team structures that are optimally suited to the team's mission (Levchuk, Pattipati, & Kleinman, 1998; MacMillan et al., 2001). Participation in the A2C2 program has given us a sense of how the design of a team's structure affects the team's need to coordinate for effective performance and how the need for coordination affects the communication that is necessary for team cognition. *Team structure*, in this context, refers not just to the lines of authority in the team (who reports to whom) but also to how the team divides its tasks and responsibilities and controls its resources (including information) to perform its mission.

We turn next to a discussion of two of our experiments on team structure, using the empirical relationships that were found in each experiment to construct an explanatory framework that links team structure to team performance through its effects on coordination and communication.

EXPERIMENT 1: JOINT TASK FORCE COMMAND TEAM WITH A STRUCTURE OPTIMIZED FOR ITS MISSION

The first experiment compares team performance, coordination, and communication behaviors under two different team structures, one that was optimized for the mission and one that reflects a more traditional Joint Task Force (JTF) organizational structure.

Optimized and Traditional Team Structures

As part of the A2C2 research program, a team at the University of Connecticut (Levchuk, Pattipati, & Kleinman, 1998, 1999) developed an organizational structure for a JTF team optimized for accomplishing a mission that involved an air- and sea-based operation to regain control of an allied country that had been taken over in a hostile invasion by a neighboring country. The mission involved the coordination of land-, sea-, and air-based forces to perform a sequence of operational tasks (e.g., take the beach, advance on the airport, take the airport) in the face of opposition by the enemy. Many of the tasks were sequentially interdependent (i.e., one had to be completed before another could be started), and most required the simultaneous use of several different types of resources (e.g., sensor and weapon platforms) for successful completion. The mission was to be accomplished by a six-person JTF command team.

The optimized team structure developed for the experiment was based primarily on two optimization objectives: simultaneously minimizing the coordination required to accomplish the mission and balancing workload across the team. These multiple objectives act to constrain each other, because the workload-balancing objective prevents the assignment of all tasks to only a few team members to minimize the coordination requirements.

Coordination is defined here by the need for team members to combine the resources under their control to successfully accomplish each task. Because almost all tasks in the mission required the use of multiple types of resources, reducing the need for coordination resulted in an organizational structure in which each team member controlled most, if not all, of the resources needed to accomplish a specific task. Team members were therefore able to act independently to accomplish many tasks because all of the resources needed for the task were under their direct control. In the experiment, this optimized organizational structure was compared with a more "traditional" JTF team structure, developed by subject matter experts, in which similar resources were controlled by the same node without explicit consideration of the need to coordinate their use in the mission.

The optimized team structure in this experiment allocated the team's resources so that team members could act more independently, thus reducing the need for coordination. One might argue that, at the extreme, such a design approach would result in a collection of independent individuals that was no longer a team in the usual sense of the word. The constraints of the team's mission were such that this was not a possibility, however. Many of the team's tasks could not be done independently by one team member because of the workload associated with them. Even under the optimized design, there was considerable need for coordination—it was simply less under the optimized structure than under the traditional design.

Performance Differences Under the Two Structures

The two team structures were "played out" in a simulation-based experiment, with 10 six-person teams of military officers from the Naval Postgraduate School in Monterey (E. E. Entin, 1999). Each team participated under both architectures, with the order counterbalanced to control for learning effects. Two types of summary performance measures were used in the experiment: simulation-based measures, which come directly from the simulation testbed, and observer-based measures, which were prepared by subject matter expert observers rating team behavior during the experiment sessions. For both types of performance measures, the performance of the six-person team using the structure that had been optimized for the mission was superior to the performance of the six-person team using the more traditional team structure that was developed by subject matter experts. The mean for the mission outcome measure under the optimized structure ($M = 83.7$, $SD = 2.14$) was significantly higher than the mean for the traditional structure ($M = 78.5$, $SD = 5.21$), $t(16) = 1.82$, $p < .05$. The mean for the observer's overall rating for the optimized structure ($M = 5.32$, $SD = 0.53$) was also significantly higher than the mean for the traditional structure ($M = 4.33$, $SD = 0.73$), $t(17) = 2.26$, $p < .05$.

Effects of Structure on Coordination

The optimized team structure was designed to achieve its results by minimizing the need for coordination (defined as the need for team members to work together to accomplish a task because each one controlled different resources needed for the task), and the results show that it was successful in this goal. Teams using the optimized structure achieved superior performance while taking significantly fewer coordination actions during the mission, as measured by the coordination rate. The mean coordination rate for the optimized structure ($M = 0.66$, $SD = 0.22$) was significantly lower than the mean for the traditional structure ($M = 1.12$, $SD = 0.31$), $t(17) = 3.55$, $p < .05$. As might be expected given the lower need for coordination, there was also significantly less communication (a lower communication rate) for teams using the optimized structure ($M = 6.30$, $SD = 1.53$) than for teams using the traditional structure ($M = 7.61$, $SD = 1.82$), $t(18) = 1.71$, $p < .05$.

Communication Anticipation Ratio

The optimized team structure also seems to have resulted in more *efficient* communication as measured by the anticipation ratio. The mean for the optimized structure ($M = 4.21$, $SD = 1.91$) was significantly higher than the mean for the traditional structure ($M = 2.67$, $SD = 1.26$), $t(17) = 1.72$, $p < .05$. This measure is based on a classification of verbal communications by the team members into information requests and information transfers (as distinguished from other categories), computing a count of each type and calculating the ratio of the latter to the former. Under the optimized structure, team members communicated less overall, and relatively more of those communications were information transfers rather than requests for information.

Mutual Organizational Awareness

Associated with the higher anticipation ratio, team members in the optimized structure had a more accurate awareness of the tasks being performed by other members of the team. The accuracy of the team's mutual organizational awareness was calculated on the basis of the results of a questionnaire administered to participants after each experiment session. Participants were asked to "think back" to a specified memorable point in the scenario (e.g., the team had just completed taking the north beach) and to name the task they were performing at that time using 12 predefined task categories as well as naming the tasks that each other team member was doing at that time. The average agreement between participants' self-ratings of tasks performed and the ratings of the other team members provides a measure of how accurately the team members as a whole understood what each of the other team members were doing. The percentage of tasks correctly estimated in the optimized condition ($M = 37.4$, $SD = 14.57$) was significantly higher than the percentage correctly estimated in the traditional structure ($M = 24.5$, $SD = 10.23$), $t(17) = 1.94$, $p < .05$.

Task Load Index Workload Ratings

The workload of the team was assessed through the Task Load Index (TLX) self-report instrument (Hart & Staveland, 1998), with individual scores combined into a team workload score. To determine if the optimized team structure reduced workload, we made comparisons of the TLX data across conditions. The data show that the mean TLX score in the optimized team structure (M = 11.84, SD = 1.59) was lower than the mean for the traditional structure (M = 13.18, SD = 1.47), although the difference was only marginally significant, $t(17)$ = 1.52, p < .075, one-tailed. Note that a one-tail test is appropriate given that the optimized team structure was specifically designed to decrease communication overhead that is related to subjective workload.

Discussion: Theoretical Framework for Results of Experiment 1

In this experiment, a lower need for coordination and a lower communication rate were associated with better team performance. We suggest that a complex pattern of factors centered around communication overhead produced this result, as shown in Figure 4.1. Task interdependence was defined by the mission—a given in the experiment—and was quite high. Almost all of the tasks required multiple types of resources for completion, and many could not be accomplished until others were completed. Task interdependence and team structure jointly determine the need for coordination within the team, defined as the need to simultaneously use resources controlled by multiple individuals to accomplish a task. The need for communication follows from the need to coordinate. The optimal team structure resulted in less need for coordinated use of resources to accomplish tasks and, therefore, less need to communicate.

Team cognition requires communication, but communication has a cost in time and effort. Because less communication was required to accomplish the mission successfully under the optimized structure, team members experienced lower workload (as measured by the TLX score) and were able to devote more effort to understanding the roles and actions of the other team members (increased mutual awareness). This improved understanding led to more efficient communication (anticipation ratio) based on a better mental model of teammates' activities. Overall, team members in the optimized structure communicated less, and, when they did communicate, they communicated more efficiently, contributing to better overall team performance.

EXPERIMENT 2: HUMANITARIAN ASSISTANCE AIRLIFT TEAM USING FUNCTIONAL AND DIVISIONAL TEAM STRUCTURES

This second experiment provides another perspective on the effects of team structure on the communication necessary for effective team cognition (Miller, Price, Entin, Rubineau, & Elliott, 2001; Price, Miller, Entin, & Rubineau, 2001). The experimental task was a humanitarian airlift mission in which teams of three participants planned and carried out an air drop of food and medical supplies at predetermined target locations (refugee sites).

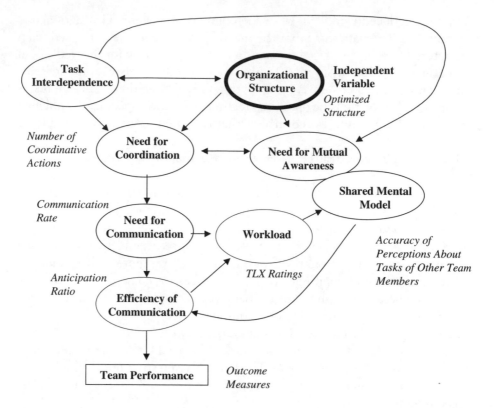

Figure 4.1. Theoretical framework for results of Experiment 1 (measures shown in italics). TLX = Task Load Index.

There were three types of aircraft involved: food supply planes, medical supply planes, and Combat Air Patrol (CAP) planes that served as a defensive escort for the mission. The team coordinated to plan and carry out the airlift. Thirty-six university students served as participants in teams of three.

Divisional and Functional Organizational Structures

Like Experiment 1, this experiment also tested different organizational structures and examined the effects of team structure on team processes and performance. Two organizational structures were used: a functional structure and a divisional structure. In a divisional structure, work units are constructed so that each unit possesses the skills or resources required to complete a product or task. Work units are therefore capable of working relatively autonomously. In a functional structure, work units focus on one type of skill or resource. Thus multiple units are required to complete most tasks or products.

The distinction between divisional and functional structures in industry dates back to the organizational behavior distinctions and changes made in the 1980s in the context of adaptability to market demands and competition. In particular, when production began to require more rapid adaptation to deal with competitors, organizational design theorists began to describe the benefits of moving from the strict hierarchies associated with the divisional structure common to most U.S. firms. With the move to product focus, although losing the economies of scale, firms were able to address competition by rapidly adapting to market demands.[1]

Following the team research of Hollenbeck et al. (1999), we applied the conceptual differentiation between functional and divisional structures, originally developed in a broader organizational context, to the functioning of a three-person team. In the experiment, the divisional structure was defined by having each of the three team members control some of each of the three types of planes needed for the airlift. In the functional structure, the food, medicine, and CAP planes were controlled by three different individuals so that all tasks required coordination.

Note that the divisional and functional structures have some similarity to the two structures described in the previous experiment, with the functional structure being more similar to the traditional JTF structure, and the divisional structure more similar to the optimized JTF structure. However, the optimized JTF structure allocated resources to individuals on the basis of the requirements of the mission, whereas the divisional structure simply allocated some resources of each type to each team member. In this experiment, the availability of resources and the amount of resources allocated to each team member were key factors that affected the need for coordination (pooling of resources to accomplish tasks) under the two structures. Organizational structure was varied as a within-teams variable in the experiment, with each team performing under both structures in counterbalanced order.

Hollenbeck and associates (Hollenbeck et al., 1999; Moon et al., 2000) have found that the effectiveness of teams using the divisional and functional structures depends on the nature of the tasks to be accomplished and the uncertainty in the situation. When the situation is uncertain or unpredictable, the divisional structure works well. In more predictable situations, the functional structure is more efficient.

We suggest that task interdependence and adequacy of resources are also key factors that *interact* in the effectiveness of the two structures. If team members in the divisional structure have adequate resources to handle tasks on their own, then this structure, which minimizes the need for coordination, should be more effective. If team members in the divisional structure lack sufficient resources to handle tasks alone, however, then they will need to coordinate and may be at a disadvantage because of their lack of experience in coordination. In the functional structure, team members must always coordinate to accomplish tasks that require multiple types of resources. This

---

[1]We are indebted to Steve Fiore and Eduardo Salas for this historical perspective.

structure will therefore generate more need for coordination than the divisional structure, if the team members in the divisional structure have adequate resources to handle the tasks independently.

The interaction of the mission and the organizational structures and the resource allocation in the experiment was such that many of refugee sites, but not all of them, could be handled independently by the team members in the divisional condition. For some sites, none of the team members in the divisional condition had sufficient resources to handle the site by themselves and coordination was required. In the functional condition, the team members always needed to coordinate to handle a site.

Mission Planning With Electronic Collaborative Tools

A second major purpose of the experiment, in addition to testing team structures, was to evaluate the effect of electronic collaborative planning tools on the planning processes of the team. Planning medium—defined as the presence or absence of electronic tools for collaborative planning—was a second independent variable in the experiment, varied as a between-teams variable. In one condition, the participants conducted their planning session using an electronic whiteboard showing a map of the targeted area for the airlift. As they developed their plan, they were able to capture it by making electronic annotations on the shared whiteboard. In the other condition, participants used a paper map covered with a clear plastic sheet to conduct map-and-grease-pencil planning similar to that currently conducted in many military operations. The major advantage of electronic collaboration tools is, of course, their ability to support collaboration for teams who are physically distributed in location. In this initial experiment, however, the team members in both conditions were physically colocated to assess the effects of the tools on the planning process independent of the location of the team members.

Performance Differences by Condition

The performance of the teams in the experiment was measured by task accuracy: success in delivering the required amount of supplies to each of the refugee sites. Percentage task accuracy was measured by the percentage of times that the team managed to deliver 100% of the needed supplies to each of the refugee sites. With this measure, team performance was more accurate for the functional ($M = 83.9$, $SD = 15.04$) than for the divisional condition ($M = 77.14$, $SD = 17.28$), $t(10) = 1.92$, $p < .05$. Using a slightly different measure (average percentage task accuracy), task accuracy was also higher when the electronic whiteboard was used for planning ($M = 52.8$, $SD = 4.62$) than for the paper-based planning condition ($M = 48.04$, $SD = 7.03$), $t(10) = 1.83$, $p < .05$.

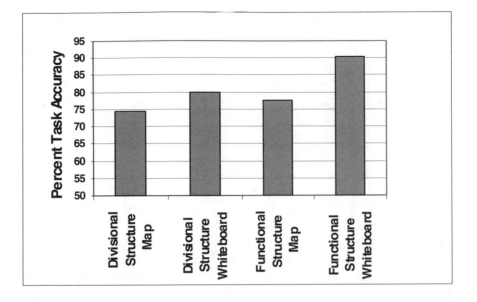

Figure 4.2. Team performance (percentage task accuracy) by divisional and functional team structure and by planning condition.

We have some evidence, as shown in Figure 4.2, that the electronic planning medium was more advantageous for teams in the functional condition. The performance of the functional teams using the electronic whiteboard (M = 90.31, SD = 7.67) was somewhat higher than the performance of functional teams using the paper map (M = 77.49, SD = 18.45), although the difference is only marginally significant, $t(10)$ = 1.38, $p < .10$.[2] There was no significant difference by planning medium for teams using the divisional structure.

Coordination Success

Analysis of the coordination patterns and the communication during planning for the two team structures sheds some light on these effects. Overall, the functional structure required that team members coordinate use of their resources more frequently than the divisional structure. However, the requirements of the mission and the organizational structure interacted to require a certain amount of coordination in the divisional structure—that is, there were numerous sites for which no one team member had the resources needed to handle the site independently. When team members in the divisional structure needed to coordinate, they did so with much less success

---

[2]These means combine the effects of a within-teams variable (structure) and a between-teams variable (planning condition). We used a pooled error term to test these contrasts, following the procedures of Winer (1962).

than teams in the functional structure, as measured by the percentage of the team members required to complete a coordinated task who actually participated in that task. For example, if the resources of two team members were needed to complete the task, and only one team member attempted to perform the task, the value of the measure is 50%. The mean for the coordination success measure (percentage of required team members who participated in each task) was higher for the functional structure ($M = 95.36$, $SD = 4.30$) than for the divisional structure ($M = 84.35$, $SD = 10.77$), $t(10) = 3.63$, $p < .05$.

The divisional structure, as it was implemented with resources available, and given the mission requirements, seems to have put the teams at a disadvantage in this experiment. Overall, the divisional team structure required less coordination than the functional structure, but this did not give the structure an advantage for the mission. The coordination that was required for the divisional teams seems to have been more difficult for them. The functional teams achieved better performance than the divisional teams even though they needed to coordinate more frequently to achieve that performance.

Collaboration During Planning

In this experiment, we implemented a measure of the extent to which the teams communicated in a collaborative manner during planning. During the planning process, both the verbal and written (graphic as well as text) communications of the team members were coded by number and type. Communications during planning were later categorized into those that represented collaborative intentions (e.g., paraphrasing or acknowledging others' ideas) and those that did not (e.g., proposing a new idea). Using this measure of collaborative communication during planning, we found that the planning sessions conducted using the electronic whiteboard involved more collaborative communication ($M = 84.02$, $SD = 6.52$) than those conducted with the paper map ($M = 79.33$, $SD = 5.18$), $t(10) = 1.74$, $p < .05$. This was the case for both organizational structures.

We suggest that the more collaborative planning process that was associated with the use of the electronic whiteboard contributed to the team's ability to coordinate successfully and, therefore, to the better performance of the teams in the functional structure/electronic whiteboard condition. The collaborative planning process, as supported by the electronic whiteboard, gave the functional teams an advantage in carrying out their coordinated activities during mission execution. The divisional teams, in contrast, apparently did not benefit from collaborative planning in such a way that they were able to carry out their coordinated tasks effectively—they performed less well during the mission.

Discussion: Theoretical Framework for Results of Experiment 2

In Experiment 2, we saw again how the team's structure, in particular, the allocation of resources to team members, interacted with the resource demands of the tasks to be performed by the team to affect the need for coordination among the team members. However, there was an additional factor in this experiment that we had not previously studied in assessing the effects of structure on performance—the presence of an electronic planning tool that changed the collaborative interaction of the teams during the premission planning process. Collaborative planning played a key role in allowing the teams using the functional structure to accomplish the coordination required. Teams that planned using the electronic whiteboard exhibited more collaborative communication during their planning, and this collaboration during planning was apparently more beneficial to the teams in the functional structure that needed a high degree of coordination to complete the mission successfully.

Figure 4.3 shows a theoretical framework for understanding the results of Experiment 2. As in Experiment 1, we suggest that the organizational structure and the interdependence of the tasks drive the need for coordination. In this experiment we have a direct measure of the success of the coordinated actions, and more successful coordination is associated with better team performance as measured by task accuracy. We suggest that the presence of the electronic whiteboard, through its effect on increasing collaborative communication during planning, contributed to that coordination success. The need for coordination was affected by the nature of the mission tasks and the team's structure, and the success of the needed coordination was affected by the nature of the team's preplanning activity.

Effective preplanning has been shown to increase a team's shared mental model and subsequent coordinated team performance (Stout et al., 1999), and we expect that the more collaborative planning process that was facilitated by the electronic whiteboard may have led to a better shared mental model among the members of the functional teams (this was not directly measured in Experiment 2). We also expect that the functional teams may have been able to communicate more efficiently during the mission because of their better shared mental model, and that this efficiency of communication allowed them to achieve a higher level of performance even though their team structure required more coordination than was needed under the divisional structure. Therefore, we would expect to see a higher anticipation ratio for teams using the functional structure and the collaborative planning tool. The anticipation ratio was not measured in this experiment, however.[3]

---

[3]Communications data (counts by type of communication) were coded by observers (in real time) only during premission planning, not during mission performance.

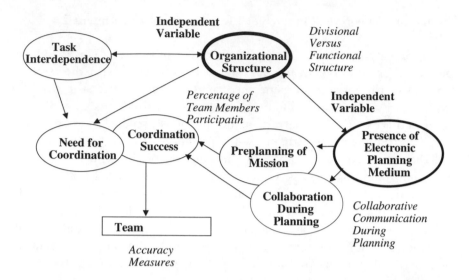

Figure 4.3. Theoretical framework for results of Experiment 2 (measures shown in italics).

SUMMARY: THEORETICAL FRAMEWORK LINKING TEAM STRUCTURE TO COMMUNICATION AND PERFORMANCE

In both of the experiments described here, we saw how the organizational structure used by the team (in particular, the way that the team's resources were allocated and controlled) interacted with the requirements of the tasks to be performed to generate requirements for coordination. In Experiment 1, the available resources were adequate for implementing an optimized structure that allowed team members to function relatively independently, reducing the coordination needed for successful performance. In Experiment 2, resources were not adequate for team members in a divisional structure to handle all tasks independently. Although the overall need for coordination was lower in the divisional structure (fewer tasks required the coordinated use of resources), the teams using this structure performed less well than teams using a structure that required more coordination.

We believe that the workload associated with communication (the communication overhead) was a critical factor in the performance of teams under the different organizational structures. In the first experiment, the optimized structure successfully reduced the need for coordination and the volume of communication necessary to achieve this coordination. We suggest that the reduced workload associated with less need for communication allowed team members to develop a better awareness of the tasks of others on the team (better mutual awareness) and, based on that awareness, to communi-

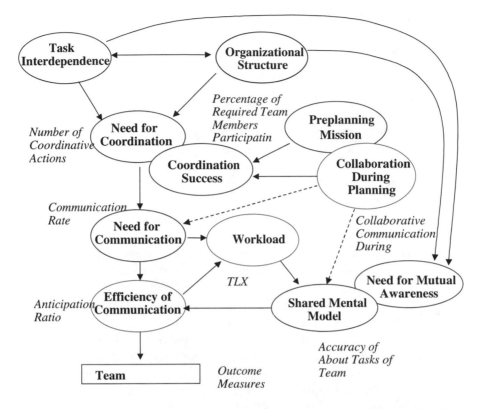

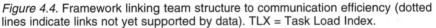

Figure 4.4. Framework linking team structure to communication efficiency (dotted lines indicate links not yet supported by data). TLX = Task Load Index.

cate more efficiently (higher anticipation ratio). Teams communicated less frequently, and also more efficiently, in the optimized structure.

In the second experiment, we saw effects of both collaborative premission planning and team structure on performance. Even though teams using a functional structure needed to coordinate more to accomplish the mission, they were able to achieve a higher level of performance, apparently as a result of more collaborative premission planning. We suggest that collaborative premission planning may have increased the team's shared mental model and mutual awareness, allowing them to communicate more efficiently, although this was not directly measured in Experiment 2.

The two experiments reported in this chapter examined different factors and used different measures and so are able to provide empirical evidence to support two different, but overlapping, theoretical constructs. In Figure 4.4 we combine these two constructs into a single overall framework that shows how team structure, given a particular task configuration, affects performance through its effects on required coordination and communication overhead. The framework shown in Figure 4.4 is suggested but not yet established—it is provided as a possible explanation for the empirical relationships among variables that were found in the two experiments.

The framework suggests the following relationships:

- The structure of the team (in particular, the control of resources and the allocation of tasks to team members) interacts with the nature of the team's tasks to generate the need for coordination among team members and the need for mutual awareness. If the team members have the resources to act relatively independently in many situations, they will have less need to coordinate their actions and may have less need to be aware of the activities of others.
- The need for coordination drives the need for communication among team members.
- To the extent that team members need to coordinate, better mutual awareness allows them to do so more efficiently, that is, with a lower communication overhead.
- Lower need for communication and more efficient communication are associated with lower workload.
- The ability to collaboratively preplan the mission results in better mutual organizational awareness (knowledge of tasks being performed by other team members), and this awareness allows team members to communicate more efficiently (lower communication overhead).
- More efficient communication among team members (lower communication overhead) results in better team performance. This reduction in communication overhead can be created in multiple ways, such as by restructuring the team to reduce the need for coordination or by activities that increase mutual awareness and shared mental models among team members, such as collaborative premission planning.

We plan to focus our future research on the links that are suggested in Figure 4.4 but not yet empirically validated, shown as dotted lines in the figure. We have evidence that changing the team's structure affects the need for coordination, the need for communication, and the efficiency of communication; and that better mutual awareness is associated with more efficient communication (lower communication overhead). However, rearranging team responsibilities to reduce the need for coordination may be neither desirable nor practical in many circumstances. We saw two different patterns associated with superior performance in the two experiments—one case in which the teams that needed to coordinate *less* during the mission performed better, and one in which the teams that needed to coordinate *more* during the mission performed better if they collaborated more during premission planning. We suspect that communication overhead is an important factor in these different patterns, and we need to better understand how to reduce that overhead. We believe that premission collaborative planning achieves its effect on performance by increasing the team's mutual awareness and thereby reducing communication overhead, but we do not yet have direct evidence for that belief. In the future, we hope to more firmly establish the means by which collaborative premission planning supports effective coordination during the mission.

REFERENCES

Bolstad, C. A., & Endsley (1999). Shared mental models and shared displays: An empirical evaluation of team performance. In *Proceedings of the 43rd Meeting of the Human Factors and Ergonomics Society* (pp. 213–217). Santa Monica, CA: Human Factors and Ergonomics Society Press.

Bolstad, C. A., & Endsley (2000). The effect of task load and shared displays on team situation awareness. In *Proceedings of the 44th Meeting of the Human Factors and Ergonomics Society* (pp. 189–193). Santa Monica, CA: Human Factors and Ergonomics Society Press.

Bowers, C. A., Jentsch, F., Salas, E., & Braun, C. C. (1998). Analyzing communication sequences for team training needs assessment. *Human Factors, 40*, 672–679.

Cannon-Bowers, J., Salas, E., & Converse, S. (1993). Shared mental models in expert team decision making. In N. J. Castellan, Jr. (Ed.), *Individual and group decision making* (pp. 221–246). Hillsdale, NJ: Erlbaum.

Dwyer, D. J., Fowlkes, J. E., Oser, R. L., Salas, E., & Lane, N. E. (1997). Team performance measurement in distributed environments: The TARGETS methodology. In M. T. Brannick, E. Salas, & C. Prince (Eds.), *Team performance assessment and measurement* (pp. 137–153). Mahwah, NJ: Erlbaum.

Entin, E. B., & Entin, E. E. (2000). Assessing team situation awareness in simulated military missions. In *Proceedings of the Human Factors and Ergonomics Society 44th Annual Meeting* (pp. 73–77). San Diego, CA: Human Factors and Ergonomics Society Press.

Entin, E. B., Entin, E. E., & Serfaty, D. (2000). *Organizational structure and adaptation in the joint command and control domain* (No. TR-915). Burlington, MA: ALPHATECH, Inc.

Entin, E. E. (1999). Optimized command and control architectures for improved process and performance. In *Proceedings of the 1999 Command and Control Research and Technology Symposium* (pp. 116–122). Washington, DC: Department of Defense C4ISR Cooperative Research Program.

Entin, E. E., & Serfaty, D. (1999). Adaptive team coordination. *Human Factors, 41*, 312–325.

Entin, E. E., Serfaty, D., & Deckert, J. C. (1994). *Team adaptation and coordination training* (No. TR-648-1). Burlington, MA: ALPHATECH, Inc.

Entin, E. E., Serfaty, D., & Kerrigan, C. (1998). Choice and performance under three command and control architectures. In *Proceedings of the 1998 Command and Control Research and Technology Symposium*, Monterey, CA.

Fiore, S. M., Salas, E., & Cannon-Bowers, J. A. (2001). Group dynamics and shared mental model development. In M. London (Ed.), *How people evaluate others in organizations: Person perception and interpersonal judgment in industrial/organizational psychology* (pp. 309–336). Mahwah, NJ: Erlbaum.

Foushee, H. C. (1984). Dyads and triads at 35,000 feet: Factors affecting group process and aircrew performance. *American Psychologist, 39,* 885–893.

Fowlkes, J., Lane, N., Salas, E., Franz, T., & Oser, R. (1994). Improving the measurement of team performance: The TARGETS methodology. *Military Psychology, 6,* 47–61.

Hart, S. G. & Staveland, L. E. (1988). Development of NASA-TLX (Task Load Index): Results on empirical and theoretical research. In P. A. Hancock & N. Meshkati (Eds.), *Human mental workload. Advances in psychology, 52* (pp. 139–183). Amsterdam: North-Holland.

Hollenbeck, J. R., Ilgen, D. R., Moon, H., Shepard, L., Ellis, A., West, B., & Porter, C. (1999, April/May). *Structural contingency theory and individual differences: Examination of external and internal person-team fit.* Paper presented at the 31st Annual Convention of the Society for Industrial and Organizational Psychology, Atlanta, GA.

Johnston, J. A., Smith-Jentsch, K. A., & Cannon-Bowers, J. A. (1997). Performance measurement tools for enhancing team decision making. In M. T. Brannick, E. Salas, & C. Prince (Eds.), *Team performance assessment and measurement* (pp. 311–327). Mahwah, NJ: Erlbaum.

Kiekel, P. A., Cooke, N. J., Foltz, P. W., & Shope, S. M. (2001). Automating measurement of team cognition through analysis of communication data. In M. J. Smith, G. Salvendy, D. Harris, & R. J. Koubek (Eds.), *Usability evaluation and interface design* (pp. 1382–1386). Mahwah, NJ: Erlbaum.

Kleinman, D. L., & Serfaty, D. (1989, April). *Team performance assessment in distributed decisionmaking.* Paper presented at the Simulation and Training Research Symposium on Interactive Networked Simulation for Training, University of Central Florida, Orlando, FL.

Landauer, T. K., Foltz, P. W., & Laham, D. (1998). An introduction to latent semantic analysis. *Discourse Processes, 25,* 259–284.

Levchuk, Y., Pattipati, C., & Kleinman, D. (1998). Designing adaptive organizations to process a complex mission: Algorithms and applications. In *Proceedings of the 1998 Command and Control Research and Technology Symposium* (pp. 11–32). Washington, DC: Department of Defense C4ISR Cooperative Research Program.

Levchuk, Y., Pattipati, C., & Kleinman, D. (1999). Analytic model driven organizational design and experimentation in adaptive command and control. In *Proceedings of the 1999 Command and Control Research and Technology Symposium* (pp. 11–32). Washington, DC: Department of Defense C4ISR Cooperative Research Program.

MacMillan, J., Paley, M. J., Levchuk, Y. N., Entin, E. E., Freeman, J., & Serfaty, D. (2001). Designing the best team for the task: Optimal organizational structures for military missions. In M. McNeese, E. Salas, & M. Endsley (Eds.), *New trends in cooperative activities* (pp. 284–299). Santa Monica, CA: Human Factors and Ergonomics Society Press.

McIntyre, R. M., & Salas, E. (1995). Team performance in complex environments: What we have learned so far. In R. Guzzo & E. Salas (Eds.), *Team effectiveness and decision making in organizations* (pp. 9–45). San Francisco: Jossey-Bass.

Miller, D., Price, J. M., Entin, E. E., Rubineau, B., & Elliott, L. (2001). Does planning using groupware foster coordinated team performance? In *Proceedings of the Human Factors and Ergonomics Society 45th Annual Meeting* (pp. 390–394). San Diego, CA: Human Factors and Ergonomics Society Press.

Moon, H., Hollenbeck, J., Ilgen, D., West, B., Ellis, A., Humphrey, S., & Porter, A. (2000). Asymmetry in structure movement: Challenges on the road to adaptive organization structures. In *Proceedings of the 2000 Command and Control Research and Technology Symposium* (pp. 11–32). Washington, DC: Department of Defense C4ISR Cooperative Research Program.

Orasanu, J. M. (1990). *Shared mental models and crew decision making* (CSL Report No. 46). Princeton, NJ: Princeton University, Cognitive Science Laboratory.

Orasanu, J. M. (1993). Decision making in the cockpit. In E. Wiener, B. Kanki, & R. Helmreich (Eds.), *Cockpit resource management* (pp. 137–172). San Diego, CA: Academic Press.

Orasanu, J. M., & Fischer, U. (1992). Team cognition in the cockpit: Linguistic control of shared problem solving. In *Proceedings of the 14th Annual Conference of the Cognitive Science Society* (pp. 189–194). Hillsdale, NJ: Erlbaum.

Orasanu, J. M., & Salas, E. (1993). Team decision making in complex environments. In G. A. Klein, J. M. Orasanu, R. Calderwood, & C. E. Zsambok (Eds.), *Decision making in action: Models and methods* (pp. 327–345). Norwood, NJ: Ablex.

Price, J. M., Miller, D. L., Entin, E. E., & Rubineau, B. (2001). Collaborative planning and coordinated team performance. In *Proceedings of the 2001 Command and Control Research and Technology Symposium*. Washington, DC: Department of Defense C4ISR Cooperative Research Program.

Sanderson, P., & Fisher, C. (1994). Exploratory sequential data analysis: Foundations. *Human-Computer Interaction, 9,* 251–317.

Serfaty, D. (1996). Adaptive architectures for command and control: An overview. In *Proceedings of the 1996 Command and Control Research and Technology Symposium* (pp. 272–274). Washington, DC: Department of Defense C4ISR Cooperative Research Program.

Serfaty, D., Entin, E. E., & Johnston, J. (1998). Team adaptation and coordination training. In J. A. Cannon-Bowers & E. Salas (Eds.), *Decision making under stress: Implications for training and simulation* (pp. 221–245). Washington, DC: American Psychological Association.

Smith-Jentsch, K. A., Zeisig, R. L., Acton, B., & McPherson, J. A. (1998). Team dimensional training: A strategy for guided self correction. In J. A. Cannon-

Bowers & E. Salas (Eds.), *Decision making under stress: Implications for training and simulation* (pp. 271–312). Washington, DC: American Psychological Association.

Stout, R. J., Cannon-Bowers, J. A., Salas, E., & Milanovich, D. M. (1999). Planning, shared mental models, and coordinated performance: An empirical link is established. *Human Factors, 41,* 61–71.

Urban, J. M., Weaver, J. L., Bowers, C. A., & Rhodenizer, L. (1996). Effects of team workload and structure on team processes and performance: Implications for complex team training. *Human Factors, 38,* 300–310.

Winer, J. B. (1962). *Statistical principles in experimental design.* New York: McGraw-Hill.

5

ADVANCES IN MEASURING TEAM COGNITION

NANCY J. COOKE, EDUARDO SALAS,
PRESTON A. KIEKEL, AND BRIAN BELL

Teams have become an integral and essential social component in organizations. There is no doubt that there are more businesses, industries, and agencies implementing team-based systems than ever before. Organizations believe that teams, teamwork, and effective team functioning can provide a competitive edge. Teams are, after all, dispatched to tackle difficult and complex problems. Why? Organizations think teams hold the solution to many problems. The perception is that teams can manage stress, teams can adapt and be flexible, teams can make better decisions, and teams can be more productive than individuals. So, teams are a popular commodity in organizations.

While the evidence of the efficacy of teams remains open, social scientists have begun to provide much needed answers to this issue. In fact, the amount of research effort and resources aimed at understanding what comprises effective team performance is overwhelming. Military, human factors,

This work was supported by Air Force Office of Scientific Research (AFOSR) Grant F49620-01-0261 and Office of Naval Research Grant N00014-00-1-0818 to Nancy J. Cooke and by AFOSR Grant F4620-01-0214 to Eduardo Salas. We thank Janie DeJoode, Jamie Gorman, Heather Jiron, Rebecca Keith, Harry Pedersen, Steven Shope, and Natasha Sutherlin for their contributions to the research described here. We also thank an anonymous review for helpful suggestions.

social, cognitive, and industrial/organizational psychologists have been studying teams for decades (see Guzzo & Shea, 1992; Levine & Moreland, 1990). And so progress has been made. We understand better what teams do, how they do it, why they do it, and how we can improve what they do. We can now identify the behaviors (i.e., skills) and attitudes that teams need to be effective (see Salas & Cannon-Bowers, 2000). Moreover, there is evidence that this leads to better performance (see Cannon-Bowers & Salas, 1998; Guzzo & Salas, 1995; Hackman, 1990). But we also know that teams "think." That is, team members possess knowledge that allows them to function effectively as a team, even during periods of high workload (Orasanu, 1990). This knowledge is as important as skills and attitudes; in some cases, these cognitive abilities are more important. Team cognition has also been linked to team performance (Stout, Cannon-Bowers, & Salas, 1996). Unfortunately, our understanding of team cognition is limited because it is difficult to capture or measure team cognition. Therefore, to fully understand team performance as well as the contribution of team cognition to effective team functioning, we must measure team cognition, which is the motivation behind this chapter.

Why do we need to measure team cognition? First, measures of team cognition provide a window to some of the factors underlying team acquisition and performance of a complex skill and can thus be valuable in diagnosing team performance successes and failures. Second, with an understanding of team cognition, training and design interventions can target the cognitive underpinnings of team performance. The ability to assess team cognition and predict team performance has far-reaching implications for evaluating progress in training programs and diagnosing remediation needs during training. If one can measure the cognitive structures and processes that support task performance, then one can use this information to predict the time course of skill acquisition and the asymptotic levels of performance once skill has been acquired. Finally, understanding the cognition underlying team performance has implications for the design of technological aids to improve team performance not only in training but, more importantly, in actual task environments.

We have organized this chapter into six sections. We first discuss the nature of team cognition. We then highlight some of the limitations of measures, followed by a brief discussion of some new approaches to measuring team cognition. Next, we outline some validation procedures and what we have learned so far about team cognition. We conclude with a few remarks about the future of team cognition.

WHAT IS TEAM COGNITION?

Teams perform cognitive tasks. That is, they detect and recognize pertinent cues, make decisions, solve problems, remember relevant information, plan, acquire knowledge, and design solutions or products as an integrated unit. But, is team cognition anything more than the sum of the cognition of the individual team members? Yes, our position, which serves as the basis for our approach to measuring team cognition, holds that team cognition is more than the sum of the cognition of the individual team members. Instead, team cognition emerges from the interplay of the individual cognition of each team member and team process behaviors.

We see these two intertwined aspects of team cognition—individual cognition of team members and team process behaviors—as analogous to cognitive structures and cognitive processes at the individual level. For example, individual knowledge may be, in principal, described in terms of a knowledge structure, but the effective application of that knowledge structure requires processes such as retrieval and pattern recognition that act on that structure. In a similar way, team members interact through communication, coordination, and other process behaviors and in doing so transform a collection of individuals' knowledge to team knowledge that ultimately guides action. In other words, the outcome of this transformation is effective team cognition. Figure 5.1 graphically represents this view of team cognition.

As is represented in Figure 5.1, our work to date has focused predominantly on team *knowledge*, which we view as central to team *cognition*. Parallel to research on individual expertise (e.g., Chase & Simon, 1973; Glaser & Chi, 1988), accounts of effective team performance highlight the importance of team knowledge. For instance, Cannon-Bowers and Salas (1997) proposed a framework that integrates many aspects of team cognition in the form of teamwork competencies. They categorized competencies required for effective teamwork in terms of knowledge, skills, and attitudes that are either specific or generic to the task and specific or generic to the team. Similarly, a team's understanding of a complex and dynamic situation at any one point in time (i.e., team situation awareness) is supposedly influenced by the knowledge that the team possesses (Cooke, Stout, & Salas, 1997; Stout et al., 1996). These distinctions between long-term knowledge and knowledge that is associated with a dynamic or fleeting understanding of the situation are reflected in our framework, as are distinctions between knowledge about the task (i.e., taskwork knowledge) and knowledge about the team (e.g., teamwork knowledge). We also acknowledge that there are many other distinctions that could be made in regard to knowledge type (e.g., declarative, procedural, strategic) that are not reflected in this framework.

Another critical distinction that is depicted in the framework of Figure 5.1 is among different levels or metrics of team knowledge. Individual team members have knowledge that can be aggregated or summed. We use the term *collective* to portray the aggregation of individual knowledge. Collective metrics are distinct from holistic metrics of team knowledge. In our view, the team knowledge resulting from team process behaviors is *effective* knowledge that guides team action and that is, therefore, reflected in outcome measures.

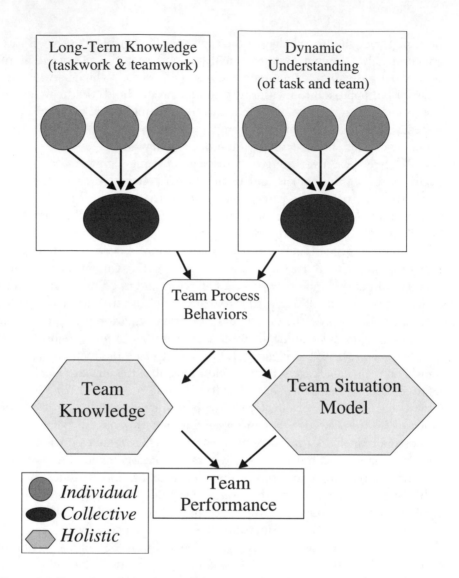

Figure 5.1. Team knowledge framework.

Eliciting or assessing team knowledge at this *holistic* level is analogous to focusing on an individual's effective knowledge revealed in his or her actions. Thus, team knowledge at this holistic level is team member knowledge that has been processed or integrated in some way through team behaviors such as communication, coordination, or leadership. For example, team members in a military aviation setting may collectively have information about an impending threat, but without adequate communication, and therefore integration or fusion of the requisite pieces of information, the holistic knowledge would be lacking and the team would fail to act on the impending threat. Holistic metrics of team knowledge more directly reflect our definition of team cognition in that it emerges from the interplay of individual team knowledge and team process behaviors.

Although specific characteristics of our framework may be novel, the proposal that team cognition exists is not. The concept of transactive memory assumes that two or more individuals can share the task of remembering by using each other as memory storage components (Wegner, 1986). Further, concepts such as distributed cognition (Hutchins, 1991) and common ground in discourse (Clark & Schaefer, 1987; Wilkes-Gibbs & Clark, 1992) also presume that cognitive tasks can be shared among two or more individuals. There has also been significant theoretical work delineating cognitive constructs at the team level, such as team decision making, shared mental models, and team situation awareness (Cannon-Bowers, Salas, & Converse, 1993; Orasanu, 1990; Stout et al., 1996). The interest in such concepts is based on the hypothesized relation between team cognition and team performance that suggests that team performance can be better understood and ultimately predicted by measuring and understanding team cognition. We agree that these team cognition constructs are key to understanding team performance. However, when we examine the way in which these constructs are measured in light of our framework (see Figure 5.1), we identify a number of measurement limitations. These limitations and our approaches to address them are the topic of the remainder of this chapter.

LIMITATIONS OF MEASURES OF TEAM COGNITION

The assessment and understanding of team cognition (i.e., team mental models, team situation awareness, team decision making) require psychometrically sound measures of the constructs that constitute team cognition. However, measures and methods targeting team cognition are sparse and fail to address some of the more interesting aspects of team cognition (Cooke, Salas, Cannon-Bowers, & Stout, 2000). In particular, we have identified several issues that need to be addressed to adequately measure team cognition. These measurement needs are presented in Exhibit 5.1 and are discussed in turn.

Holistic Versus Collective Measurement

Traditional measures of team knowledge (e.g., measures of shared mental models) are based on the elicitation of knowledge from individuals on the team, which is then aggregated (e.g., averaged) to generate a representation of the team's knowledge. Thus, this aggregate represents the collective level of Figure 5.1 and thus is devoid of the influences of team process behaviors (e.g., communication, coordination, situation awareness).

To what extent does team knowledge differ when measured at the collective versus the holistic level? How do collective and holistic knowledge

EXHIBIT 5.1
Team Cognition Measurement Needs

1. Measures that target the holistic level, rather than the collective level, of team cognition.
2. Measures of team cognition suited to teams with different roles.
3. Methods for aggregating individual data to derive collective knowledge.
4. Measures of team knowledge that target the more dynamic and fleeting situation models.
5. Measures that target different types of team knowledge (e.g., strategic, declarative, procedural knowledge, or taskwork vs. teamwork knowledge).
6. The extension of a broader range of knowledge elicitation methods to the problem of eliciting team cognition.
7. The streamlining of measurement methods to better automate them and embed them within the task context.
8. The validation of newly developed measures.

compare in terms of their ability to predict team performance? Based on the framework in Figure 5.1, we predict that holistic knowledge, by virtue of its direct link to team performance, would be a better predictor of team performance compared with collective knowledge. Can team knowledge measured at the collective level be transformed in some way to better reflect the holistic level? How can knowledge be elicited or measured at the holistic level? We have begun to address this latter question that we view as a prerequisite to answering the others.

Heterogeneous Versus Homogeneous Measurement

Traditional measures of team cognition or team knowledge reflect an underlying assumption of homogeneous cognition or knowledge among members of a team. For instance, many measures of shared mental models are based on averaging responses elicited from individual team members. Not only is aggregation focused at the collective rather than the holistic level, but typical aggregation metrics such as averaging assume that what is being measured (e.g., taskwork knowledge) varies only quantitatively. That is, knowledge is a matter of degree or the extent to which a core set of facts is mastered. Further, typical measures of shared mental models are based on an assumption that shared knowledge among team members is the same as similar knowledge among team members.

In contrast, it is possible to conceive of team members as a collection of "apples and oranges," each having very different knowledge, skills, and attitudes that the member brings to the task. Indeed, this characterization of team members is central to a common definition of team offered by Salas, Dickinson, Converse, and Tannenbaum (1992). They define *team* as "a distinguishable set of two or more people who interact dynamically, interdependently, and adaptively toward a common and valued goal/object/mission, who have each been assigned specific roles or functions to perform, and who have a limited life span of membership" (p. 4). Thus, teams, unlike some groups, have differentiated responsibilities and roles (Cannon-Bowers et al., 1993). This division of cognitive labor is quite common (e.g., surgery, battlefield command) and enables teams to tackle tasks too complex for any individual. In this context, shared knowledge may be likened to sharing a piece of pie (i.e., each team member has a different but complementary piece) rather than sharing in the sense of a belief or value (i.e., in which the belief or value is identical for all team members). This heterogeneous nature of teams is a feature that has been neglected by current measurement practices (e.g., Langan-Fox, Code, & Langfield-Smith, 2000). It also poses a challenge to measuring team knowledge or shared mental models.

Need for Improving Aggregation Methods

Traditional aggregation procedures (e.g., averaging) associated with collective metrics assume homogeneity with respect to team member knowledge. For instance, a good example of a team for whom a simple averaging of individual scores is inappropriate is a structured team, in which every member has a different role. In an operating room we would not simply average scalpel-wielding performance, as the anesthesiologist would likely have a 0, regardless of how well he or she anesthetizes. There is a need for more principled aggregation approaches suited to heterogeneous teams, such as process-oriented methods for aggregating individual knowledge to attempt to predict holistic knowledge (e.g., the social decision scheme literature; Davis, 1973; Hinsz, 1999). Essentially, these strategies consist of assessing how a team might combine their individual scores into a team score, based on what we know about their team process.

Dynamic Fleeting Knowledge Versus Long-Term Static Knowledge

Also, as portrayed in Figure 5.1, we conceive of team knowledge as both background knowledge that is long-lived in nature and a more dynamic and fleeting understanding that a team member has of a situation at any one point in time. Indeed, many applied researchers have highlighted the importance of this latter kind of cognition, often termed *situation awareness* (Durso & Gronlund, 1999; Endsley, 1995b; Sarter & Woods, 1991). There has also been a growing appreciation of the importance of team situation awareness, or that rapidly changing information that a team uses to understand and make decisions in a rapidly evolving environment (Cooke, Stout, & Salas, 2001; Salas, Prince, Baker, & Shrestha, 1995). This dynamic, fleeting knowledge is a challenge to measure at the individual level compared with the more stable knowledge associated with most knowledge elicitation methods (Adams, Tenney, & Pew, 1995; Endsley, 1995a; Fracker, 1991; Salas et al., 1995; Sarter & Woods, 1995; Taylor & Selcon, 1994; Vidulich, 1989). Thus, measures of team knowledge have focused primarily on long-term team knowledge, at the expense of the more dynamic knowledge associated with situation awareness.

Need for Broader Focus on Different Knowledge Types

The measurement of team cognition has tended to focus on the knowledge constructs of shared mental models (Cannon-Bowers et al., 1993; Klimoski & Mohammed, 1994; Kraiger & Wenzel, 1997) and, to a lesser extent, team processes involved in team decision making and communication. As previously mentioned, there have been a few recent attempts to measure knowledge associated with situation awareness. However, even within the area of long-term team knowledge (and situation awareness as well) there are a number of other distinctions that have largely been ignored. For instance, Cannon-Bowers, Tannenbaum, Salas, and Volpe (1995) distinguished between taskwork and teamwork knowledge. Taskwork knowledge is knowledge about the individual and team task, whereas teamwork knowledge is knowledge about the roles, requirements, and responsibilities of team members. Others have distinguished among strategic, procedural, and declarative knowledge (Stout et al., 1996). These theoretical distinctions have yet to be captured by measures of team knowledge, which should in turn put these distinctions to the test.

Need for Broader Application of Knowledge Elicitation Methods

Cooke (1994) outlined the various knowledge elicitation techniques that have been applied to individual knowledge elicitation, and Cooke, Salas, et al. (2000) described how these techniques can be applied to knowledge elicitation at the team level. In summary, the varieties of knowledge elicitation methods can be categorized into one of four categories: (a) observations, (b) interviews and surveys, (c) process tracing, and (d) conceptual methods. Those methods that have been used to elicit team knowledge relevant to shared mental models or situation awareness have been typically restricted to interview and survey methods and, to a lesser extent, conceptual methods. The application of a broader spectrum of knowledge elicitation methods to the problem of measuring team knowledge could open the door to the measurement of varieties of team knowledge previously untapped. As is described in what follows, we have begun to explore the application of process tracing techniques at the team level through the opportunistic use of team communications.

Need for Automated and Embedded Measures

There are several reasons why it is particularly advantageous to have automated and embedded measures in team research. Most of them trace back to the fact that applied research on team tasks tends to be more complex and has more variables and measures. As task complexity increases, it becomes more disruptive to interrupt and administer a questionnaire or interview an expert. Moreover, as the size of the team increases, the time needed to query all team members increases. So, essentially, even fairly efficient measures can become difficult to administer and retain when the flow of the task is more fragile, when there are multiple team members being queried, and when multiple measures are being taken. Automating measures and embedding them within the task can reduce task disruption due to measurement, along with experimenter measurement errors and experimenter resources. Automated and embedded measures in applications also allow for real-time monitoring of team behavior for immediate intervention.

Need for Validation

The units used in team research are typically not items on a questionnaire but rather single team-level measures. It is therefore unlikely that there will be enough observations to conduct certain standard psychometric tests, such as Cronbach alpha for reliability. On the other hand, test–retest reliability is a possibility if there are multiple trials on which the measure is taken. Also, if the measure is the judgment of more than one person, then interrater reliability remains viable.

Two approaches are readily taken to assess validity. First, if there are repeated trials in which a measure is taken, it can be determined if the measure shows an acquisition curve that corresponds to the team's learning of the task. The measure should show either a power curve or an inverse linear curve. The second strategy is to show criterion validity to some other measure, such as performance.

SOME NEW APPROACHES TO MEASURING TEAM COGNITION

In this section we describe the approaches that we have taken in an effort to begin to address the limitations of measures of team knowledge described above.

Holistic Knowledge Measurement

The approach we have taken to holistically assessing knowledge is to have the team (three members in this case) collaborate on their responses to queries that would otherwise have been administered individually. For instance, when we ask individuals to make pairwise relatedness ratings of pertinent concepts in the task, we immediately follow this procedure with asking the team to make their ratings, this time reaching a verbal consensus on each value they assign. For each concept pair, the rating entered in the prior session by each team member is displayed on the computer screen of every team member. The three team members discuss each pair until consensus is reached.

We have assumed that this assessment at the team level would capture not only the collective knowledge of the team members but also the process behaviors of the team that are used in coming to consensus on the ratings. For instance, if a team has a particularly persuasive—but wrong—team member, then their team score is accurately reflected as being too close to that misinformed score. The same process takes place during actual task performance, for better or for worse. Because of the inclusion of team process in the ratings, it was hypothesized that the consensus ratings would be better predictors of team performance than the aggregate taskwork ratings.

It is possible, however, that the consensus measure is not a good estimate of holistic knowledge. The conformity demanded by the measure may induce process behavior different from task-related process, and the public nature of the consensus may overshadow private disagreements. Whether such discrepancies result in output that is a good predictor, or at least a better predictor of performance than collective measures, awaits empirical results.

We have devised similar holistic rating procedures for measures of fleeting situation awareness knowledge, for knowledge of interaction among team members (i.e., teamwork knowledge), and for knowledge of the functioning of the task itself (i.e., taskwork knowledge). Order of presentation between holistic and individual cannot be randomized, because of the carryover effects of achieving consensus. So the challenge is to keep the task short enough to minimize fatigue or boredom effects.

Metrics for Heterogeneous Teams

To assess knowledge of heterogeneous teams, we have computed knowledge accuracy metrics that are role-specific. A referent or "answer key" is generated by the experimenters for each role, by only considering what knowledge a team member in that role should be expected to know to do his or her job well. Individual query responses are scored not only against a key representing overall knowledge but also against role-specific keys. In this way, measures of role or positional accuracy, as well as interpositional accuracy (i.e., interpositional knowledge, or knowledge of roles other than their own) can be determined. Effective performance can ultimately be characterized in terms of degree of knowledge homogeneity among team members.

Aggregation of Team Data

If measures are not collected at the team or holistic level but at the individual level, then how can the individual measures best be used to estimate holistic, team-level scores? Here we label as *collective* any a priori aggregation scheme, whether based on central tendency (i.e., attempting to choose the "typical" score for the team), dispersion (i.e., assessing dissimilarity among team members), or anything else. A more empirically driven collective approach attempts to find a function that combines individual scores to best predict team scores. We are in a particularly good position to do this when we have data collected both at the individual and at the holistic (team consensus) level.

Our framework for thinking about team cognition (see Figure 5.1), as well as work of others (e.g., Steiner, 1972), suggests that we should attempt to correct our collective estimates so that they reflect change in individual scores due to process loss (or possibly gain). For instance, one could compute central tendency corrected for dispersion by making aggregation contingent on the result of cluster analysis (Everitt, 1993) or other similarity methods. Aggregation methods based on team process are relatively ideographic, in that there will be a different combination rule for every team, depending on what their process is like.

Social decision scheme theory (SDS; Davis, 1973; Hinsz, 1999; see also chap. 3, this volume) takes this ideographic attempt to estimate holistic scores as its explicit focus. SDS attempts to combine individual decision making in such a way that it predicts the actual team decision among discrete alternatives. Combination rules are proposed based on theories about how specific groups interact rather than on a single nomothetic rule applied to all teams, as the traditional collective approach does. Theories about team process are tested by determining how well the theoretical combination of scores under an SDS matches the actual decision.

In our work, to identify strategies that teams use to come to consensus in a knowledge rating task, we examined the three individual and one team response for each item within a knowledge measure as a single response set. Each response set can be classified according to one of five rules that map individual responses onto the team response. For example, in the context of the pairwise relatedness ratings used to measure taskwork knowledge, we can identify response sets in the following categories (TM = team member):

1. all agreed (e.g., TM1 = 5, TM2 = 5, TM = 5, Team = 5)
2. majority (2 out of 3) rules (e.g., TM1 = 4, TM2 = 4, TM3 = 3, Team = 4)
3. leader emerges (e.g., TM1 = 3, TM2 = 0, TM3 = 1, Team = 3 or TM1 = 4, TM2 = 4, TM3 = 2, Team = 2)
4. mid rating (e.g., TM1 = 0, TM2 = 3, TM3 = 5, Team = 2 or TM1 = 0, TM2 = 3, TM3 = 5, Team = 3)
5. different from each, and not middle rating (e.g., TM1 = 5, TM2 = 2, TM3 = 4, Team = 0)

Process strategies identified through these or similar data could then be used to aggregate other individual measures taken on the same teams. Interestingly, in our analyses we found that teams used a variety of strategies; however, there was no connection between the strategy they used and team performance. In particular, teams used *majority rules* and the *leader emerges* strategies frequently. In addition, they used the fifth "nonstrategy" fairly often, which led us to question the degree to which team members took the consensus rating task seriously.

Measuring Broader Varieties of Team Knowledge

In our approaches to measuring team knowledge, we discriminate among varieties of knowledge that we target. For instance, we have developed some strategies for measuring team situation awareness, or more specifically, the dynamic situation model that teams create. This is distinguished from the longer term background knowledge that experienced team members bring to the task. Within the long-term knowledge category, we have additionally distinguished methods that elicit teamwork knowledge from those that elicit taskwork knowledge. In this section we describe these efforts.

We, like others (e.g., Endsley, 1995b), view the team process of situation assessment as distinct from the outcome of this process, which is the knowledge that is embodied in the team situation model. We focus on the latter here. We view the team situation model as the team's understanding of a specific situation at any one point in time (Cooke, Stout, & Salas, 2001). As suggested in Figure 5.1, the situation model is a product of situation assessment and other team process behaviors and individual situation models of each team member.

In our measurement of the team situation model, we have extended situation awareness query methods such as Situation Awareness Global Assessment Technique (SAGAT; Endsley, 1990) and Situation Present Assessment Method (SPAM; Durso et al., 1998) to the team situation. Most of our measures have relied on the SPAM method in which the environmental cues remain present (i.e., the display is not frozen or blank as required by the SAGAT method) and queries focus on future events or present events not immediately apparent from perusal of a single display.

We typically query each individual on the team about aspects of the task environment in the present or future (e.g., how many targets will your team manage to successfully photograph by the end of this mission?). Queries are either triggered by events or presented at randomly determined times. Individual responses are either written or oral; in the case of oral responses, team members are queried in random order within a 5-minute interval. Team accuracy can be estimated through aggregation of individual accuracy scores, though recently, we have begun to present queries to the team as a whole for a consensual response. We also examine the similarity or agreement of individual responses as another measure of the team situation model. In addition to implementing a holistic procedure, we have recently addressed the issue of repeating the same situation awareness queries across multiple missions.

We have explored a number of off-line (apart from the task) methods of assessing taskwork and teamwork knowledge of individuals and the team as a whole. Although we have assessed taskwork knowledge using multiple-choice test items pertinent to the task and by having team members analyze the task in terms of goals, subgoals, and objectives, the most successful approach thus far has relied on pairwise relatedness estimates of task-relevant concepts. That is, individual team members rate concepts like *airspeed* and *altitude* in terms of their overall relatedness in the task context. The concepts, which typically number 10 to 15, are carefully selected as representative of critical task concepts. In addition, selected concept pairs are hypothesized to discriminate between team members with low and high taskwork knowledge or between team members with different task roles. After rating data are collected, the results can also be used to further identify pairs that empirically discriminate individuals and teams.

We have used Pathfinder network scaling as a means of meaningfully reducing the quantitative ratings to a graphical structure (Schvaneveldt, 1990). The Pathfinder procedure also offers a means of comparing two or more resulting network structures quantitatively, thereby allowing comparisons of taskwork knowledge of two or more individuals or teams (aggregate networks based on average ratings of team members). This also allows comparisons of team or individual networks to a referent to determine knowledge accuracy. As mentioned previously, we have also extended this particular measure of taskwork knowledge to allow for holistic measurement and to address heterogeneous teams.

Our approach to measuring teamwork knowledge has also focused (until recently) on individual measurement and aggregation. In general, we elicit from individual team members their understanding of information requirements within a given scenario. The measure has evolved from a task in which team members used index cards to represent team members and information links between team members to a questionnaire in which team members read a scenario and check relevant items in a list where each items refers to a team member passing a specific type of information to another team member. Most of our data on the teamwork measure, however, come from a more open-ended questionnaire in which team members first indicate who is talking to whom in a given scenario and then describe the content of the communication. This measure can also be scored for intrateam similarity as well as accuracy.

Using Communication as a Window to Team Cognition

We have proposed a general methodological approach for semiautomatically assessing team cognition using communication data (Kiekel, Cooke,

Foltz, & Shope, 2001). The approach rests on the premise that analyzing communication data is a means of assessing team cognition. If teams are to be the unit of analysis under our holistic definition, we will need to measure behaviors exhibited by the team as a whole. Just as we use think-aloud verbal protocols to make inferences about individual cognition, so we have used the communication inherent in the collaboration process to assess team cognition in a holistic way. In this respect, team cognition is easier to measure than individual cognition; teams need not interrupt their process to think aloud, because they are always "thinking aloud" in some sense. With a newly formed team, team cognition begins as the sum of individual cognition. Then, as the team thinks (interacts), dynamic changes occur in the team mind as a natural result of the interaction. Effects of this process on performance depend on the type of task (Steiner, 1972). Thus, an analysis of team communication provides a window through which to view team cognition.

The need for automation in measurement and analysis is sparked by the time-consuming process of achieving reliable results with communication data. Such data are often voluminous and rich in contextual information. We have approached two aspects of communication data: communication flow from team member to team member and communication content. For communication flow, we have recorded frequency of speech by each team member at each second or at smaller specified intervals. We have developed and used several methods, especially sequential methods, for addressing these data. For instance, we have developed Clustering Hypothesized Underlying Models in Sequence (CHUMS; Kiekel, Cooke, Foltz, Gorman, & Martin, 2002) to cluster adjacent time units, so we can look for pattern changes (e.g., in amount of speech by each person). Another example is our use of Procedural Networks (ProNet; Cooke, Neville, & Rowe, 1996) to determine which speech events tend to co-occur in time (e.g., pilot begins speaking, navigator interrupts, pilot finishes speaking).

To analyze content data, we have quantified the actual content of the speech, both manually and using latent semantic analysis (LSA; Landauer, Foltz, & Laham, 1998). LSA is a model of human language that can be used to code content and to determine similarity among utterances. It works by assessing co-occurrence of words within a large representative corpus of the language (e.g., encyclopedias, text books, transcripts). It first defines a matrix of the frequency of co-occurrence of each word with each other word. Co-occurrence is defined as two words occurring in the same paragraph. Then this rudimentary knowledge of the language is generalized to semantic knowledge. LSA extracts latent dimensions underlying the co-occurrence matrix by singular value decomposition (the machinery behind principal-components analysis and factor analysis). LSA then retains the first 300–400 dimensions (however many the user chooses), so that each word is quantified by a vector in 300–400 dimensional space. Each utterance is a vector made of the mean of its words. These vectors each have length, which is akin to the amount of meaning in an utterance. Furthermore, utterances can be correlated by taking their cosine. Using LSA, we have looked at variables such as the continuity of similarity from one utterance to the next, similarity of the whole team's dialogue to other teams whose performance score was known, and overall internal consistency of the team's communication, defined by the mean of the similarity matrix among all utterances.

Automating and Embedding Measures

We have approached the goal of automated and task-embedded knowledge measures along several fronts. There is still much to do. For instance, our measures of taskwork and teamwork knowledge are still collected offline. The teamwork measures are paper-based questionnaires, and although the taskwork relatedness ratings are collected via computer, the sheer number of ratings required for a pairwise ratings task where N is equal to the number of concepts is $(N \times (N-1))/2$. This translates to 45 ratings for 10 concepts and 190 for 20. Consequently, as concepts are added, the task becomes tedious quickly and requires streamlining.

Alternatively, our team situation awareness measures represent progress along this front. We are firm believers in embedded measures of situation awareness, as it is necessary to measure that knowledge in the context of the situation at the moment when momentary understanding occurs. So, we have successfully embedded our team situation awareness measures in the task and have even generated somewhat automated and online probe sheets as cues for the experimenters.

Possibly our greatest contribution in the area of automation and task-embedded measures has resulted from the work described previously in which we use team communications as an automatically generated and task-embedded think-aloud task at the team level. We can then infer team cognition or team knowledge from this team think-aloud.

VALIDATING NEW MEASURES OF TEAM COGNITION

Our approach has been to validate the measures described previously through experimentation in which we examine the changes in the measure with skill acquisition and the degree to which the measure is predictive of performance. Experimentation occurs in the context of Synthetic Task Environments (STEs), laboratory abstractions of operational tasks such as Navy helicopter rescue missions (Cooke, 1998; Cooke et al., 2003), and Uninhabited Air Vehicle (UAV) ground operations (Cooke, Kiekel, & Helm, 2001; Cooke, Shope, & Kiekel, 2001).

Looking at the changes in acquisition curves across trials provides at least two pieces of information. First, it is a means of validating the measure, as measures of knowledge or skill gained in the course of the experimental trials should show a learning curve with repeated trials and covary with skill acquisition. Second, testing postasymptote trials against one another can assess reliability for any given measure. If it is known that the team is at asymptote, then any variation in the same team on the same score must be due to unreliability.

Team process and cognitive or knowledge measures can be judged for validity on the basis of how well they predict performance. Whether the prediction needs to be a direct or an indirect prediction of performance (a path that leads through another variable) depends on the constructs under consideration. Further, when team performance is affected by manipulations of various types (e.g., workload changes, communication mode changes), it is expected that such variations in performance should also be reflected in underlying cognitive and behavioral constructs that support this performance. For example, when workload demands of the task are increased, team performance typically declines, and this decline should similarly be apparent from the measures of relevant cognitive and behavioral constructs.

WHAT HAVE WE LEARNED ABOUT TEAM COGNITION?

We have conducted several team experiments in which we measure team knowledge in addition to team performance and process (Cooke, 1998; Cooke, Kiekel, & Helm, 2001; Cooke, Kiekel, et al., 2000; Cooke et al., 2003; Cooke, Shope, et al., 2001). We measure team performance using composite scores based on task outcomes, and we measure team process behaviors using observer ratings of process behaviors along dimensions such as communication, coordination, and decision making or by using a behavioral checklist in which target behaviors are associated with event triggers in the context of the task. These performance and process measures serve as criterion values for our team knowledge predictors. Newly developed or modified measures of team knowledge are then applied in these experiments and evaluated in terms of their ability to predict team performance and process and to reflect any other experimental manipulations thought to influence team knowledge, such as team task experience and training regime.

As previously mentioned, our experiments were performed in the context of synthetic task environments. Findings that were replicated in at least three of the four studies are reported next. Note that although these findings appear to generalize across our two synthetic tasks, the extent to which they generalize to other teams, team tasks, and work domains is an empirical question for further research.

Taskwork Knowledge Is Predictive of Team Performance

Across our studies we have generally found that taskwork knowledge, measured after individual task training, is predictive of team performance.

That is, teams with members who understand the task immediately or soon after training tend to be high-performing teams. For example, in one of our UAV studies (Cooke, Kiekel, & Helm, 2001), taskwork knowledge measured after training and the first mission predicted team performance on the 2nd mission, $r(9) = .839$, $p < .01$, and the 10th mission, $r(8) = .725$, $p < .05$. However, there are a few caveats to this generalization, even within the context of our studies.

First, this finding is true when taskwork knowledge is measured using taskwork relatedness ratings (i.e., team members rate pairs of task-relevant concepts for relatedness and these ratings are analyzed using the Pathfinder network scaling algorithm) and, to a lesser extent, the consensus version of the ratings targeting holistic taskwork knowledge. For instance, in the same UAV study mentioned previously (Cooke, Kiekel, & Helm, 2001), taskwork knowledge accuracy as based on the individual taskwork ratings predicted team performance on the first four missions with correlations ranging from .535 to .839 ($df = 9$), whereas when taskwork knowledge accuracy is based on the consensus ratings correlations with team performance on the same missions ranged from .352 to .549 ($df = 9$). Accuracy using these rating measures is based on comparison with a referent network indicating pairs that should or should not be related. The ability of taskwork knowledge to predict team performance, however, does not hold when measured more directly using multiple-choice tests or unstructured questionnaires requiring goal and task decomposition.

This does not imply that these more direct methods are invalid. Alternatively, it may be that our implementation of them is flawed. Indeed, our multiple-choice questions have tended to be too easy and thus not very sensitive, whereas the goal and task decomposition exercise was so open-ended that it produced a wide range of mainly terse and vague responses that were very difficult to score. So, although we have had the most success with the relatedness rating task, team knowledge of the task may be measured adequately using other methods implemented in a different way. However, we believe that the relatedness ratings task works (i.e., is sensitive to team performance differences) because of its indirect nature. Judgments are made more easily than explicit facts are recalled, and seemingly minor discrepancies in some judgments may reflect the difference between an expert and a novice (Schvaneveldt et al., 1985). Also, in many ways, the similarity of two sets of relatedness estimates, or two resulting networks, seems more in line with the idea of shared mental models. Although we would not expect two individuals with "shared mental models" to know the identical facts and rules in regard to a task (as measured by more direct tests of knowledge), it seems reasonable that they would have the same perspective on a task, reflected in similar relatedness judgments.

The second caveat to the finding that taskwork knowledge is predictive of team performance is that with the application of our heterogeneous knowledge metrics we are getting a better idea of the precise nature of that knowledge. In the UAV context, teams that are high performing have members who each understand the task as a whole (i.e., the big picture) and from the perspective of each team role or position. For instance, for good UAV teams, the Air Vehicle Operator understands the task from all perspectives in that he or she provides ratings that are accurate in regard to the Air Vehicle Operator referent, as well as the referents associated with the Payload Operator, and DEMPC (i.e., Data Exploitation, Mission Planning, and Communications Operator) roles. In a UAV study, for instance (Cooke, Kiekel, & Helm, 2001), correlations between team performance and interpositional taskwork knowledge based on ratings and comparisons with role referents ranged from .232 to .613 for the first four missions and .555 to .677 for the last three missions. In other words, good teams have interpositional knowledge of taskwork. So, for these highly interdependent team tasks that we have studied, it is not just a matter of becoming expert at a single task, but also of understanding the other roles well enough to provide "accurate" relatedness ratings of task concepts relevant to these other roles.

Finally, one other finding has emerged that has direct support in one of the helicopter studies and indirect support in several other studies. Specifically, there appears to be a sequential constraint on the acquisition of taskwork versus teamwork knowledge. In a cross-training study (Cooke et al., 2003), we attempted to short-cut traditional cross-training in which all team members are given complete training in each role. We compared this full cross-training condition that emphasized taskwork with a condition in which team members were cross-trained not in the other tasks themselves but on teamwork information. That is, information about the responsibilities and information requirements associated with each team role was conveyed through notes and charts. We hypothesized that because this latter condition preserved what we believed to be the essence of cross-training, it should take less time and be at least as successful in terms of team performance relative to full cross-training.

Contrary to our expectations, full cross-trained teams showed marginal benefits in terms of team performance but significant taskwork and teamwork knowledge benefits. That is, full cross-trained teams had more interpositional knowledge than other teams in regard to both taskwork and teamwork knowledge (see Cooke et al., 2003, for details). Further analyses suggested that the acquisition of teamwork knowledge (trained explicitly in the abbreviated training condition) was facilitated by a prior understanding of taskwork knowledge (conveyed in the full cross-training condition). In other words, team members need to understand what is done before they understand who does it. But, why did we see only marginal performance benefits with full cross-training? It appears that for this task, unlike the UAV task, taskwork knowledge specialization, not interpositional knowledge, is associated with high-performing teams. Thus, cross-training may be at odds with the knowledge requirements of this task. These interesting possibilities regarding knowledge requirements and sequential constraints in the acquisition of taskwork and teamwork knowledge were only revealed through our measurement of team knowledge, and thus provide support for the diagnostic power of the measurement of team cognition.

Team Situation Awareness Is Predictive of Team Performance

In our studies we have also found that team situation awareness is a consistently good predictor of team performance. Teams with high situation awareness tend to be better performing teams. For instance in a UAV study (Cooke, Kiekel, & Helm, 2001), team accuracy scores on situation awareness probes (averaged across 10 missions) were correlated with team performance (also averaged across the 10 missions), $r(11) = .88$, $p < .0001$. In addition, team situation awareness is one type of knowledge that continues to improve after training with team task experience. For instance, Cooke, Kiekel, and Helm (2001) found that team situation awareness accuracy and intrateam similarity improve across missions and parallel skill acquisition on the task. This might be expected as the knowledge and expectations that are tied to specific mission situations cannot be conveyed in our factual tutorials as well as through direct exposure to the situation.

In some cases the correlation between team situation awareness and team performance has been so high—for example, the $r(11) = .88$ referenced above—that we have questioned the validity of our measure. It is possible that through repeated exposure to situation awareness queries, team members acquire situation awareness that focuses on information relevant to the queries, thus artificially inflating their situation awareness accuracy. However, if this is the case, then it is the acquisition of this "test knowledge," rather than situation awareness, that is associated with high team performance. Indeed, our most recent results suggest that accuracy on repeated situation awareness queries is more highly correlated with team performance than in accuracy on nonrepeated queries. This suggests that the situation awareness that we measure that is developing and mirroring performance is constrained to the specific task and experimental situation.

Teamwork Knowledge Changes With Experience

In our studies we have also seen a general tendency for the teams' knowledge of teamwork to increase over time. For example, Cooke, Kiekel, and Helm (2001) found that accuracy on the teamwork questionnaire increased over the four knowledge sessions (.53, .66, .71, and .65), with the largest increase paralleling the team performance acquisition function. However, discrepancies in the accuracy of teamwork knowledge do not predict team performance and, thus, this is something that teams seem to acquire uniformly with team task experience. The general pattern seems to be that the team's knowledge of taskwork is acquired early through the training tutorials (largely declarative knowledge), but this is not acquired to the same degree by all teams, and discrepancies are predictive of team performance. The more fleeting knowledge (i.e., situation awareness) and the team's knowledge of teamwork are acquired through actual task experience (largely procedural knowledge). Also, discrepancies in situation awareness but not teamwork knowledge predict performance. The sequential constraint discussed previously in regard to teamwork and taskwork knowledge may explain the different patterns of knowledge acquisition. That is, it seems important for the acquisition of taskwork knowledge to precede teamwork knowledge and so unlike situation awareness, it may not be that exposure to actual mission situations is critical to learn about teamwork. Rather the sequential constraint demands that the acquisition of teamwork knowledge wait until taskwork knowledge is mastered. In addition, it is possible that our teamwork measure (questions about information flow in the team) is not sensitive enough to reveal subtle differences among teams that are reflected by the situation awareness and taskwork measures.

Communication Consistency Predicts Team Performance

We believe that the use of communication data as a window to team cognition is not only theoretically justified but also practical given that these data can be collected unobtrusively during mission performance. The challenge is in finding methods of communication analysis that best reflect team cognition. Thus far, we have had promising results using LSA (Landauer et al., 1998) to identify similarity in segments of discourse based on semantic content. We have also used ProNet (Cooke et al., 1996) to examine patterns of communication flow among team members across a 40-minute mission. In both cases, the preliminary results (Kiekel et al., 2001) suggest that teams who perform poorly exhibit a variety of communication patterns in terms of both flow and content. This variation occurs within individual teams. In contrast, high-performing teams demonstrate consistency over time in both what they say (i.e., content) and who they say it to and when (i.e., flow). In general, the results of the semiautomated approaches to communication analysis have been successful in terms of predicting team performance. Next steps involve associating communication patterns with team characteristics or behaviors more diagnostic of cognitive or behavioral deficits or strengths (Kiekel et al., 2002).

CONCLUDING REMARKS

In this chapter we have presented our motivation for investigating team cognition, have discussed its importance, and have offered a definition of team cognition. In light of this definition, we have highlighted several limitations of traditional measurements of team cognition. Our recent research in the area begins to address some of these limitations by developing new methods or adapting older methods for measuring team cognition. Of primary importance are the development of automated and task-embedded measures and the evaluation of new measures in terms of their validity. Thus far, we have identified some valid measures of team cognition, specifically taskwork knowledge, teamwork knowledge, and the knowledge associated with team situation awareness. In four studies we find that taskwork knowledge seems to precede the acquisition of teamwork knowledge and that teams with members who understand the task from the perspectives of roles other than their own (assessed using metrics for heterogeneous teams) tend to be high-performing teams. These results seem to be specific to the task, however, as we also find in other tasks that specialization in taskwork knowledge is key to effective performance. We have also begun to develop and test holistic measures of team knowledge that approach measurement by eliciting or assessing knowledge at the team level. Finally, we are investigating team communication analysis methods because they offer the promise of automated and task-embedded measures of team cognition.

This chapter documents some small steps taken in an effort to help understand fully what comprises effective team functioning. Team cognition represents the most challenging and difficult pillar for providing a comprehensive picture of the attitudes, behavior, and cognition of teams. It is only, we believe, through theoretically driven systematic lab and field studies that focus on designing, developing, and validating sensitive, diagnostic, and useful measures of team cognition that we will contribute a much needed answer to the numerous businesses, industries, and agencies for which teams are central. We hope this chapter and the others in this volume motivate more thinking and research on this important topic.

REFERENCES

Adams, M. J., Tenney, Y. J., & Pew, R. W. (1995). Situation awareness and the cognitive management of complex systems. *Human Factors, 37,* 85–104.

Cannon-Bowers, J. A., & Salas, E. (1997). Teamwork competencies: The interaction of team member knowledge skills and attitudes. In O. F. O'Neil (Ed.), *Workforce readiness: Competencies and assessment* (pp. 151–174). Hillsdale, NJ: Erlbaum.

Cannon-Bowers, J. A., & Salas, E. (Eds.). (1998). *Making decisions under stress: Implications for individual and team training.* Washington, DC: American Psychological Association.

Cannon-Bowers, J. A., Salas, E., & Converse, S. (1993). Shared mental models in expert team decision making. In J. Castellan, Jr. (Ed.), *Current issues in individual and group decision making* (pp. 221–246). Hillsdale, NJ: Erlbaum.

Cannon-Bowers, J. A., Tannenbaum, S. I., Salas, E., & Volpe, C. E. (1995). Defining team competencies and establishing team training requirements. In R. Guzzo & E. Salas (Eds.), *Teams: Their training and performance* (pp. 101–124). Norwood, NJ: Ablex.

Chase, W. G., & Simon, H. A. (1973). Perception in chess. *Cognitive Psychology, 4*, 55–81.

Clark, H. H., & Schaefer, E. F. (1987). Collaborating on contributions to conversations. *Language and Cognitive Processes, 2*, 19–41.

Cooke, N. J. (1994). Varieties of knowledge elicitation techniques. *International Journal of Human-Computer Studies, 41*, 801–849.

Cooke, N. J. (1998). *Measures of team knowledge* (Report No. N61339-97-M-0507, submitted to Naval Air Warfare Center Training Systems Division, Orlando, FL). Las Cruces, NM: Cooke.

Cooke, N. J., Kiekel, P. A., & Helm, E. (2001). Measuring team knowledge during skill acquisition of a complex task. *International Journal of Cognitive Ergonomics, 5*, 297–315.

Cooke, N. J., Kiekel, P. A., Salas, E., Stout, R., Bowers, C., & Cannon-Bowers, J. (2003). Measuring team knowledge: A window to the cognitive underpinnings of team performance. *Group Dynamics: Theory, Research, and Practice, 7*(3), 179–199.

Cooke, N. J., Neville, K. J., & Rowe, A. L. (1996). Procedural network representations of sequential data. *Human-Computer Interaction, 11*, 29–68.

Cooke, N. J., Salas, E., Cannon-Bowers, J. A., & Stout, R. (2000). Measuring team knowledge. *Human Factors, 42*, 151–173.

Cooke, N. J., Shope, S. M., & Kiekel, P. A. (2001). *Shared-knowledge and team performance: A cognitive engineering approach to measurement* (Tech. Rep. No. F49620-98-1-0287 for AFOSR Grant). Las Cruces, NM: Cooke.

Cooke, N. J., Stout, R., & Salas, E. (1997). Expanding the measurement of situation awareness through cognitive engineering methods. In *Proceedings of the Human Factors and Ergonomics Society 41st Annual Meeting* (pp. 215–219). Santa Monica, CA: Human Factors and Ergonomics Society.

Cooke, N. J., Stout, R. J., & Salas, E. (2001). A knowledge elicitation approach to the measurement of team situation awareness. In M. McNeese, M. Endsley, & E. Salas (Eds.), *New trends in cooperative activities: System dynamics in complex settings* (pp. 114–139). Santa Monica, CA: Human Factors and Ergonomic Society.

Davis, J. H. (1973). Group decision and social interaction: A theory of social decision schemes. *Psychological Review, 80*, 97–125.

Durso, F. T., & Gronlund, S. D. (1999). Situation awareness. In F. T. Durso, R. S. Nickerson, R. W. Schvaneveldt, S. T. Dumais, D. S. Lindsay, & M. T. H. Chi (Eds.), *Handbook of applied cognition* (pp. 283–314). London: Wiley.

Durso, F. T., Hackworth, C. A., Truitt, T. R., Crutchfield, J., Nikolic, D., & Manning, C. A. (1998). Situation awareness as a predictor of performance in en route air traffic controllers. *Air Traffic Control Quarterly, 5*, 1–20.

Endsley, M. R. (1990). A methodology for the objective measure of situation awareness. In *Situational awareness in aerospace operations* (No. AGARD-CP-478, pp. 1/1–1/9). Neuilly-Sur-Seine, France: NATO, Advisory Group for Aerospace Research and Development.

Endsley, M. R. (1995a). Measurement of situation awareness in dynamic systems. *Human Factors, 37,* 65–84.

Endsley, M. R. (1995b). Toward a theory of situation awareness in dynamic systems. *Human Factors, 37,* 32–64.

Everitt, B. S. (1993). *Cluster analysis* (3rd ed.). New York: Halsted Press.

Fracker, M. L. (1991). *Measures of situation awareness: Review and future directions* (Tech. Rep. No AL-TR-1991-0128). Wright Patterson Air Force Base, OH: Air Force Systems Command.

Glaser, R., & Chi, M. T. H. (1988). Overview. In M. T. H. Chi, R. Glaser, & M. J. Farr (Eds.), *The nature of expertise* (pp. xv–xxviii). Hillsdale, NJ: Erlbaum.

Guzzo, R. A., & Salas, E. (Eds.). (1995). *Team effectiveness and decision-making in organizations.* San Francisco: Jossey-Bass.

Guzzo, R. A., & Shea, G. P. (1992). Group performance and intergroup relations in organizations. In M. D. Dunnette & L. M. Hough (Eds.), *Handbook of industrial and organizational psychology* (Vol. 3, 2nd ed., pp. 269–313). Palo Alto, CA: Consulting Psychologists Press.

Hackman, R. A. (Ed.). (1990). *Groups that work (and those that don't): Creating conditions for effective team work.* San Francisco: Jossey-Bass.

Hinsz, V. B. (1999). Group decision making with responses of a quantitative nature: The theory of social decision schemes for quantities. *Organizational Behavior and Human Decision Processes, 80,* 28–49.

Hutchins, E. (1991). The social organization of distributed cognition. In L. B. Resnick, J. M. Levine, & S. D. Teasley (Eds.), *Perspectives on socially shared cognition* (pp. 283–307). Washington, DC: American Psychological Association.

Kiekel, P. A., Cooke, N. J., Foltz, P. W., Gorman, J., & Martin, M. (2002). Some promising results of communication-based automatic measures of team cognition. In *Proceedings of the Human Factors and Ergonomics Society 46th Annual Meeting* (pp. 298–302). Santa Monica, CA: Human Factors and Ergonomics Society.

Kiekel, P. A., Cooke, N. J., Foltz, P. W., & Shope, S. M. (2001). Automating measurement of team cognition through analysis of communication data. In M. J. Smith, G. Salvendy, D. Harris, & R. J. Koubek (Eds.), *Usability evaluation and interface design* (pp. 1382–1386). Mahwah, NJ: Erlbaum.

Klimoski, R., & Mohammed, S. (1994). Team mental model: Construct or metaphor. *Journal of Management, 20,* 403–437.

Kraiger, K., & Wenzel, L. H. (1997). Conceptual development and empirical evaluation of measures of shared mental models as indicators of team effectiveness. In M. T. Brannick, E. Salas, & C. Prince (Eds.), *Performance assessment and measurement: Theory, methods, and applications* (pp. 63–84). Mahwah, NJ: Erlbaum.

Landauer, T. K., Foltz, P. W., & Laham, D. (1998). An introduction to latent semantic analysis. *Discourse Processes, 25*, 259–284.

Langan-Fox, J., Code, S., & Langfield-Smith, K. (2000). Team mental models: Techniques, methods, and analytic approaches. *Human Factors, 42*, 242–271.

Levine, J. M., & Moreland, R. L. (1990). Progress in small group research. *Annual Review of Psychology, 41*, 585–634.

Orasanu, J. (1990). *Shared mental models and crew decision making* (Tech. Rep. No. 46). Princeton, NJ: Princeton University, Cognitive Science Laboratory.

Salas, E., & Cannon-Bowers, J. A. (2000). The anatomy of team training. In S. Tobias & J. D. Fletcher (Eds.), *Training and retraining: A handbook for business, industry, government, and the military* (pp. 312–335). New York: Macmillan Reference.

Salas, E., Dickinson, T. L., Converse, S. A., & Tannenbaum, S. I. (1992). Toward an understanding of team performance and training. In R. W. Swezey & E. Salas (Eds.), *Teams: Their training and performance* (pp. 3–29). Norwood, NJ: Ablex.

Salas, E., Prince, C., Baker, D. P., & Shrestha, L. (1995). Situation awareness in team performance: Implications for measurement and training. *Human Factors, 37*, 123–136.

Sarter, N. B., & Woods, D. D. (1991). Situation awareness: A critical but ill-defined phenomenon. *International Journal of Aviation Psychology, 1*, 45–57.

Sarter, N. B., & Woods, D. D. (1995). How in the world did we ever get into that mode? Mode error and awareness in supervisory control. *Human Factors, 37*, 5–19.

Schvaneveldt, R. W. (1990). *Pathfinder associative networks: Studies in knowledge organization*. Norwood, NJ: Ablex.

Schvaneveldt, R. W., Durso, F. T., Goldsmith, T. E., Breen, T. J., Cooke, N. M., Tucker, R. G., & DeMaio, J. C. (1985). Measuring the structure of expertise. *International Journal of Man-Machine Studies, 23*, 699–728.

Steiner, I. D. (1972). *Group processes and productivity*. New York: Academic Press.

Stout, R., Cannon-Bowers, J. A., & Salas, E. (1996). The role of shared mental models in developing team situation awareness: Implications for training. *Training Research Journal, 2*, 85–116.

Taylor, R. M., & Selcon, S. J. (1994). Situation in mind: Theory, application, and measurement of situational awareness. In R. D. Gilson, D. J. Garland, & J. M. Koonce (Eds.), *Situational awareness in complex systems* (pp. 69–77). Daytona Beach, FL: Embry-Riddle Aeronautical University Press.

Vidulich, M. A. (1989). The use of judgment matrices in subjective workload assessment: The subjective workload dominance (SWORD) technique. In *Proceedings of the Human Factors Society 33rd Annual Meeting* (pp. 1406–1410). Santa Monica, CA: Human Factors and Ergonomics Society.

Wegner, D. M. (1986). Transactive memory: A contemporary analysis of the group mind. In B. Mullen & G. Goethals (Eds.), *Theories of group behavior* (pp. 185–208). New York: Springer-Verlag.

Wilkes-Gibbs, D., & Clark, H. H. (1992). Coordinating beliefs in conversation. *Journal of Memory and Language, 31*, 183–194.

6

EXPLICIT VERSUS IMPLICIT COORDINATION MECHANISMS AND TASK DEPENDENCIES: ONE SIZE DOES NOT FIT ALL

J. ALBERTO ESPINOSA, F. JAVIER LERCH, AND ROBERT E. KRAUT

Teams are important units of organizational work because they bring diverse expertise, skills, and resources to complex tasks that may be too large or complex for a single individual to undertake. However, as projects and teams grow in size and complexity, tasks and member dependencies become more numerous and more complex, thus increasing the need for team coordination. Effective teams manage these dependencies using a number of explicit and implicit coordination mechanisms and processes. Teams coordinate explicitly using task programming mechanisms (e.g., schedules, plans, procedures) or by communicating (e.g., orally, in writing, formally, informally, interpersonally, in groups). We call these mechanisms *explicit* because team members use them purposely to coordinate. However, teams can also coordinate *implicitly* (i.e., without consciously trying to coordinate) through team cognition, or knowledge that team members share about the task and

This research was partially supported by the National Science Foundation Grant No. ISS-9812123 and by Lucent Technologies.

about each other. This shared knowledge helps team members understand what is going on with the task and anticipate what may happen next and which actions team members are likely to take, thus helping them coordinate. In this chapter we discuss the interplay between explicit and implicit coordination mechanisms and how they jointly affect team coordination and performance.

Because dependencies can be managed in more than one way, teams will make decisions on which explicit coordination mechanisms to use. However, the use of such explicit mechanisms both influence (e.g., by interacting, by sharing documents) and are influenced by the existing level of team cognition (e.g., members with shared knowledge may communicate less frequently and more efficiently). Consequently, it is important that we understand how explicit and implicit coordination mechanisms complement and interact with each other. We also discuss in this chapter the need to understand the nature of the multiple dependencies involved in a task to figure out which mechanisms can be more effective in helping teams coordinate. Different mechanisms, whether explicit or implicit, will have varying degrees of effectiveness for different tasks and for different stages of a given task. On the one hand, team communication may be very important for complex intellective tasks in which task dependencies are somewhat uncertain or for the early stages of a task, when team members are still unfamiliar with the task and with each other. On the other hand, team communication may not be so important for more mechanical tasks (e.g., assembly line) in which dependencies are more predictable or for the late stages of a task, once team members know each other or once they have implemented division of labor schemes.

Throughout this chapter we focus on asynchronous (i.e., non-real-time) and geographically dispersed task contexts. This is an important distinction because most of the literature on team cognition has focused on synchronous (i.e., same-time) and co-located teams (e.g., flight crews, medical emergency units). However, work arrangements and the nature of the resulting dependencies will vary substantially depending on whether the team is separated by time or by distance. We begin our discussion by describing a unified framework of team coordination that incorporates both explicit and implicit coordination mechanisms. Next we discuss the importance of identifying key dependencies and coordination types for a given task. Finally, we summarize our conclusions. Throughout our discussion, we present examples and results from our empirical studies with (a) decision (asynchronous) teams that managed simulated companies for Carnegie Mellon University's Management Game course (Espinosa, Carley, Kraut, Lerch, & Fussell, 2002) and (b) large-scale, geographically distributed software development teams from a Fortune 500 telecommunications company (Espinosa, 2002; Espinosa et al., 2001; Espinosa, Kraut, et al., 2002). We refer in this chapter to the first teams as the *decision teams* and to the second teams as the *software teams*.

THEORETICAL FRAMEWORK

In this section we propose and describe a theoretical framework (illustrated in Figure 6.1) to study the effects of team cognition on team coordination and performance. This framework has three important properties. First, it is an input–process–output model, which is appropriate for the study of teams (Kraemer & Pinsonneault, 1990; McGrath, 1991; McGrath & Hollingshead, 1994). Input variables in the framework represent task, team, and context factors that give rise to different work arrangements and dependencies. Teams manage these dependencies using a mix of coordination mechanisms. The effective management of these dependencies influences the team's state of coordination, which in turn affects team performance. Second, the framework includes both explicit and implicit coordination mechanisms, which, as we discuss later in the chapter, need to be modeled jointly because they may complement, affect, or interact with each other in their effect on team coordination. Finally, the framework relates to how task dependencies originate (i.e., the need to coordinate) and how these dependencies are managed (i.e., the act of coordinating). In this section, we provide the theoretical foundations of the framework. We first define coordination and then describe the framework by discussing how coordination affects performance, how implicit and explicit coordination mechanisms affect team coordination, and how input variables (i.e., task, team, and context) influence the mix of coordination mechanisms used by a team. We then offer an integrated view of our theoretical framework. We discuss the third property of the framework in the next section of this chapter in which we relate the different elements of the framework to the underlying task dependencies.

Coordination Defined: Managing Dependencies

We draw from the research literature on coordination theory to define coordination as the effective management of dependencies among subtasks, resources (e.g., equipment, tools), and people (Malone & Crowston, 1990, 1994). If things can be done totally independently, then there is nothing to coordinate. Conversely, when multiple individuals, subtasks, and resources need to interact in a synchronized fashion to carry out a joint task, it gives rise to dependencies among them. Team members can perform their individual responsibilities competently and still be very uncoordinated with the rest of the team if the respective dependencies among their subtasks are not well managed. We use this view of coordination from the perspective of managing dependencies throughout this chapter to explain how different elements of the proposed framework fit together. This definition of coordination is useful when conducting research because it helps define concepts and develop measures. For example, coordination can be viewed as both a process (i.e., coordinating) and an outcome (i.e., coordination success). The

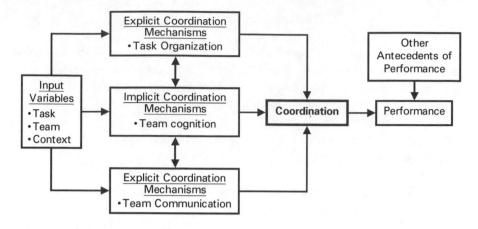

Figure 6.1. Theoretical framework.

process of coordinating can be defined as the activities carried out by team members when managing dependencies. For instance, when a software team convenes a debriefing meeting so that all parties can share the status of their respective tasks, they are managing the dependencies involved in developing software as a team by communicating with each other about what is going on with their individual task assignments. Coordination as an outcome (i.e., coordination success) can be defined as the extent to which dependencies have been effectively managed. For example, a software team will be well coordinated if all software parts for a given project work well together, are delivered on schedule, and are produced according to the established software process (i.e., technical, temporal, and software process dependencies have been effectively managed).

Coordination: An Antecedent of Team Performance

Performance is an outcome of utmost interest in team research. Team coordination is useful to the extent that it leads to team performance, but coordination is not always important for performance. For example, coordination may not be so important for team problem-solving tasks in which a "eureka" type solution exists, which is evident to all members when one member figures it out. If members of a team can work independently and if there are no task dependencies, then there is nothing to coordinate and, consequently, coordination will not affect performance (Malone & Crowston, 1994; Thompson, 1967; VanDeVen, Delbecq, & Koenig, 1976). In contrast, more complex tasks with substantial dependencies can indeed benefit from coordination. However, even if coordination is necessary for performance, it may not always be sufficient to ensure performance. First of all, some task dependencies are more critical to performance than others. A team may be doing a great job at managing some task dependencies that are important but not critical for task performance (e.g., delivering software on time) while not paying much attention to other dependencies that are critical for task performance (e.g., delivering high-quality and error-free software). For instance, in our study with software teams some technical and project managers described situations in which they had implemented software product features in a very effective and productive manner, only to find out later on that these features had been removed from the product because they were not what the client wanted or what the market needed. Similar "feature churn" problems have been documented in other studies (Crowston & Kammerer, 1998). Similarly, in our study with decision teams we found that the effect of task coordination (e.g., avoiding duplication of work, having clear assignment of tasks) on performance is indirect, mediated by functional strategy coordination (e.g., finance strategy well coordinated with production strategy).

Second, there may be other antecedents of performance that are unrelated to coordination, which may hinder or enhance performance. For example, in our study with decision teams we found some evidence that strategy coordination had a positive effect on team performance, but it only explained a small percentage of variance. Instructors of the Management Game simulation course indicated that in addition to having coordinated strategies, successful teams also have sound functional strategies (i.e., finance, marketing, and operations) and a good understanding of the competitive environments in which their simulated firms operate.

Explicit Coordination Mechanisms:
The Classic Organizational Theory View

A coordination mechanism is one that helps teams manage dependencies. For example, simple things in a person's daily life such as a traffic light and a flight schedule can be viewed as coordination mechanisms because they help the person manage dependencies with other drivers and the airlines, respectively. Consequently, explicit coordination mechanisms can be defined as those mechanisms explicitly used by a team for the purpose of managing task dependencies. Explicit coordination mechanisms and processes have been studied in the classical organizational research literature for several years. This literature suggests that teams coordinate explicitly by using task organization mechanisms or by communicating. March and Simon (1958) suggested that teams use task organization (or *task programming*) mechanisms for the most routine aspects of the task because the respective dependencies are more predictable, and thus can be more easily managed in a programmed way (see also Thompson, 1967). Examples of these mechanisms include division of labor, tools, schedules, plans, manuals, and specifications.

When routines change or when the task has very little or no routine aspects, task organization mechanisms are less effective because dependencies can no longer be managed in a programmed way. March and Simon

(1958) suggested that teams resort to communication (i.e., coordination by feedback) in such cases. For example, a software project schedule may be rendered useless if several deliverable deadlines have already been missed or if there has been a crisis (e.g., a major hardware failure) that calls for rescheduling. When these things happen, the team needs to communicate to cope with the changing situation or to implement different coordination mechanisms more suitable to the new situation. Coordination by communication can be interpersonal or in groups. It can also be formal or informal. For instance, an empirical study with software teams at an organization found that teams not only coordinated by communicating formally through meetings and documents but also did a substantial amount of coordination informally during encounters in public places such as water coolers and hallways (Kraut & Streeter, 1995).

This discussion underscores the fact that different coordination mechanisms may be more suitable for different tasks. Furthermore, the same task may require the use of different coordination mechanisms over time. Studies conducted at Carnegie Mellon have analyzed software student teams developing small applications for external clients and found that these teams changed the mix of coordination mechanisms they used over time (Wholey, Kiesler, & Carley, 1996). For example, Wholey et al. found that teams communicate more intensely at the beginning. The study also found that (a) successful teams only communicated moderately toward the end; (b) unsuccessful novice teams communicated too little, whereas unsuccessful expert teams communicated too much; and (c) division of labor was an effective task organization mechanism only toward the end of the task, once team members knew each other's skills well.

Implicit Coordination Mechanisms: A More Recent View From Team Cognition Research

More recent research in team cognition suggests that as team members interact with each other and gain expertise with the task, they develop shared knowledge about the task and the team, which helps them coordinate implicitly (Cannon-Bowers, Salas, & Converse, 1993; Klimoski & Mohammed, 1994; Levesque, Wilson, & Wholey, 2001). For example, team members coordinate implicitly by providing necessary information to each other without having to ask (Entin & Serfaty, 1999; Kleinman & Serfaty, 1989). Such implicit coordination has been referred to as the "synchronization of member actions based on unspoken assumptions about what others in the group are likely to do" (Wittenbaum & Stasser, 1996, p. 23). Consequently, we define implicit coordination mechanisms as those that are available to members from team cognition that enable them to explain and anticipate task states and member actions, thus helping them manage task dependencies.

There are a number of different streams of research that have studied these implicit coordination mechanisms. A survey by Cannon-Bowers and Salas (2001) identified over 20 team cognition labels and constructs described and studied in the literature, including shared (or team) mental models (Cannon-Bowers et al., 1993; Klimoski & Mohammed, 1994; Kraiger & Wenzel, 1997; Rouse, Cannon-Bowers, & Salas, 1992; Rouse & Morris, 1986), team situation awareness (Endsley, 1995; Wellens, 1993), transactive memory (Liang, Moreland, & Argote, 1995; Wegner, 1986), mutual knowledge (Cramton, 2001; Fussell & Krauss, 1992; Krauss & Fussell, 1990), and collective mind (Weick & Roberts, 1993). These constructs are conceptually distinct, but they share the commonality that some form of knowledge similarity or knowledge complement helps team members explain other members' actions, understand what is going on with the task, develop accurate expectations about future member actions and task states, and communicate meaning efficiently because of shared vocabulary and more common ground. All of this improves coordination.

Team cognition research has focused primarily on developing theoretical foundations, but there has been a paucity of empirical studies. Fortunately, this is beginning to change. For example, a study of dyads working in a flight simulation task found that shared mental models have a positive, but indirect effect on team performance, mediated by team process (e.g., coordination; Mathieu, Goodwin, Heffner, Salas, & Cannon-Bowers, 2000). Also, most of the research in shared cognition has focused on real-time and co-located teams. But because time and distance separation provide fewer opportunities for members to interact and acquire shared knowledge, team cognition is much more difficult to develop in asynchronous and geographically dispersed environments, thus the importance of conducting research in these contexts. Fortunately, new research is beginning to emerge in these contexts. For instance, a recent study of large-scale software developers found that "administrative" (i.e., explicit) coordination positively affects team performance, but it also found that knowing where expertise is located in the team has a positive and significant effect on team effectiveness and efficiency, above and beyond the effects of administrative coordination (Faraj & Sproull, 2000). Another study conducted with consulting teams composed of MBA students working on 3-month long projects in actual client organizations found preliminary evidence that transactive memory is positively correlated with team coordination (Lewis, 2003). Yet another study with software requirements teams at two organizations found that explicit management of dependencies helped understand why teams were coordinated, but only up to a certain point, and that teams that exhibited a "collective mind" (Weick & Roberts, 1993)—that is, "individuals developing a shared understanding of the group's task and each other"—were more coordinated (Crowston & Kammerer, 1998, p. 238).

Our research with decision teams has also found that shared mental models have a positive effect on task coordination (i.e., management of general task dependencies—e.g., avoiding duplication of work, tasks are clearly assigned) and strategy coordination (i.e., management of functional strategy dependencies—e.g., finance, operations, and marketing strategies; Espinosa, Carley, et al., 2002). Observations in a related study with two distributed decision teams (i.e., students from a Mexican university and from Carnegie Mellon University working on the same team) suggested that these teams were uncoordinated at the beginning, but that they became progressively more coordinated over time as they became more familiar with the task and with each other.[1] Analysis from our field research with software teams has also found evidence that organized shared knowledge (i.e., shared mental models) of key concepts, processes, and products, knowing who knows what in the team (i.e., transactive memory), and knowing what is happening with the task (i.e., task awareness) and who is around (i.e., presence awareness) help teams coordinate, particularly when teams are geographically distributed (Espinosa, 2002; Espinosa, Kraut, et al., 2001).

In sum, as team members develop experience with the task and interact with each other, they develop team cognition that helps them coordinate implicitly. But team communication and the use of task organization mechanisms affect how team cognition develops. In turn, the strength and type of team cognition developed influences which task organization mechanisms are used by the team (and how they are used) and how they communicate.

Input Variables: Effect on Mix of Implicit and Explicit Coordination Mechanisms

As the following discussion suggests, a team will use a mix of coordination mechanisms that it deems most suitable to manage task dependencies in a given context. As Table 6.1 shows, task, team, and context variables influence the number, complexity, and types of dependencies that are present in the task and, consequently, which coordination mechanisms are used by team members to manage these dependencies. For example, decision and software teams in our studies faced different types of dependencies. Decision teams had dependencies on general task activities (e.g., avoiding duplicate work, task assignments) and functional strategy dependencies (e.g., synchronizing finance and operations strategies), whereas software teams faced technical (i.e., software parts working well together), temporal (i.e., parallel activities completed on time), and software process dependencies (i.e., activities carried out according to the formal process).

---

[1]Students from each site visited the other site twice during the semester and also had video conference meetings.

TABLE 6.1
Tasks, Teams, and Dependencies

Variable	Decision team	Software team
Task	Decision making	Large-scale software development for telecommunications products
Teams	Simulated management teams	Software teams
Dependencies	General task activities— clear assignment of tasks, no redundancies	Technical—integration of software parts Temporal—per schedule
	Among functional strategies—integration of finance, marketing and operational strategies	Software process—according to the established software process
Coordination	Activity and functional strategy coordination	Technical, temporal and process coordination
Complexity	Moderate	Very high
Context	Same place Different time	Different place Different time

Team variables also influence the types of dependencies present. For instance, larger teams are likely to have more numerous and complex dependencies than smaller teams. Also, teams with a long history of working together may be more experienced at managing team member dependencies. Finally, context variables also influence the types of dependencies present in the task. Things such as technology and organizational processes can impose structure and restrictions that affect how teams interact and carry out their tasks. For example, teams that are co-located are likely to use a different mix of coordination mechanisms than teams that are geographically distributed and whose interaction is mediated by communication technologies. Similarly, teams working in real-time contexts (e.g., flying an airplane, operating on a patient) are likely to use a different mix of coordination mechanisms than teams working on asynchronous tasks (e.g., strategic planning, large-scale software development). We now explore in more detail how input variables change the nature of dependencies.

An Integrated Framework: Explicit and Implicit Coordination

Our discussion suggests the integration of the classical organizational view of team coordination with newer views from team cognition research. As we discuss next, every task is different, and the nature of dependencies present influences which mix of coordination mechanisms can better help teams coordinate. Teams working on familiar and routine tasks and larger teams may benefit more from task organization mechanisms (i.e., plans, schedules, programs, tools, etc.). Teams working on less familiar tasks and in uncertain conditions and smaller teams may benefit more by coordinating through communication. In addition, as the task progresses and as team members interact over time, their team cognition will gradually become stronger and, while team members may continue to use some explicit coordination mechanisms, they will probably begin to substitute other explicit mechanisms with implicit mechanisms. Explicit mechanisms that consume more time and effort (e.g., formal meetings, written reports) are more likely to be substituted, particularly when teams are under time pressure.

Consequently, team studies that focus on explicit coordination mechanisms need to take into account team members' use of implicit coordination mechanisms. Furthermore, the interplay between explicit and implicit coordination mechanisms may give rise to complementary and interaction effects. For example, the effect that a new software version management system may have on coordination in software development may be different for a new team than for one who has been working together in the same task domain for several years. For example, the introduction of a new software modeling tool had noticeably different effects on teams at two sites we studied. Team members at one site had a long history of working together and little turnover, and had developed paradigms and methods deeply rooted in tradition. This group had great difficulty adapting to the new tool, and many indicated that the tool did not help them coordinate. The team at the other site had only been in existence for approximately 3 years and had a high turnover rate. Most developers at this other site indicated that the new tool helped them coordinate. Similarly, studies of team coordination that focus on team cognition need to take into account the team's use of explicit coordination mechanisms. For example, a software team that does not use a configuration management system for software version control may need to rely more on shared task knowledge than a team that uses such systems. In sum, we suggest the use of an integrated framework of team coordination that incorporates both implicit and explicit coordination mechanisms, as illustrated in Figure 6.1.

DIFFERENT TYPES OF DEPENDENCIES AND COORDINATION: ONE SIZE DOES NOT FIT ALL

In a nutshell, the framework proposed above suggests that task, team, and context variables influence the nature of dependencies present in a task, which in turn affect the mix of coordination mechanisms necessary to manage these dependencies effectively. To the extent that these dependencies are important for performance, coordination will affect team performance. However, as suggested in other studies, figuring out which coordination mechanisms are most effective in managing the various dependencies requires an understanding of these dependencies (Crowston & Kammerer,

1998). While some argue that shared mental models or transactive memory can improve coordination and performance, we argue that there may be important complementarities, tradeoffs, and interactions between implicit and explicit mechanisms. Consequently, if key dependencies can be managed effectively with explicit coordination mechanisms alone, then team cognition may not improve coordination noticeably. For example, configuration management systems (i.e., version control systems) in large-scale software projects use a library metaphor in which software is "checked out," updated, and then "checked in," thus facilitating parallel development by multiple programmers who may not even know each other. Modern configuration management systems automatically protect all parts of the software code that are affected by the software part that was checked out so that developers do not interfere with each other, and they also contain features to manage workflow (Grinter, Herbsleb, & Perry, 1999). Such systems make communication and team cognition less important when coordinating small modifications to the software (Espinosa, 2002). However, these tools may not be sufficient to coordinate larger modifications because dependencies are more complex, so communication and team cognition can indeed provide incremental benefits.

This discussion illustrates the importance of understanding the nature of the dependencies involved in a task before we can truly learn which mechanisms help teams coordinate and perform. This is particularly important for complex tasks like management decisions and large-scale software development in which dependencies are numerous and complex. For instance, our study with software teams found that there are three main types of coordination problems in this domain stemming from the specific dependencies involved: technical, temporal, and software process. Technical coordination problems arise because of inadequate management of technical dependencies among software parts that need to work well together when integrated. Temporal coordination problems arise because temporal dependencies are inadequately managed when software parts or related subtasks are not completed according to schedule in a synchronized manner. Software process coordination problems arise when process dependencies are inadequately managed because some team members do not adhere to the established software process or to procedures agreed on at meetings.

Because of the importance of understanding dependencies when studying team cognition and coordination, we have reformulated our framework, as illustrated in Figure 6.2, to bring attention to the fact that different coordination mechanisms will have different effects on different types of coordination, which in turn will have different effects on team performance—that is, *one size does not fit all*. The following discussion explores the relationship between dependencies and the different elements of the framework. Once again, we start the discussion with the dependent variable of interest (i.e., team performance) and proceed backward through the framework.

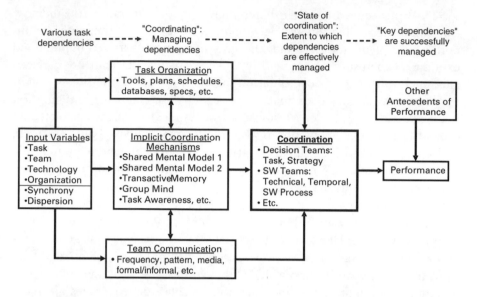

Figure 6.2. Reformulated theoretical framework.

Effect of (Which Type of) Coordination on Performance: Key Dependencies Managed Effectively

If the purpose of a coordination mechanism is to help teams reach higher levels of performance, it is imperative that we understand not only which dependencies are present in the task but also which ones are more critical to performance. Team cognition can only be effective in helping teams coordinate if it helps the team manage important task dependencies. Teams may be highly coordinated and still perform poorly because other antecedents of performance are weak. For example, a software team with well-coordinated task activities but whose members have little knowledge of the application domain for which they are writing software will probably produce poor-quality software (Curtis, Krasner, & Iscoe, 1988). Also, some dependencies may be more important to performance than others. Although many dependencies may be adequately managed, some other dependencies that are key to performance may not be managed well. For instance, a software team with high technical and temporal coordination will deliver error-free software on time but will not be considered an effective team if important features needed by clients have not been implemented.

Our research with decision teams has also shown that teams with poor task activity coordination (e.g., duplication of efforts, the left hand not knowing what the right hand is doing, unclear work assignments) do not perform well, but it has also shown that good task activity coordination is insufficient for performance. However, we did find that good functional strategy coordination was a strong predictor of team performance because the decision task involved in this study required the successful integration of functional strategies into a cohesive company strategy. Once again, team cognition in this case can be more effective if it involves shared knowledge of aspects of the task that are very important to performance. Also, the performance variance explained by strategy coordination was small, suggesting that other types of coordination or other variables (e.g., sound functional strategies, understanding the competition) were important too, and that the difference in performance may be affected by different types of coordination. For example, in our studies with decision teams, we found that strategy coordination affected objective financial performance but it did not directly affect performance measured with external board evaluations. The effect of strategy coordination on board evaluations was mediated by financial performance.

Effect of Coordination Mechanisms on Coordination: Managing Dependencies Effectively

Different mechanisms will have varying degrees of effectiveness in helping members manage the various types of dependencies present. Therefore, well-coordinated teams will not necessarily be those that have strong team cognition but rather those who adopt an effective mix of mechanisms for the coordination needs of the task in which they are engaged. Consequently, when we study the effect of team cognition on coordination, it is important to answer these questions: (a) Which types of team cognition are we studying? (b) Which types of coordination are involved? and (c) Which other types of explicit coordination mechanisms are being used by the team?

Consistent with the classical view of explicit coordination, our research with decision teams shows that teams with high task coordination made heavy use of a central file-sharing facility to routinely exchange documents that contain information on simulation inputs and presentations for their board of directors. They also relied on face-to-face and electronic communications for less routine aspects of the task such as discussion of work assignments and key decisions to be made. It is interesting to note that the same explicit coordination factors were used by teams with high strategy coordination, except for the file-sharing system, probably because it did not help them integrate functional strategies, which were done mostly by communicating. Shared mental models of the task and shared mental models of the team were concurrently correlated with both task and strategy coordination, but when the proper regression models were formulated, the effect of shared mental model of the team disappeared. This suggests that once the use of all explicit coordination mechanisms is accounted for, only the shared mental model of the task has an effect on coordination in this domain (i.e., decision task, co-located and asynchronous), thus highlighting the importance of considering the effects of all coordination mechanisms used. In contrast, both shared mental models had significant and positive effects in another study with flight simulation teams (Mathieu et al., 2000), suggesting that managing both task and member dependencies is important for coordination for co-located, synchronous tasks.

Similarly, experiences from our research with software teams suggest that technical personnel (e.g., software developers, testing engineers) are more concerned with technical coordination because they want to ensure that the different parts of the software they are developing integrate well. Therefore, they rely heavily on software tools (e.g., modeling tools, change management system) and formal documents (e.g., interface specifications) and communicate heavily when they encounter unusual situations or errors that need to be repaired. Technical coordination problems tend to appear when team members do not have organized shared knowledge (i.e., shared mental models) about the products being developed and the functions being implemented. In contrast, technical and project managers are more concerned with temporal and software process coordination because they want to ensure that things are done in a timely manner, per project schedules, and that things are carried out as specified by the formal software process established. These managers rely more on planning, project management, and software process documents. They also have more frequent meetings because the nature of the dependencies they have to manage is mostly nonroutine. Also, process coordination problems tend to appear when managers do not have organized shared knowledge about the established software process, which leads to confusion, duplication of work, and priority conflicts, among other things.

Effect of Input Variables on Use of Coordination Mechanisms: Nature of Dependencies

When conducting research on team cognition and coordination, we need to understand how task, team, and context variables influence the types of dependencies present in a task. This is important for a number of reasons. First, some findings may be limited to the particular type of task, team, or context of the study because the nature of dependencies will be different outside of those boundaries. Second, different types of coordination mechanisms may be more effective at managing different types of dependencies. For example, team members experienced with the task and who have a long history of working together are more likely to rely on team cognition (e.g., shared mental models, transactive memory) than team members without such experience, who can only rely on task organization mechanisms and communication. Finally, some task, team, and context variables cannot be changed easily (e.g., type of task, organizational culture), whereas some others may be more easily changed through interventions (e.g., training, new member recruitment, technology, geographic location). Consequently, it may be easier to solve some coordination problems by changing the nature of dependencies through task, team, and context interventions than by forcing teams to use different coordination mechanisms.

We now discuss how task, team, and four context variables can affect the nature of dependencies present. Two of the context variables we discuss, technology and organization, are important input variables used in team research because they have substantial effects on how teams interact. The other two context variables, synchrony and dispersion, are essential in the study of teams mediated by information technologies because time separation (i.e., real time vs. different time) or distance separation (co-located vs. dispersed) has a substantial effect on how teams organize their work and interact (Bullen & Bennett, 1993).

The Task

The nature of the task really matters when studying team interaction and performance (McGrath, 1991). It affects which types of dependencies are present. For example, a team assembling parts in a mechanical task will face different dependencies than a medical team with a variety of specialists trying to diagnose a patient. For instance, research on problem-solving teams has shown that when team members believe that a demonstrable solution exists (i.e., an intellective task), it changes how information is sampled from team members, compared with when they believe that a demonstrable solution does not exist (i.e., a judgment task; Stasser & Stewart, 1992).

The Team

Many team variables can affect the nature of dependencies present. For example, how long or how often the team has worked or trained together in the past, the team composition (e.g., homogeneity, expertise), member acquisition practices (e.g., labor markets, socialization), and team size will affect team cognition development (Cannon-Bowers et al., 1993; Klimoski & Mohammed, 1994; Levesque et al., 2001; Rentsch & Klimoski, 2001). Teams that have worked together for a long time may have well-developed team cognition mechanisms and work practices that help them minimize dependencies. Not only can team variables affect team cognition development, but they also influence which explicit coordination mechanisms its members use. For example, the number and complexity of dependencies in software development increase exponentially as the size of the team increases and it makes it difficult to coordinate and communicate (Brooks, 1995). So, larger teams are more likely to rely on task organization mechanisms (e.g., software tools, manuals, specifications, schedules), whereas smaller teams are more likely to rely on team communication (VanDeVen et al., 1976). Other studies with software teams have also found that project size and task uncertainty make coordination more difficult (Espinosa, 2002; Kraut & Streeter, 1995) but that teams that use formal routines reduce some of the resulting negative effects (Sproull & Kiesler, 1991).

Context

Technology. Communications and other technologies can affect how teams interact (McGrath & Hollingshead, 1994). For example, a study of relationships between technologists and radiologists at two hospitals found that new technologies changed the nature of individual roles, which in turn had a substantial effect on how technologists and radiologists interacted (Barley, 1990). Other research studies have also suggested that information technologies affect dependencies, information flow, and workflow among collaborators (Grinter et al., 1999; Sproull & Kiesler, 1991). For instance, smaller software projects do not always utilize configuration management systems, which creates member dependencies when different developers need to work on the same part of the software code. In contrast, large-scale software projects use such systems, which enable multiple developers to work on the same part of the software code simultaneously without having to interact with each other (i.e., the system handles this for them), which reduces member dependencies.

Organization. Organizational factors (e.g., culture, structure, standard procedures) also affect how teams interact. In fact, some research studies suggest that organizations are social systems that affect (and are affected by) how technologies are used (DeSanctis & Poole, 1994; Orlikowski, 1992, 1996), all of which can affect the types of dependencies present in a task.

Synchrony and Geographic Dispersion. Teams can operate synchronously (i.e., same time or real time) or asynchronously (i.e., different time) and can be either co-located (i.e., same place) or geographically dispersed (i.e., different place), thus creating four possible modes of team interaction that need to be considered when researching teams (Bullen & Bennett, 1993). Consequently, synchrony and geographic dispersion need to be considered when studying team cognition because they can generate different work arrangements with different resulting sets and types of dependencies. Asynchronous and geographically dispersed teams have fewer opportunities to interact, communicate less spontaneously, and use leaner communication media (e.g., electronic mail, telephone). Consequently, time and distance separation will not only make it more difficult for team members to develop and use shared cognition to coordinate, but it will also affect the mix of explicit and implicit mechanisms that they will use to coordinate. So, although research in same-time and same-place contexts has yielded useful theoretical foundations and empirical support for the positive effects of team cognition (Liang et al., 1995; Mathieu et al., 2000; Stout, Cannon-Bowers, & Salas, 1999), we do not know if these findings extend to different-time and different-place contexts.

Fortunately, as we discussed earlier, new empirical research studies are beginning to emerge in different-time and same-place contexts (i.e., asynchronous, co-located), which are beginning to show evidence of the positive effects of team cognition on performance (Crowston & Kammerer, 1998; Espinosa, 2002; Espinosa, Carley et al., 2002; Faraj & Sproull, 2000; Lewis,

2003) and helping to identify anecedents of team cognition (Levesque et al., 2001; Rentsch & Klimoski, 2001). Our study with decision teams found a positive effect of the shared mental model of the task but found no effect of the shared mental model of the team. Our explanation for this is that the shared mental model of the team is perhaps important in high-paced, real-time tasks like a flight simulation because this shared model helps team members explain and anticipate each other's actions, which helps manage member dependencies, which are key to performance in these contexts. Conversely, management decision teams are asynchronous, so having shared knowledge of the task is perhaps more important for managing the respective task dependencies than having a well-developed shared mental model of the team.

However, there is almost no empirical research in different-place contexts (i.e., geographically dispersed). Our research studies try to fill this gap by focusing specifically on different-place or different-time contexts. For example, our research with software teams (i.e., asynchronous, dispersed) found that dependencies and coordination needs are very different for co-located than for dispersed teams, but that having organized shared knowledge about key concepts, processes, and products (i.e., shared mental models) and knowing who knows what in the team (i.e., transactive memory) helped teams coordinate, thus reducing some of the coordination problems associated with geographic distance. We also found that software development time was reduced when team members have shared familiarity with prior software projects and with the same parts of the software code, and that this effect was stronger for geographically distributed teams than for co-located teams.

As discussed previously, research in team cognition can benefit by taking into account the task context, particularly synchrony and geographic dispersion. Research findings are likely to differ depending on time and distance separation because the nature of the dependencies present will change. In fact, interventions that change the synchrony or dispersion of a task can have substantial effects on coordination. For instance, although a field study of global software teams found that there are more complex dependencies and coordination challenges when development is done across sites than when it is done at a single site (Herbsleb, Mockus, Finholt, & Grinter, 2001), a related prior study also found that large-scale software development is often distributed in ways that reduce dependencies across sites, such as (a) develop all related software functions (e.g., call handling, billing) at a single site; (b) develop software for similar parts of the software product (e.g., base station controllers) at a single site; (c) keep similar software development phases (e.g., testing) at a single site; and (d) develop a core product at a single site and customize it for specific client needs at a site near the client (Grinter et al., 1999).

CONCLUSIONS

Our arguments and examples in this chapter bring attention to the fact that it is important to consider explicit coordination mechanisms and task dependencies when studying team cognition. Results from empirical studies in team cognition will be more useful if they limit the scope and validity of the study to particular contexts involving the use of a given set of explicit coordination mechanisms. At the same time, if the use of explicit mechanisms vary across teams, it is important to control for the use of such mechanisms. This underscores the importance of using an integrated research framework that incorporates both implicit and explicit coordination mechanisms. It is also important to understand how task, team, and context variables affect work arrangements and task dependencies when we study team coordination. Empirical findings from research studies about the effect of a particular team cognition construct on team coordination and performance will be more useful for research and practice if the specifics of the task dependencies are articulated and considered. Also, although coordination may not be a sufficient condition for effective team performance, it is certainly necessary for tasks with substantial dependencies. At the same time, teams that are highly coordinated in certain aspects of the task may not necessarily exhibit high performance levels unless other antecedents of performance are also present.

There is an increased interest these days in how different types of team cognition can influence team coordination and performance. Many team cognition constructs have been identified in the literature (Mohammed & Dumville, 2001), and although these constructs are conceptually distinct, they share some similarities. In particular, most constructs involve some form of compatible, complementary, or similar knowledge among team members (Cannon-Bowers & Salas, 2001). This team knowledge, in turn, arguably helps team members coordinate their actions with the rest of the team and communicate more effectively. Although such concepts and theories are intuitive and useful in helping us explain team coordination and performance, we still need more empirical evidence. Through our research, we have identified a set of specific areas and issues that need further development to better understand team cognition:

1. There is very little agreement or consistency in the literature about how to measure shared cognition (Cooke, Salas, Cannon-Bowers, & Stout, 2000; Lewis, 2003; Mohammed & Dumville, 2001). Further research and more consistency of methods are needed in this area to be able to compare results across studies.
2. There is very little empirical work supporting these theories and concepts. More empirical work is necessary in this area (Mathieu et al., 2000; Mohammed & Dumville, 2001). Part of the reason for this has to do with the difficulty of measuring shared cognition.
3. There is not much discussion in the literature about how the effects of team cognition may vary depending on the type of

task involved. The nature of the task and its context matter when studying team performance (McGrath, 1991). More specifically, time and distance separation make a difference when studying team coordination (Bullen & Bennett, 1993).

4. How team cognition affects coordination and performance will depend on the extent to which teams use certain explicit coordination mechanisms like collaboration tools, electronic communication, shared databases, and division of labor. More research is needed in which the effects of explicit and implicit coordination mechanisms are jointly explored.

5. Complex tasks have multiple dependencies. The management-specific task dependencies will require different types of coordination. Therefore, more research is needed to better understand (a) the various effects that specific explicit and implicit coordination mechanisms have on the effective management of different task dependencies and (b) how different types of coordination affect different aspects of team performance.

The first point about measures has been partly addressed in other studies (Cooke et al., 2000; Espinosa, 2001; Espinosa & Carley, 2001). In this chapter we have addressed the remaining four issues by focusing on two overarching themes of concern for team cognition research. The first one is the need for a research framework that incorporates explicit mechanisms (from the classical organizational research literature) and implicit coordination mechanisms (from more recent research in team cognition). The second overarching theme has to do with the need to better understand the nature of the multiple dependencies and coordination types involved in a task (i.e., one size does not fit all). Complex tasks often have many types of dependencies, some more critical than others, and certain coordination mechanisms may be more effective than others for particular types of dependencies. Conversely, one particular mechanism (e.g., shared mental model of the task) may not be equally effective in managing different dependencies. Consequently, an effective strategy for coordination success involves finding a mix of coordination mechanisms well suited for the task. Furthermore, this mix will probably need to change as the task progresses over time (e.g., communication may be more effective at the beginning of the task, whereas division of labor or shared mental models may be more effective later on). This mix will also need to change with distance separation (i.e., co-located vs. distributed).

REFERENCES

Barley, S. (1990). The alignment of technology and structure through roles and networks. *Administrative Science Quarterly, 35,* 61–103.

Brooks, F. (1995). *The mythical man-month: Essays on software engineering.* Reading, MA: Addison-Wesley.

Bullen, C., & Bennett, J. (1993). Groupware in practice: An interpretation of work experiences. In R. Baecker (Ed.), *Groupware and computer-supported cooperative work: Assisting human–human collaboration* (pp. 69–84). San Francisco: Morgan Kaufman.

Cannon-Bowers, J. A., & Salas, E. (2001). Reflections on shared cognition. *Journal of Organizational Behavior, 22,* 195–202.

Cannon-Bowers, J. A., Salas, E., & Converse, S. (1993). Shared mental models in expert team decision-making. In J. Castellan (Ed.), *Individual and group decision-making: Current issues* (pp. 221–246). Hillsdale, NJ: Erlbaum.

Cooke, N. J., Salas, E., Cannon-Bowers, J. A., & Stout, R. J. (2000). Measuring team knowledge. *Human Factors, 42,* 151–173.

Cramton, C. D. (2001). The mutual knowledge problem and its consequences for dispersed collaboration. *Organization Science, 12,* 346–371.

Crowston, K., & Kammerer, E. E. (1998). Coordination and collective mind in software requirements development. *IBM Systems Journal, 37,* 227–245.

Curtis, B., Krasner, H., & Iscoe, N. (1988). A field study of the software design process for large systems. *Communications of the ACM, 31,* 1268–1286.

DeSanctis, G., & Poole, M. S. (1994). Capturing the complexity in advanced technology use: Adaptive structuration theory. *Organization Science, 5,* 121–145.

Endsley, M. (1995). Toward a theory of situation awareness in dynamic systems. *Human Factors, 37,* 32–64.

Entin, E. E., & Serfaty, D. (1999). Adaptive team coordination. *Journal of Human Factors, 41,* 321–325.

Espinosa, J. A. (2001, August). *Shared mental models: Accuracy and visual representation.* Paper presented at the Americas Conference in Information Systems, Boston.

Espinosa, J. A. (2002). *Shared mental models and coordination in large-scale, distributed software development.* Unpublished doctoral dissertation, Carnegie Mellon University.

Espinosa, J. A., & Carley, K. (2001, August). *Measuring team mental models.* Paper presented at the Academy of Management Conference, Washington, DC.

Espinosa, J. A., Carley, K., Kraut, R. E., Lerch, F. J., & Fussell, S. (2002, December). *The effect of task knowledge similarity and distribution on asynchronous team coordination and performance: Empirical evidence from decision teams.* Workshop conducted at the Information Systems Cognitive Research Exchange, Barcelona, Spain.

Espinosa, J. A., Kraut, R. E., Lerch, F. J., Slaughter, S. A., Herbsleb, J. D., & Mockus, A. (2001, December). *Shared mental models and coordination in large-scale, distributed software development.* Paper presented at the International Conference in Information Systems, New Orleans, LA.

Espinosa, J. A., Kraut, R. E., Slaughter, S. A., Lerch, F. J., Herbsleb, J. D., & Mockus, A. (2002, December). *Shared mental models, familiarity, and coordination: A multi-*

method study of distributed software teams. Paper presented at the International Conference in Information Systems, Barcelona, Spain.

Faraj, S., & Sproull, L. (2000). Coordinating expertise in software development teams. *Management Science, 46,* 1554–1568.

Fussell, S., & Krauss, R. (1992). Coordination of knowledge in communication: Effects of speakers' assumptions about what others know. *Journal of Personality and Social Psychology, 62,* 378–391.

Grinter, R. E., Herbsleb, J. D., & Perry, D. E. (1999). The geography of coordination: Dealing with distance in R&D work. In *Proceedings of the International ACM SIGGROUP Conference on Supporting Group Work, Group 99* (pp. 306–315). New York: ACM Press.

Herbsleb, J., Mockus, A., Finholt, T., & Grinter, R. E. (2001, May). *An empirical study of global software development: Distance and speed.* Paper presented at the 23rd International Conference on Software Engineering, Toronto, Ontario, Canada.

Kleinman, D. L., & Serfaty, D. (1989, April). *Team performance assessment in distributed decision-making.* Paper presented at the Interactive Networked Simulation for Training Conference, Orlando, FL.

Klimoski, R. J., & Mohammed, S. (1994). Team mental model: Construct or metaphor. *Journal of Management, 20,* 403–437.

Kraemer, K., & Pinsonneault, A. (1990). Technology and groups: Assessment of the empirical research. In J. Galegher, R. E. Kraut, & C. Egido (Eds.), *Intellectual teamwork: Social and technological foundations of cooperative work* (pp. 375–405). Hillsdale, NJ: Erlbaum.

Kraiger, K., & Wenzel, L. (1997). Conceptual development and empirical evaluation of measures of shared mental models as indicators of team effectiveness. In M. Brannick, E. Salas, & C. Prince (Eds.), *Team performance assessment and measurement* (pp. 63–84). Hillsdale, NJ: Erlbaum.

Krauss, R., & Fussell, S. (1990). Mutual knowledge and communicative effectiveness. In J. Galegher, R. E. Kraut, & C. Egido (Eds.), *Intellectual teamwork: Social and technological foundations of cooperative work* (pp. 111–146). Hillsdale, NJ: Erlbaum.

Kraut, R. E., & Streeter, L. A. (1995). Coordination in software development. *Communications of the ACM, 38*(3), 69–81.

Levesque, L. L., Wilson, J. M., & Wholey, D. R. (2001). Cognitive divergence and shared mental models in software development project teams. *Journal of Organizational Behavior, 22,* 135–144.

Lewis, K. (2003). Measuring transactive memory systems in the field: Scale development and validation. *Journal of Applied Psychology, 88*(4), 587–604.

Liang, D., Moreland, R., & Argote, L. (1995). Group versus individual training and group performance: The mediating role of transactive memory. *Personality and Social Psychology Bulletin, 21,* 384–393.

Malone, T., & Crowston, K. (1990). What is coordination theory and how can it help design cooperative work systems. In *Proceedings of the Third Conference on Computer Supported Collaborative Work* (pp. 357–370). New York: ACM Press.

Malone, T., & Crowston, K. (1994). The interdisciplinary study of coordination. *ACM Computing Surveys, 26,* 87–119.

March, J., & Simon, H. (1958). *Organizations.* New York: Wiley.

Mathieu, J. E., Goodwin, G. F., Heffner, T. S., Salas, E., & Cannon-Bowers, J. A. (2000). The influence of shared mental models on team process and performance. *Journal of Applied Psychology, 85,* 273–283.

McGrath, J. (1991). Time, interaction and performance (TIP). *Small Group Research, 22,* 147–174.

McGrath, J., & Hollingshead, A. (1994). *Groups interacting with technology.* Thousand Oaks, CA: Sage.

Mohammed, S., & Dumville, B. C. (2001). Team mental models in a team knowledge framework: Expanding theory and measurement across disciplinary boundaries. *Journal of Organizational Behavior, 22,* 89–106.

Orlikowski, W. (1992). Learning from notes: Organizational issues in groupware implementation. In *Proceedings of the Conference on Computer Supported Collaborative Work* (pp. 362–369). New York: ACM Press.

Orlikowski, W. (1996). Improvising organizational transformation over time: A situated change perspective. *Information Systems Research, 7,* 63–92.

Rentsch, J. R., & Klimoski, R. J. (2001). Why do great minds think alike?: Antecedents of team member schema agreement. *Journal of Organizational Behavior, 22,* 107–120.

Rouse, W. B., Cannon-Bowers, J. A., & Salas, E. (1992). The role of mental models in team performance in complex systems. *IEEE Transactions on Systems, Man and Cybernetics, 22,* 1296–1308.

Rouse, W. B., & Morris, N. M. (1986). On looking into the black box: Prospects and limits in the search for mental models. *Psychological Bulletin, 100,* 349–363.

Sproull, L., & Kiesler, S. (1991). *Connections: New ways of working in the networked organization.* Cambridge, MA: MIT Press.

Stasser, G., & Stewart, D. (1992). Discovery of hidden profiles by decision-making groups: Solving a problem versus making a judgment. *Journal of Personality and Social Psychology, 63,* 426–434.

Stout, J. A., Cannon-Bowers, J., & Salas, E. (1999). Planning, shared mental models, and coordinated performance: An empirical link is established. *Human Factors, 41,* 61–71.

Thompson, J. (1967). *Organizations in action.* New York: McGraw-Hill.

VanDeVen, A. H., Delbecq, L. A., & Koenig, R. J. (1976). Determinants of coordination modes within organizations. *American Sociological Review, 41,* 322–338.

Wegner, D. (1986). Transactive memory: A contemporary analysis of the group mind. In B. Mullen & G. Goethals (Eds.), *Theories of group behavior* (pp. 185–208). New York: Springer-Verlag.

Weick, K., & Roberts, K. (1993). Collective mind in organizations: Heedful interrelating on flight decks. *Administrative Science Quarterly, 38,* 357–381.

Wellens, R. (1993). Group situation awareness and distributed decision-making: From military to civilian applications. In J. Castellan (Ed.), *Individual and group decision-making: Current issues* (pp. 267–291). Hillsdale, NJ: Erlbaum.

Wholey, D., Kiesler, S., & Carley, K. (1996). *Learning teamwork: Emergence of organization in novice software development teams.* Unpublished manuscript.

Wittenbaum, G. M., & Stasser, G. (1996). Management of information in small groups. In J. L. Nye & A. M. Brower (Eds.), *What's social about social cognition?* (pp. 3–28). Thousand Oaks, CA: Sage.

III

APPLICATIONS OF THE TEAM COGNITION CONSTRUCT

7

PROCESS MAPPING AND SHARED COGNITION: TEAMWORK AND THE DEVELOPMENT OF SHARED PROBLEM MODELS

STEPHEN M. FIORE AND JONATHAN W. SCHOOLER

As we enter the 21st century, work teams continue to be a dominant force in industry (e.g., Cannon-Bowers, Oser, & Flanagan, 1998; Guzzo & Salas, 1995). Teams are formed for a diverse range of tasks, from creating product marketing strategies to implementing change management procedures, and their life expectancy can vary from the duration of a given meeting to the duration of a corporation. Because of this prevalence of teams in industry today, many are formed without much forethought along with the expectation that only gains in productivity can result from teamwork (Hackman, 1990). The reality is that there is little guarantee of success, as many teams fail for any number of reasons (e.g., Hackman, 1998; Tanskanen,

The views herein are those of the authors and do not necessarily reflect those of their affiliated organizations. Portions of the research for this chapter were funded by an Andrew Mellon Foundation Predoctoral Fellowship to Stephen M. Fiore and by Grant No. F49620-01-1-0214 from the Air Force Office of Scientific Research to Eduardo Salas, Stephen M. Fiore, and Clint A. Bowers. We thank B. Jean Ferketish, John M. Levine, Richard L. Moreland, and two anonymous reviewers for helpful comments or discussions on this chapter.

Buhanist, & Kostama, 1998). In this chapter we link theoretical approaches from cognitive science on the nature of problem solving with research in team performance to illustrate how certain process interventions may facilitate team performance through the development of shared problem models.

The literature on team performance and shared mental models, while not lacking in theory, has far fewer methodologies that may foster their development. Only in the last few years have systematic attempts to train shared mental models been empirically examined (e.g., Marks, Zaccaro, & Mathieu, 2000; Mathieu, Heffner, Goodwin, Salas, & Cannon-Bowers, 2000; Smith-Jentsch, Campbell, Milanovich, & Reynolds, 2001). Nonetheless, in industry, armies of consultants continually apply any number of tools in their attempts to improve organizational effectiveness. Unfortunately, while the utility of such tools often seems intuitively obvious, they are typically applied at a rate that vastly outpaces the research necessary to fully capitalize on their strengths while limiting their weaknesses. Because of this, the overarching problem facing many is that much ambiguity exists about not only the appropriateness of such tools but also why they may, or may not, be effective. A systematic attempt to link theory and research from cognitive and organizational psychology may assist in not only the development of new tools based on theory but also the analysis of current tools to understand what drives their success and limit what may be their failings. Therefore, to the degree that the research community can focus attention on this issue in an attempt to maximize the utility of and minimize the costs associated with such tools, organizational effectiveness may be better fostered. As an illustration of how this may proceed, we conduct a descriptive analysis of one such tool and discuss how it may be contributing to increases in team effectiveness.

In this chapter we first review the problem-solving process and discuss how shared mental model theory has been applied to explain how teams can often overcome barriers to effective performance. We then discuss process mapping, a tool designed to assist problem-solving teams overcome some of the limitations that can lead to failure while, at the same time, capitalizing on factors that can lead to success. We argue that this tool, originally developed to assist teams in process redesign and organizational change (e.g., Rummler & Brache, 1995), is successful because it leads to the construction of a shared mental model of the problem in question (Cannon-Bowers, Salas, & Converse, 1993). Our discussion centers on the notion that, to the degree the team task requires the construction of a shared understanding, external representational tools can act as a scaffolding to facilitate the building of that shared representation.

Types and definitions of teams vary somewhat, from "interdependent collections of individuals who share responsibility for specific outcomes for their organizations" (Sundstrom, De Meuse, & Futrell, 1990, p. 120) to "two or more people who interact dynamically, interdependently and adaptively toward" a shared goal (Salas, Dickinson, Converse, & Tannenbaum, 1992, p. 4). Our discussion in this chapter focuses only on problem-solving teams. Problem-solving teams are typically established for short-term situations that require relatively rapid action be taken against specific workplace problems. Furthermore, such teams often possess a diverse membership, composed of members from a variety of functional areas (see Moreland, Levine, & Wingert, 1996, for a discussion of issues in group composition). As such, they represent a particularly challenging form of team structure given that they possess a compressed developmental life span and heterogeneous composition, the combination of which potentially exacerbates problems arising from group dynamics. In sum, although numerous definitions of teams have been offered, problem-solving teams do meet the apparent defining criteria by being composed of members with complementary skills who maintain a degree of interdependence by the fact that their overall task goal (i.e., resolution of an organizational problem) requires cooperative interaction (e.g., Fleishman & Zaccaro, 1992; Katzenbach & Smith, 1993). We next discuss the problem-solving process, emphasizing problem conceptualization and its import to team problem solving.

TEAMS AND PROBLEM CONCEPTUALIZATION

An old management axiom states that "a problem defined is half solved." Problem solving, then, could be said to involve a substantial reflective component in that successful problem resolution requires adequate problem definition. Indeed, research from cognitive science comparing expert–novice problem solving finds that experts in a particular field spend a considerable amount of time representing a problem before attempting to solve it (e.g., Chi, Glaser, & Rees, 1982). The issue of problem representation is foundational to theories of problem solving (e.g., Newell & Simon, 1972), and it becomes even more critical when talking about problem-solving teams. Specifically, because teamwork, by its very definition, involves a collaborative component, team performance is a function of the level of understanding the team shares about their task and their capabilities. Researchers in team problem solving argue that "before a decision can be made, the [team] must first recognize that a problem exists, determine its nature, and determine the desired outcome" (Orasanu, 1994, p. 256). Nonetheless, despite the criticality of fully understanding the nature of a problem prior to beginning the solution generation phase, research has long demonstrated that teams show little inclination to engage in this aspect of the problem-solving task (e.g., Hackman & Morris, 1975). Furthermore, Moreland and Levine (1992), in their article on problem identification in teams, cited a surprising paucity of research on teams and this process.

Problem-Solving Stages

Cognitive scientists have identified several distinct stages involved in problem solving, each of which requires unique approaches to be successfully resolved. For example, problem solving is said to involve a search through a hypothesis generation space and a hypothesis testing space (Klahr & Dunbar, 1988; Simon & Lea, 1974), and successful solution generation takes place through a number of interdependent processes (see also Klahr, Fay, & Dunbar, 1993; Schooler, Fallshore, & Fiore, 1995). Others have focused on the stages occurring prior to hypothesis generation. For example, problem identification or problem sensing involves initial apperception that a potential problem exists or may shortly occur (Cowan, 1986; Klein, 1993; Klein & Pierce, 2001; Klein, Pliske, Crandall, & Woods, 1999; Moreland & Levine, 1992). In such a case, stimuli in one's environment are constantly monitored, and one scans for cues suggesting abnormalities. After this stage, one would move to the problem conceptualization stage, the stage after which a problem has been recognized and prior to attempts to generate a solution. During problem conceptualization, the problem solver describes and diagnoses the problem that has been recognized.

We wish to clearly distinguish between the problem identification and problem conceptualization stages. Problem identification in teams is thought to occur only when the members realize that other team members are aware of the problem (Larson & Christensen, 1993; Moreland & Levine, 1992). In particular, "no meaningful interactive problem-solving activity can take place without members first becoming cognizant of the fact that others in the group perceive the problem" (Larson & Christensen, 1993, p. 9). Only then would problem conceptualization proceed appropriately. While not denying the criticality of the problem identification process, we focus on problem conceptualization specifically because a problem improperly conceptualized is unlikely to be solved.

Problem Conceptualization

The stage of problem conceptualization can be said to involve the construction of a *problem space*. Problem space theory, initially developed from information-processing theories of human problem solving (e.g., Newell & Simon, 1972), has only recently been applied to group interaction processes (e.g., Fiore, 2000; Fiore & Schooler, 2001; Hinsz, Tindale, & Vollrath, 1997). The problem space can be considered to be the mental space in which the problem solver must encode the

> problem elements—defining goals, rules and other aspects of the situation . . . [that] represents the initial situation presented to him, the desired goal situation, various intermediate states, imagined or experienced,

as well as any concepts he uses to describe these situations to himself. (Newell & Simon, 1972, p. 59)

Constructing the problem space is a necessary, but not sufficient, factor in team problem solving. What is mandatory for effective team problem solving is that this conceptualization is shared; that is, a team's comprehension of the critical problem components contains a substantial amount of overlap (e.g., Orasanu, 1994). Although one could argue that problem solving may be facilitated by differing problem conceptualizations (e.g., by bringing diverse viewpoints into the process), we suggest that, for team problem solving to take advantage of a heterogeneous group composition, they must first be in agreement as to what the problem is. Thus, we do not suggest that a team be homogeneous with respect to their problem-solving approaches (Janis, 1972), rather, that they share an understanding of the critical problem elements.

For a team to accurately assess their problem situation, that is, adequately search their problem space, they must overcome limitations inherent in group problem solving. For example, for the team to coordinate their efforts during the problem-solving process (and be able to take advantage of diverse input), they must share a commensurate understanding of the problem itself. Although some literature does suggest that certain conceptualization processes such as planning are not always beneficial (e.g., Wittenbaum, Vaughan, & Stasser, 1998), these findings apply primarily to tasks requiring little coordination. Similarly, some research documents that groups may engage in tacit coordination (e.g., Wittenbaum, Stasser, & Merry, 1996) rather than explicitly coordinate their processes. But, within the context of teams engaged in complex problem solving, tacit coordination or a lack of planning could lead to the construction of either an incorrect or incomplete conceptualization of the problem. From the standpoint of team cognition, our argument is that, without a shared understanding of what the problem is, not only may a team be solving the wrong problem, but they also cannot make full use of their resources, the very reason teams are assembled in the first place. We turn next to a brief discussion of the shared mental model construct and follow this with an explication of how components of shared problem models fit well with the mental model construct. We then describe how it is that process mapping helps problem-solving teams to develop shared models for the conceptualized problem.

SHARED MENTAL MODELS AND TEAM PERFORMANCE

In this section we discuss how notions of shared cognition have been applied to explain successful team performance in a variety of task situations. *Shared cognition* is the term used to describe how processes at the intraindividual level are dependent on and interact with processes at the interindividual level (e.g., Cannon-Bowers & Salas, 1990; Levine, Resnick, & Higgins, 1993). Development of shared cognition theories arose out of the social cognition movement. Although definitions vary, social cognition can be defined as "those social processes . . . that relate to the acquisition, storage, transmission, manipulation and use of information for the purpose of creating a group-level intellective product" (Larson & Christensen, 1993, p. 6). As this definition suggests, groups are sometimes considered to be information-processing units (Hinsz et al., 1997) in a manner analogous to early views of human cognition (e.g., Newell & Simon, 1972). We focus on one aspect of shared cognition—shared problem models—specifically because a growing body of research demonstrates how such models directly impact team performance.

Definitions of mental models vary somewhat, often depending on the domain in question. In the cognitive science literature, mental models are involved in the comprehension of a given phenomenon as one integrates knowledge, and they facilitate one's ability to draw inferences (e.g., Johnson-Laird, 1983); they are also thought to be the interface between procedural and declarative knowledge (e.g., Glaser & Bassok, 1989). Similar notions are proposed by human factors researchers who argue that mental models allow users to generate descriptions of a system and make predictions about future system states (e.g., Rouse, 1989). From the organizational psychology literature, mental models are said to be representations of knowledge elements in an employee's environment along with the elements' interrelations (Klimoski & Mohammed, 1994; Mohammed & Dumville, 2001). In the team training literature, researchers argue that, through effective training and teamwork (e.g., cross-training, information transfer), a "shared" understanding of a task situation develops (e.g., Cannon-Bowers et al., 1993; Stout, Cannon-Bowers, & Salas, 1996). Notions of shared understanding have recently come to the forefront of research on teams because efficient and effective team performance is often shown to be related to the degree that team members agree on, or are aware of, task, role, and problem characteristics (Cannon-Bowers et al., 1993; Fiore, Salas, & Cannon-Bowers, 2001; Marks et al., 2000; Mathieu et al., 2000). For example, shared problem or task models consist of situation- and task-appropriate strategies for interpreting and acting on a variety of task situations (e.g., Klimoski & Mohammed, 1994; Orasanu & Salas, 1993), and they are thought to facilitate team coordination.

Defining Shared Mental Models

Although the exact nature of shared mental models is still in debate, a number of critical factors have been identified and we focus on three of these factors directly relevant to effective performance for problem-solving teams. More specifically, reviews of the literature concerning team mental models note that several factors need to be present to make the claim for a shared mental model (e.g., Cannon-Bowers et al., 1993; Klimoski & Mohammed, 1994). To have a shared model for a team task means to be aware of the following: problem structure, the roles and skills of the team as they pertain to the problem, and the shared awareness that each member of the team possesses this knowledge. We suggest that the successful development of these components within problem-solving teams will facilitate the overall problem conceptualization process.

First is the notion of a shared problem structure. A shared problem structure can be considered to consist of overlapping organized knowledge held by team members (e.g., Resnick, 1991). This can consist of organized declarative or procedural knowledge concerning the problem and decision rules associated with the problem (Cannon-Bowers et al., 1993). Thus, when a team possesses awareness of the problem *structure*, they are more likely to later develop an effective problem *solution* (e.g., Maier, 1967).

Second is the notion that shared mental models consist of an understanding of each team member's roles and skills. This has been labeled *interpositional* knowledge, and an absence of such knowledge is linked to failures in team effectiveness (Volpe, Cannon-Bowers, Salas, & Spector, 1996). Furthermore, the success of cross-training programs, or training designed to encourage compatible mental models with respect to team member roles and responsibilities, has been linked to increases in shared interpositional knowledge (e.g., Blickensderfer, Cannon-Bowers, & Salas, 1998; Marks et al., 2000; Mathieu et al., 2000). To the degree that the team is fully aware of member idiosyncrasies (e.g., Moreland & Levine, 1992), the unique capabilities of each team member can be fully exploited. Thus, this may help the team overcome information-sharing problems sometimes experienced during team interaction (e.g., Hollingshead, 1996; Stasser, Stewart, & Wittenbaum, 1995; Straus, 1996) and is similar to notions of "transactive memory systems" proposed by Moreland and colleagues (e.g., Liang, Moreland, & Argote, 1995; Moreland & Argote, 2003; Moreland & Myaskovsky, 2000).

The aforementioned issues relate directly to our third factor, specifically, a shared understanding of the problem requires explicitly defining the problem (e.g., articulating plans and strategies), and it ensures that all participants are solving the same problem. This has been described as the development of a shared problem model and is linked to effective team communication whereby members become equally aware that the team understands the problem (Orasanu, 1994). Furthermore, the team explicitly negotiates their shared understanding of the problem, a step argued to be critical for truly shared mental models (Levine et al., 1993).

Summary

As the brief review highlights, the development of shared mental models attenuates some of the interaction problems teams sometimes experience.

In the next section we link these components of shared mental models to an instantiation of shared problem models. We do so with an example of a popular management tool and demonstrate how certain limitations inherent in teamwork can be overcome through the use of this tool. Our overall goal is to show how theoretical and applied research can be productively intermixed in a way conducive to organizational effectiveness. Furthermore, while the use of problem-solving tools is continuously touted in industry, theoretical accounts of why they work (or do not work) are lacking. As such, this chapter represents an attempt to clarify how one such tool (i.e., process mapping) can facilitate problem conceptualization and subsequent problem solving. We now turn to a discussion of process mapping, a tool widely used in industry (e.g., Rummler & Brache, 1995) to help cross-functional teams on the initial stages of their problem solving.

PROCESS MAPPING AND PROBLEM-SOLVING TEAMS

Although the utility of shared mental models is clear with respect to teams operating in dynamic environments with a high degree of interdependence, we suggest that such models are critical in any team environment. In particular, we argue that many teams work under the unwarranted assumption that they have a shared understanding of their team task. Because they may have either only partial shared understanding or an understanding lacking in any agreement, their ability to effectively work through a problem is severely hindered. We suggest that process mapping works as a problem-solving tool because it leads to the construction of a shared mental model of the problem. Specifically, process mapping scaffolds team cognition in that it facilitates the scanning of the problem space, ensuring that all elements are accounted for, agreed on, and thus, properly addressed.

Process mapping was initially developed to assist teams in process redesign being implemented in the context of organizational improvement (e.g., Rummler & Brache, 1995). Essentially, the technique involves developing a representation of the work flow involved with a given process. In this context, a process is defined as "any combination of people, machines, materials, and methods that is aimed at manufacturing a product or performing a service" (Symons & Jacobs, 1997, p. 71). Thus, process maps are representational charts that fully delineate the process and are descriptive models of a process rather than normative models (although normative models are later defined as the problem-solving process continues).

Initially, process mapping requires the assembly of cross-functional teams, with members selected from every department involved in a given process. The first step is the creation of what is known as the "as is" map, a map detailing the process in its current incarnation. Such a map consists of a visual representation of the personnel or departments involved in the process, along with an articulation of the steps along the process. Constructing this "as is" map is typically a lengthy process because it involves classification of not only every phase of the process but also any illogical, missing, or redundant steps in the process (termed *disconnects*). Thus, the "as is" map represents the critical step in the problem conceptualization stage. Only after the team is agreed that all steps and all disconnects have been labeled do they then focus on what is called the "should be" map. This map is the idealized representation of the new process in which the disconnects have been removed. The overall goal of the construction of the "as is" and "should be" maps is an attempt to eliminate nonvalue-added steps, wherein the remaining steps are redefined for more efficiency; that is, the "should be" map represents the normative model of the process.

Across differing industrial sectors, the data suggest that this tool significantly improves the efficiency of a given process by reducing throughput time. For example, in product development processes, cycle time has been reduced anywhere from 39% to 75% (Anjard, 1996). Manufacturing reengineering efforts using process maps have also shown dramatic effects (Aldowaisan & Gaafar, 1999) with efforts by one process improvement team leading to a reduction in product installation time by 50% (Mason, 1997). Through the use of process mapping to simplify manufacturing procedures, one team found that errors were decreased to 2% of their initial level (Symons & Jacobs, 1997). Furthermore, in some situations, improvements in administrative or service processes can be as high as 90% (see Loew & Hurley, 1995, for a discussion).

PROCESS MAPPING AND PROCESS MAPS AS SHARED MENTAL MODELS

In this section we illustrate how, in the construction of the process map, the team may actually develop a shared problem model for the process in question. We do this by illustrating how it is that process mapping may help teams overcome situations typically hindering group performance (e.g., Gersick & Hackman, 1990; Gigone & Hastie, 1997; Hackman, 1990, 1998). We argue that process mapping facilitates communication among team members and leads to more effective scanning of the problem environment, ensuring that all elements are accounted for and properly addressed, facilitating the problem conceptualization process. Further, we show how components from the more standard definitions of shared mental models (e.g., team roles) fit well within the context of shared models for problem-solving teams.

Problem Structure

The development of a process map represents the development of an organized means with which to conceptualize work flow. As all team members contribute to the map with their unique knowledge base, a detailed representation develops. Specifically, process mapping helps team members flesh out a typically limited understanding of the process in question. While individual team members may possess fairly well-developed knowledge structures with respect to their aspect of a given process, their overall knowledge is, at best, incomplete and, at worst, inaccurate. For example, after process mapping sessions, problem-solving team members have noted, "most people think that they know the whole picture of what goes on in the company . . . After [cross-functional process mapping], you realize that there is a lot more to it than you thought" (Loew & Hurley, 1995, p. 58). Thus, the joint development of the map allows team members the opportunity to elaborate on their understanding of the entire process.

This aspect of process mapping makes it an ideal intervention for overcoming problems due to a tendency for teams to focus more on solution generation than problem conceptualization. In certain situations management may actually encourage this tendency; that is, management may desire solutions to their problems be identified by the team rather than a better understanding of the problem (e.g., Anjard, 1996). But, by focusing the team on the process and the problems inherent in the process (i.e., the disconnects), process mapping teams are forced to forgo discussion of solutions. Thus, we suggest that, in the collaborative construction of the map, participants are required to explicitly define the problem, ensuring that all members are conceptualizing the same problem.

In sum, process mapping provides an enabling structure that allows the team to capitalize on multiple inputs (see Hackman, 1990, 1998). Process mapping creates an environment in which a diverse team can share their knowledge in a way that promotes performance and teamwork. This is particularly important in the context of problem-solving teams because such teams are often ad hoc and will benefit from a structure that scaffolds their communication as they construct their maps.

Team Member Roles and Skills

As the team engages in the initial phases of process mapping, the unique contribution of each individual to the process is made explicit as the map is developed. Specifically, a fundamental purpose of process mapping is to introduce team members to the roles and responsibilities of those involved in a process. Because teams often have the inability to realize who has the knowledge that is most relevant to the problem at hand and how to communicate what is important about the problem (e.g., Serfaty, Entin, & Johnston, 1998), this represents a critically effective aspect of process mapping. Research from studies in the identification of expertise (e.g., Bottger, 1984) shows that groups often fail to determine members of the group who possess critical task knowledge and skills. For example, when interacting teams successfully identified members possessing the most task-relevant expertise, they performed at or near their full potential (Libby, Trotman, & Zimmer, 1987). Nonetheless, many studies illustrate the surprising inability of groups to identify those members possessing the most expertise (e.g., Bottger, 1984; Yetton & Bottger, 1982). Furthermore, organizations too often suffer from a limited understanding of the idiosyncratic skills of employees in differing departments. With process mapping, as the cross-functional team articulates the steps in the process, they are forced to identify which department (and corresponding team member) is involved in that step. This makes explicit not only the capabilities of each team member but also their responsibilities for a given stage in the process.

Process mapping is additionally beneficial because it facilitates information sharing by guiding the transfer of information that takes place during group discussion. A number of studies suggest that group members are more likely to discuss the information they hold in common (i.e., transfer similar data) and not the information they hold that is unique (e.g., Hollingshead, 1996; Stasser et al., 1995; Straus, 1996). Indeed, much research demonstrates that "pooling diverse sets of data via face-to-face discussion [is] more difficult than it seems on casual reflection" (Wittenbaum & Stasser, 1996, p. 6). By means of process mapping, not only do team members pool their resources, that is, contribute their idiosyncratic knowledge, but they also are intimately aware of each other's resources. Thus, with an increase in information sharing, the likelihood of synergistic effects improves as unique information may be brought to bear.

In sum, with process mapping the team is better able to adequately sample items for discussion, particularly when such items are not evenly distributed across the team. For example, after process mapping sessions, problem-solving team members have noted that the initial mapping stages provide "team members a far better understanding of . . . each person's role within the process. This leads to respect and often breaks down barriers that exist departmentally" (Loew & Hurley, 1995, p. 58). This identification of personnel and departmental roles along each step of the process allows team members the opportunity to appropriately acknowledge roles and skills.

Shared Problem Understanding

Overall, this collaborative construction of the process map requires that participants explicitly define their understanding of the process and associated problems, thus facilitating problem conceptualization. This is analogous to what shared mental model theorists have described as *emergent cognition* (e.g., Carley, 1997), or the notion that only as one articulates one's understanding or awareness of a given process does it truly become known to oneself and to others. Thus, the act of making knowledge explicit facilitates the development of not only one's own mental model but also a shared mental model.

More importantly, process mapping forces the team to explicitly negotiate their shared understanding of the process, a step argued to be critical for truly shared mental models (Levine et al., 1993). Others have similarly argued that problem conceptualization at the level of the team only becomes a reality when there is a shared awareness that the group accurately perceives the problem (Larson & Christensen, 1993). For example, after process mapping sessions, problem-solving team members have noted that "the 'as is' map aligns the whole group. It allows you to look at the overall picture of where you've been" (Loew & Hurley, 1995, p. 57). Only after the team agrees on the constructed "as is" map will they move to creating the idealized map, that is, begin solution generation (Mason, 1997).

Last, because a process map is an external representation, it is a concrete manifestation of the team's conceptualization of the problem. Research in collaborative problem solving has demonstrated the substantial benefit of external representation aids. Such studies use augmented displays that allow collaborators to visually articulate abstract concepts and manipulate these task artifacts as the problem-solving process proceeds (e.g., Miller, Price, Entin, Rubineau, & Elliott, 2001; Suthers, 1998). Representation tools, then, are useful because they provide a visual baseline, using a "near universal language," and are thus understandable across departments (Mason, 1997). Illustrating the effectiveness of such aids, process mapping proponents note that the map becomes a key element in team problem solving "because it is visual and people everywhere understand it. Several people in a room can look at the picture or process map and that spurs questions" (Mason, 1997, p. 67). Essentially, process maps illustrate the manner in which team task inputs and team member roles lead to process outcomes (Anjard, 1996). Thus, representational aids for the task at hand can act as a scaffolding with which the team can construct a truly shared, and concrete, depiction of the process problem.

IMPLICATIONS FOR TEAM EFFECTIVENESS

Teams will continue to be a dominant force in organizations, and, as the demand for rapid response to global changes continues to rise, so to will the use of problem-solving teams. In this chapter we suggested that problem-solving teams benefit from the development of shared problem models in a manner similar to teams in more dynamic environments (e.g., Entin & Serfaty, 1999; Serfaty et al., 1998). We identified several distinct problem-solving stages from the cognitive science literature and argued that process mapping facilitates team problem solving by assisting teams in developing a shared conceptualization of the problem. Further, we showed how more standard components of shared mental models actually fit well within the context of shared problem models.

We should note that our approach to shared mental model theory is somewhat unique. Essentially, we suggest that process mapping facilitates a form of team cognition whereby a shared problem model is developed as the team is forced to negotiate the construction of the map. Other approaches, for example, empirical studies assessing mental models, use methods such as concept mapping to assess underlying dimensions of mental models (e.g., Rentsch, Heffner, & Duffy, 1994) or train shared knowledge to facilitate team interaction (e.g., Blickensderfer et al., 1998; Smith-Jentsch, Zeisig, Acton, & McPherson, 1998). Thus, rather than attempting to assess a mental model and make a claim for its existence, we suggest that the map is the model (Jonassen, Beissner, & Yacci, 1993); that is, a process map is an external representation that depicts the shared problem model for a problem-solving team.

Essentially process mapping facilitates the aspect of initial problem solving cognitive scientists have labeled the *search phase* (e.g., Klahr & Dunbar, 1988). In the search phase, the problem solver scans the environment ensuring that all elements are accounted for and addressed. We defined this as the problem conceptualization stage, or the stage that occurs after a problem has been recognized but prior to attempts at generating solutions. Process mapping is beneficial because an adequate initial search phase can help overcome later attempts at solution generation. Process mapping forces the team to recognize deficiencies (disconnects in the "as is" map) prior to attempting to address solutions with the "should be" map. By forcing the team to make a full evaluation of the problem before any suggestions are made, all relevant elements/variables and their interactions are addressed.

By diagramming the entire flow such that interconnections are clear and all repercussions are noted, process mapping provides a means with which to accurately articulate complicated processes and can overcome limitations normally experienced when teams deal with complex problems. The issue of the accuracy versus sharedness of mental models continues to be researched (e.g., Marks et al., 2000; Mathieu et al., 2000; Mohammed & Dumville, 2001), and by providing a means with which to integrate multiple perspectives, process mapping may lead to an accurate shared problem conceptualization. Thus, because process mapping encourages a thorough investigation of the problem space, it may lead to more accurate models of the problem.

Last, we also note the implications of the process map for later problem-solving stages. After a team successfully conceptualizes the problem, they then move to solution generation. In process mapping this entails creating the idealized map (i.e., the "should be" map). The problem-solving team is tasked to "work on isolating and eliminating the irrationalities and redundancies that have crept into the process, attacking the most glaring sources of waste and error first" (Mason, 1997, p. 60). Thus, just as noted by shared mental model theorists (Klimoski & Mohammed, 1994), accurate shared representations of the problem are also important in the later problem-solving stages. Only when problem elements have been identified, properly conceptualized, and agreed on can problem solving proceed effectively.

Some caveats to note concerning the use of process maps include the time required for process mapping. Depending on the complexity of the issue, process mapping can take anywhere from one to several days. But a crucial benefit of process mapping is that no real training is required; the procedure can be learned relatively easily, often in less than a day (e.g., Selander & Cross, 1999). Nonetheless, it may require a skilled group leader or facilitator if the team is inexperienced in the technique. Thus, as in early research on group interaction, in which leaders or facilitators have been documented to benefit group problem solving (e.g., Fiedler, Chemers, & Mahar, 1976; Maier, 1967), process mapping requires such direction (see also Gregory & Romm, 2001). Indeed, as we have argued with respect to process maps, others note that leaders or facilitators are effective when they direct interventions that prompt group members to examine their current problem-solving processes (Gersick & Hackman, 1990; Maier, 1967; Oxley, Dzindolet, & Paulus, 1996), that is, focus on conceptualizing the problem or their approach, *not* the solution.

CONCLUSIONS

The success of process mapping in overcoming interaction problems suggests that there are tools in existence, or tools to be developed, that can begin to truly take advantage of team resources. Heretofore, teams have typically been operating in an additive fashion whereby collective efforts are merely the sum of individual efforts. The question then becomes, what are other tools that are consistently applied in organizations (e.g., cause-and-effect diagrams; Pfadt, 1999), and are they successfully addressing problems experienced by problem-solving teams?

Although the focus of this chapter has been in decomposing the factors that lead to effective team problem solving by means of process mapping, there are two outcomes to be taken from this analysis. The first outcome concerns the research community and how it is that similar analyses can foster a better understanding of the potential causes of performance outcomes when analyzing team cognition. In particular, a closer examination of the many tools in use in industry (e.g., Ishikawa, 1985) is warranted if we are truly going to contribute to a better understanding of organizational interventions. By deconstructing the procedures associated with such tools and identifying their relation to empirically validated performance constructs, researchers may be able to suggest either improvements to existing tools or innovations that provide entirely new approaches to team interaction. Specifically, it is unlikely that such tools would have proliferated had they not demonstrated some measurable success. Therefore, our point is that it behooves us to better analyze current tools to understand what drives their success and limit what may be partial failures. The second outcome concerns the organizational community and how it can benefit from such analyses. Organizational practitioners, who should encourage constructive assessment of these tools, will benefit from an understanding of how they work and when they are best applied.

We conclude that the challenge facing organizational and cognitive psychologists is to fully address the often overlooked difficulties associated with team problem solving and suggest that much needs to be done if we are to truly realize the synergistic potential involved in teamwork. In addition to designing theoretically derived methods for overcoming team processes hindering effective performance, researchers should also more fully analyze the many problem-solving tools being applied to identify their strengths and weaknesses. With a more systematic approach, we can maximize the utility of organizational interventions by more fully delineating the situations for which they are most beneficial.

REFERENCES

Aldowaisan, T. A., & Gaafar, L. K. (1999). Business process reengineering: An approach for process mapping. *Omega: The International Journal of Management Science, 27*, 515–524.

Anjard, R. P. (1996). Process mapping: One of three, new, special quality tools for management, quality and all other professionals. *Microelectronics and Reliability, 36*, 223–225.

Blickensderfer, E., Cannon-Bowers, J. A., & Salas, E. (1998). Cross training and team performance. In J. A. Cannon-Bowers & E. Salas (Eds.), *Making decisions under stress: Implications for individual and team training* (pp. 299–311). Washington, DC: American Psychological Association.

Bottger, P. C. (1984). Expertise and air time as bases of actual and perceived influence in problem-solving groups. *Journal of Applied Psychology, 69*, 214–221.

Cannon-Bowers, J. A., Oser, R., & Flanagan, D. L. (1998). Work teams in industry: A selected review and proposed framework. In J. A. Cannon-Bowers & E. Salas (Eds.), *Making decisions under stress: Implications for individual and team training* (pp. 329–354). Washington, DC: American Psychological Association.

Cannon-Bowers, J. A., & Salas, E. (1990, April). *Cognitive psychology and team training: Shared mental models in complex systems.* Paper presented at the annual meeting of the Society for Industrial and Organizational Psychology, Miami, FL.

Cannon-Bowers, J. A., Salas, E., & Converse, S. (1993). Shared mental models in expert team decision making. In N. J. Castellan, Jr. (Ed.), *Current issues in individual and group decision making* (pp. 221–246). Hillsdale, NJ: Erlbaum.

Carley, K. M. (1997). Extracting team mental models through textual analysis. *Journal of Organizational Behavior, 18,* 533–558.

Chi, M. T. H., Glaser, R., & Rees, E. (1982). Expertise in problem solving. In R. J. Sternberg (Ed.), *Advances in the psychology of human intelligence* (pp. 7–75). Hillsdale, NJ: Erlbaum.

Cowan, D. A. (1986). Developing a process model of problem recognition. *Academy of Management Review, 11,* 763–776.

Entin, E. E., & Serfaty, D. (1999). Adaptive team coordination. *Human Factors, 41,* 312–325.

Fiedler, F. E., Chemers, M. M., & Mahar, L. (1976). *Improving leadership effectiveness: The leader match concept.* New York: Wiley.

Fiore, S. M. (2000). *Problem space and problem solving failure: Cognitive mechanisms in the explanation of process loss in group problem solving.* Unpublished doctoral dissertation, University of Pittsburgh.

Fiore, S. M., Salas, E., & Cannon-Bowers, J. A. (2001). Group dynamics and shared mental model development. In M. London (Ed.), *How people evaluate others in organizations: Person perception and interpersonal judgment in industrial/organizational psychology* (pp. 309–336). Mahwah, NJ: Erlbaum.

Fiore, S. M., & Schooler, J. W. (2001). Convergent or divergent problem space search: The effect of problem structure on group versus individual problem solving. In *Proceedings of the 45th Annual Meeting of the Human Factors and Ergonomic Society* (pp. 483–487). Santa Monica, CA: Human Factors and Ergonomics Society.

Fleishman, E. A., & Zaccaro, S. J. (1992). Toward a taxonomy of team performance functions. In R. W. Swezey & E. Salas (Eds.), *Teams: Their training and performance* (pp. 31–56). Norwood, NJ: Ablex.

Gersick, C., & Hackman, J. R. (1990). Habitual routines in task-performing groups. *Organizational Behavior and Human Decision Processes, 47,* 65–97.

Gigone, D., & Hastie, R. (1997). Proper analysis in the accuracy of group judgments. *Psychological Bulletin, 121,* 149–167.

Glaser, R., & Bassok, M. (1989). Learning theory and the study of instruction. *Annual Review of Psychology, 40,* 631–666.

Gregory, W. J., & Romm, W. J. (2001). Critical facilitation: Learning through intervention in group process. *Management Learning, 32,* 453–467.

Guzzo, R. A., & Salas, E. (Eds.). (1995). *Team effectiveness and decision making in organizations.* San Francisco: Jossey-Bass.

Hackman, J. R. (1990). *Groups that work (and those that don't): Creating conditions for effective teamwork.* San Francisco: Jossey-Bass.

Hackman, J. R. (1998). Why teams don't work. In R. S. Tindale (Ed.), *Theory and research on small groups: Vol. 4. Social psychological applications to social issues* (pp. 245–267). New York: Plenum.

Hackman, J. R., & Morris, C. G. (1975). Group tasks, group interaction process and group performance effectiveness: A review and proposed integration. In L.

Berkowitz (Ed.), *Advances in experimental social psychology* (Vol. 8, pp. 45–99). New York: Academic Press.

Hinsz, V. B., Tindale, R. S., & Vollrath, D. A. (1997). The emerging conceptualization of groups as information processors. *Psychological Bulletin, 121,* 43–64.

Hollingshead, A. B. (1996). Information suppression and status persistence in group decision making: The effects of communication media. *Human Communication Research, 23,* 193–219.

Ishikawa, K (1985). *Guide to quality control.* Tokyo: Asian Productivity Organization.

Janis, I. L. (1972). *Victims of groupthink: A psychological study of foreign-policy decisions and fiascoes.* Boston: Houghton Mifflin.

Johnson-Laird, P. N. (1983). *Mental models: Towards a cognitive science of language, inference, and consciousness.* Cambridge, MA: Harvard University Press.

Jonassen, D. H., Beissner, K., & Yacci, M. (1993). *Structural knowledge: Techniques for representing, conveying, and acquiring structural knowledge.* Hillsdale, NJ: Erlbaum.

Katzenbach, J. R., & Smith, D. K. (1993). *The wisdom of teams: Creating the high performance organization.* Boston: Harvard Business School Press.

Klahr, D., & Dunbar, K. (1988). Dual space search during scientific reasoning. *Cognitive Science, 12,* 1–48.

Klahr, D., Fay, A. L., & Dunbar, K. (1993). Heuristics for scientific experimentation: A developmental study. *Cognitive Psychology, 25,* 111–146.

Klein, G. (1993). A recognition primed decision (RPD) model of rapid decision making. In G. Klein, J. Orasanu, R. Calderwood, & C. Zsambok (Eds.), *Decision making in action* (pp. 138–147). Norwood, NJ: Ablex.

Klein, G., & Pierce, L. G. (2001). Adaptive teams. In *Proceedings of the 6th ICCRTS Collaboration in the Information Age Track 4: C2 decision-making and cognitive analysis.* Retrieved on October 30, 2002 from http://www.dodccrp.org/6thICCRTS/

Klein, G., Pliske, R. M., Crandall, B., & Woods, D. (1999). Features of problem detection. In *Proceedings of the 43rd Annual Meeting of the Human Factors and Ergonomics Society* (pp. 133–137). Santa Monica, CA: Human Factors and Ergonomics Society.

Klimoski, R., & Mohammed, S. (1994). Team mental model: Construct or metaphor? *Journal of Management, 20,* 403–437.

Larson, J. R., & Christensen, C. (1993). Groups as problem-solving units: Toward a new meaning of social cognition. *British Journal of Social Psychology, 32,* 5–30.

Levine, J. M., Resnick, L. B., & Higgins, E. T. (1993). Social foundations of cognition. *Annual Review of Psychology, 44,* 585–612.

Liang, D. W., Moreland, R. L., & Argote, L. (1995). Group versus individual training and group performance: The mediating role of transactive memory. *Personality and Social Psychology Bulletin, 21,* 384–393.

Libby, R., Trotman, K. T., & Zimmer, I. (1987). Member variation, recognition of expertise, and group performance. *Journal of Applied Psychology, 72,* 81–87.

Loew, C., & Hurley, H. (1995). Faster product/process development through cross functional process mapping. *Production, 107,* 56–61.

Maier, N. R. F. (1967). Assets and liabilities in group problem solving: The need for an integrative function. *Psychological Review, 74,* 239–249.

Marks, M. A., Zaccaro, S. J., & Mathieu, J. E. (2000). Performance implications of leader briefings and team-interaction training for team adaptation to novel environments. *Journal of Applied Psychology, 85,* 971–986.

Mason, F. (1997). Mapping a better process. *Manufacturing Engineering, 118,* 58–68.

Mathieu, J. E., Heffner, T. S., Goodwin, G. F., Salas, E., & Cannon-Bowers, J. A. (2000). The influence of shared mental models on team process and performance. *Journal of Applied Psychology, 85,* 273–283.

Miller, D., Price, J. M., Entin, E., Rubineau, B.. & Elliott, L. (2001). Does planning using groupware foster coordinated team performance. In *Proceedings of the 45th Annual Meeting of the Human Factors and Ergonomic Society* (pp. 390–394). Santa Monica, CA: Human Factors and Ergonomics Society.

Mohammed, S., & Dumville, B. C. (2001). Team mental models in a team knowledge framework: Expanding theory and measurement across disciplinary boundaries. *Journal of Organizational Behavior, 22,* 89–106.

Moreland, R. L., & Argote, L. (2003). Transactive memory in dynamic organizations. In R. Peterson & E. Mannix (Eds.), *Understanding the dynamic organization* (pp. 135–162). Mahwah, NJ: Erlbaum.

Moreland, R. L., & Levine, J. M. (1992). Problem identification by groups. In S. Worchel, W. Wood, & J. A. Simpson (Eds.), *Group processes and productivity* (pp. 17–47). Newbury Park, CA: Sage.

Moreland, R. L., Levine, J. M., & Wingert, M. L. (1996). Creating the ideal group: Composition effects at work. In E. H. Witte & J. H. Davis (Eds.), *Understanding group behavior: Vol. 2. Small group processes and interpersonal relations* (pp. 11–35). Mahwah, NJ: Erlbaum.

Moreland, R. L., & Myaskovsky, L. (2000). Explaining the performance benefits of group training: Transactive memory or improved communication? *Organizational Behavior and Human Decision Processes, 82,* 117–133.

Newell, A., & Simon, H. A. (1972). *Human problem solving.* Englewood Cliffs, NJ: Prentice-Hall.

Orasanu, J. (1994). Shared problem models and flight crew performance. In N. Johnston, N. McDonald, & R. Fuller (Eds.), *Aviation psychology in practice* (pp. 255–285). Brookfield, VT: Ashgate.

Orasanu, J., & Salas, E. (1993). Team decision making in complex environments. In G. Klein, J. Orasanu, R. Calderwood, & C. E. Zsambok (Eds.), *Decision making in action: Models and methods* (pp. 327–345). Norwood, NJ: Ablex.

Oxley, N. L., Dzindolet, M. T., & Paulus, P. B. (1996). The effects of facilitators on the performance of brainstorming groups. *Journal of Social Behavior and Personality, 11,* 633–646.

Pfadt, A. (1999). Using control charts to analyze baseline stability: An illustrative example with "real time" data. *Journal of Organizational Behavior Management, 18,* 53–60.

Rentsch, J. R., Heffner, T. S., & Duffy, L. T. (1994). What you know is what you get from experience: Team experience related to teamwork schemas. *Group and Organization Management, 19,* 450–474.

Resnick, L. (1991). Shared cognition: Thinking as a social practice. In L. B. Resnick, J. M. Levine, & S. D. Teasley (Eds.), *Perspectives on socially shared cognition* (pp. 1–20). Washington, DC: American Psychological Association.

Rouse, W. B. (1989). *Advances in man-machine systems research* (Vol. 5). Greenwich, CT: JAI Press.

Rummler, G. A., & Brache, A. P. (1995). *Improving performance: How to manage the white space on the organization chart* (2nd ed.). San Francisco: Jossey-Bass.

Salas, E., Dickinson, T. L., Converse, S. A., & Tannenbaum, S. I. (1992). Toward an understanding of team performance and training. In R. W. Swezey & E. Salas (Eds.), *Teams: Their training and performance* (pp. 3–29). Norwood, NJ: Ablex.

Schooler, J. W., Fallshore, M., & Fiore, S. M. (1995). Putting insight into perspective. In R. J. Sternberg & J. E. Davidson (Eds.), *The nature of insight* (pp. 559–587). Cambridge, MA: MIT Press.

Selander, J. P., & Cross, K. F. (1999). Process redesign: Is it worth it? *Management Accounting, 80,* 40–45.

Serfaty, D., Entin, E., & Johnston, J. H. (1998). Team adaptation and coordination training. In J. A. Cannon-Bowers & E. Salas (Eds.), *Making decisions under stress: Implications for individual and team training* (pp. 221–245). Washington, DC: American Psychological Association.

Simon, H. A., & Lea, G. (1974). Problem solving and rule induction: A unified view. In L. Gregg (Ed.), *Knowledge and cognition* (pp. 105–128). Hillsdale, NJ: Erlbaum.

Smith-Jentsch, K. A., Campbell, G. E., Milanovich, D. M., & Reynolds, A. M. (2001). Measuring teamwork mental models to support training needs assessment, development, and evaluation: Two empirical studies [Special issue]. *Journal of Organizational Behavior, 22,* 179–194.

Smith-Jentsch, K. A., Zeisig, R. L., Acton, B., & McPherson, J. A. (1998). Team dimensional training. In J. A. Cannon-Bowers & E. Salas (Eds.), *Making decisions under stress: Implications for individual and team training* (pp. 271–297). Washington, DC: American Psychological Association.

Stasser, G., Stewart, D. D., & Wittenbaum, G. M. (1995). Expert roles and information exchange during discussion: The importance of knowing who knows what. *Journal of Experimental Social Psychology, 31,* 244–265.

Stout, R. J., Cannon-Bowers, J. A., & Salas, E. (1996). The role of shared mental models in developing team situational awareness: Implications for training. *Training Research Journal, 2,* 85–116.

Straus, S. G. (1996). Getting a clue: The effects of communication media and information distribution on participation and performance in computer-mediated and face-to-face groups. *Small Group Research, 27,* 115–142.

Sundstrom, E., de Meuse, K. P., & Futrell, D. (1990). Work teams: Applications and effectiveness. *American Psychologist, 45,* 120–133.

Suthers, D. (1998, April). *Representations for scaffolding collaborative inquiry on ill-structured problems*. Paper presented at the American Educational Research Association annual meeting, San Diego, CA.

Symons, R. T., & Jacobs, R. A. (1997). Multi-level process mapping: A tool for cross-functional quality analysis. *Production and Inventory Management Journal, 38*, 71–75.

Tanskanen, T., Buhanist, P., & Kostama, H. (1998). Exploring the diversity of teams. *International Journal of Production Economics, 56–57*, 611–619.

Volpe, C. E., Cannon-Bowers, J. A., Salas, E., & Spector, P. E. (1996). The impact of cross-training on team functioning: An empirical investigation. *Human Factors, 38*, 87–100.

Wittenbaum, G. M., & Stasser, G. (1996). Management of information in small groups. In J. L. Nye & A. M. Brower (Eds.), *What's social about social cognition? Research on socially shared cognition in small groups* (pp. 3–28). Thousand Oaks, CA: Sage.

Wittenbaum, G. M., Stasser, G., & Merry, C. J. (1996). Tacit coordination in anticipation of small group task completion. *Journal of Experimental Social Psychology, 32*, 129–152.

Wittenbaum, G. M., Vaughan, S. I., & Stasser, G. (1998). Coordination in task-performing groups. In R. S. Tindale & L. Heath (Eds.), *Theory and research on small groups: Vol. 4. Social psychological applications to social issues* (pp. 177–204). New York: Plenum.

Yetton, P. W., & Bottger, P. C. (1982). Individual versus group problem solving: An empirical test of a best-member strategy. *Organizational Behavior and Human Decision Processes, 29*, 307–321.

8

IMPACT OF PERSONNEL TURNOVER ON TEAM PERFORMANCE AND COGNITION

JOHN M. LEVINE AND HOON-SEOK CHOI

Work teams are a ubiquitous feature of modern organizations and have a major impact on organizational effectiveness (e.g., Hackman, 1998; Ilgen, 1999; Sundstrom, 1999). This is not surprising, because teams typically possess more task-relevant knowledge and skills than do individual workers. Moreover, team members can share information, engage in coordinated actions to achieve common goals, redistribute responsibilities in light of new task demands, and motivate one another to work hard. Despite these advantages, however, teams do not always perform as well as they might. As Steiner (1972) observed, teams' actual productivity often falls below their potential productivity because of process losses due to low member motivation or poor

Preparation of this chapter was supported by Contract N00014-90-6-1664 from the Office of Naval Research and Contract DASW01-00-K-0018 from the Army Research Institute. The views, opinions, and/or findings contained in this chapter are those of the authors and should not be construed as an official Department of the Army position, policy, or decision.

Thanks are extended to Alan Lesgold and Franziska Tschan for help in developing the experimental paradigm and to Sherrie Britt, Daniel Grech, Justina Jander, and Joel Thurston for assisting in data collection and analysis. We are particularly grateful to Gareth Gabrys for his help in writing the Network-Based Air Traffic Control program and managing the data collection.

response coordination. Motivation and coordination problems can have many causes, including inadequate training (Salas, Bowers, & Edens, 2001) and managerial mistakes, such as giving teams too much or too little authority and failing to provide teams with organizational support (Hackman, 1998).

Work teams are small groups of a special kind. Team members share common task goals, are interdependent for achieving these goals, engage in ongoing information exchange and response coordination, and are differentiated in terms of roles and responsibilities (Salas, Dickinson, Converse, & Tannenbaum, 1992). Like other kinds of small groups, teams face several challenges, which include regulating the number and type of people who belong to the group; maintaining the group's status system and norms; reducing tensions between members; adapting to the group's physical, social, and temporal environments; and facilitating group decision making and productivity (Levine & Moreland, 1998). The difficulties associated with meeting these challenges explain why team performance is often disappointing (cf. Guzzo & Salas, 1995; Hackman, 1998; Salas et al., 2001; Turner, 2001).

TEMPORAL ASPECTS OF TEAM LIFE: MEMBERSHIP CHANGE

Teams are not static entities but instead change in dynamic ways over time. To clarify the determinants of team performance, it is therefore necessary to consider temporal aspects of team life, which include team formation and dissolution, team development (i.e., changes in the team as a whole), team socialization (i.e., changes in the relationship between the team and each of its members), temporal aspects of team task performance (e.g., action synchronization, activity scheduling), team learning under stable conditions, and team adaptation to unstable conditions, such as changing membership (Arrow, McGrath, & Berdahl, 2000; Levine & Moreland, 1994; McGrath & O'Connor, 1996). In this chapter, we focus on how teams respond to membership change, which occurs when new members enter an existing team or a subset of current members exits the team.[1] Although turnover is more common in some teams than others, it is inevitable in all teams that exist for any period of time. A number of studies examining the effects of turnover in groups and organizations have been conducted. In the following discussion, we focus primarily on small group research, mentioning organizational research where appropriate.

One method of studying membership change in groups involves gradually replacing old members with new members. This *generational* paradigm

---

[1]We restrict our discussion of entry to cases in which new members join an *existing* team to differentiate this process from team formation, which occurs when people come to together to create a new team. Similarly, we restrict our discussion of exit to cases in which a *subset* of current members leaves a team to differentiate this process from team dissolution, which occurs when all current members leave, thereby ending the team's existence.

has been used to investigate such diverse phenomena as norm persistence, leadership, and group performance (Kenny, Hallmark, & Sullivan, 1993). It has been found that norms persist over several generations, during which old members gradually leave the group and new ones join (Jacobs & Campbell, 1961), and that more arbitrary norms decay faster than less arbitrary ones (MacNeil & Sherif, 1976). Other generational studies have shown that, over time, groups develop leadership systems based on seniority and become more proficient in carrying out their tasks (Insko et al., 1982; Insko et al., 1980).

Studies of membership change using other paradigms have demonstrated that change sometimes facilitates group and organizational performance. For example, Arrow and McGrath (1993) found that student groups meeting over a semester wrote better essays when they experienced membership change than when they did not. In addition, Ziller, Behringer, and Goodchilds (1962) discovered that groups with changing memberships were more creative than groups with stable memberships. Moreover, Rogelberg, Barnes-Farrell, and Lowe (1992) found that "stepladder" groups, in which a dyad that had worked together was joined by a third and then a fourth member, produced higher quality decisions than did conventional four-person groups, in which all members worked together from the beginning. Finally, there is evidence that turnover can have beneficial effects on performance in organizational settings (e.g., Virany, Tushman, & Romanelli, 1992).

The notion that membership change enhances group performance is consistent with research on the effects of member diversity and member transfer. In regard to member diversity, evidence suggests that heterogeneous groups, in which members differ on such dimensions as demographic characteristics, abilities, and educational and functional backgrounds, are often more creative than homogeneous groups (Argote & Kane, 2003). Though diversity does not always improve group performance (Milliken, Bartel, & Kurtzberg, 2003; Moreland, Levine, & Wingert, 1996), to the extent that membership change increases diversity and creativity facilitates performance, membership change should be beneficial. In regard to member transfer, evidence indicates that moving members from one group to another is often, though not always (e.g., Gruenfeld, Martorana, & Fan, 2000), an effective way of transferring knowledge within and between organizations (Argote & Kane, 2003). Because the infusion of new knowledge frequently improves group performance, research on member transfer suggests that membership change can have productive consequences.

However, turnover does not always enhance group and organizational performance (e.g., Goodman & Leyden, 1991; Moreland, Argote, & Krishnan, 1998). This is because, in order for turnover to have positive effects, it must outweigh the substantial benefits that group members derive from working together (Argote & Kane, 2003). Such experience makes it easier for members to recognize one another's strengths and weaknesses, to anticipate one another's actions, and to develop efficient transactive memory systems. In addition, it improves members' motivation and ability to share information and their willingness to express disagreement. Although "too much" experience working together can harm group members' performance (e.g., Kim, 1997), there is little doubt that at least a modicum of shared experience is necessary for good collective performance. If so, then the appropriate question becomes not whether membership change is inherently better or worse than stability, but rather what conditions increase and decrease the value of such change (cf. Abelson & Baysinger, 1984).

Several factors have been shown to affect the impact of turnover on group and organizational performance. One such factor is the time course of membership change. Trow (1960) found that while a group's overall level of turnover did not systematically affect its performance, increases in the rate of turnover harmed performance. Curvilinear relationships between turnover and performance have also been obtained, both at the small group (Glaser & Klaus, 1966) and organizational (Argote, Epple, Rao, & Murphy, 1997) levels. Another factor that can influence the impact of turnover is member ability. Trow (1960) and Naylor and Briggs (1965) found that groups performed better when new members were superior to the people they replaced (i.e., more intelligent or skilled) than when they were inferior (see also Argote et al., 1997).

Additional determinants of turnover effects include the way in which members interact with one another, the structure of the group, and the complexity of the task. For example, turnover causes more problems when group members work interactively rather than independently (Naylor & Briggs, 1965) and when the group has low rather than high structure (Carley, 1992; Devadas & Argote, 1995). Regarding task complexity, turnover is more problematical when the task is routine rather than challenging (Argote, Insko, Yovetich, & Romero, 1995), presumably because task knowledge changes more slowly for routine than for challenging tasks, and hence the departure of experienced members is more costly in the former case. It is also worth noting that the effects of turnover on performance can be rather subtle. For example, even when turnover does not directly affect group performance, it can undermine a leader's effectiveness in weighting subordinates' judgments (Hollenbeck et al., 1995).

The conditions under which turnover has positive versus negative effects on group performance have been addressed in two recent theoretical analyses. The first, by Levine and his colleagues, dealt with the phenomenon of newcomer innovation in work groups (Levine, Choi, & Moreland, 2003; Levine, Moreland, & Choi, 2001; see also Levine & Moreland, 1985). Although newcomers often interfere with group performance, for example by forcing oldtimers to expend time and energy in socialization activities (Levine & Moreland, 1999; Moreland & Levine, 1989), they can also improve this performance by introducing innovations that help the team work more effectively. According to Levine et al. (2003), such innovation is the result of an implicit or explicit negotiation between newcomers and oldtimers, both of whom play an active role during the socialization phase of group membership. In discussing how newcomers' characteristics and behaviors affect their ability to produce innovation, Levine et al. (2003) emphasized newcomers' motivation to introduce change into the team they are entering, their ability to generate ideas that can enhance team performance, and their ability to convince oldtimers to accept these ideas. They argued, for example, that newcomers' motivation to introduce change varies positively with their belief that they can develop good ideas for solving team problems and their perception that their innovation efforts will be rewarded. In discussing how team characteristics affect newcomers' ability to produce innovation, Levine et al. suggested that innovation efforts will be more effective in some teams than in others. For example, they argued that newcomers will find it easier to exert influence in teams that are open rather than closed to new members, understaffed rather than adequately staffed, in earlier rather than later stages of development, and performing poorly rather than well.

The second analysis, by McGrath and his colleagues (e.g., Arrow & McGrath, 1993, 1995; McGrath & O'Connor, 1996), had a broader goal, namely to provide a general theory of membership dynamics. They argued that the nature and impact of membership change depend on such factors as the kind of group involved, its status and role systems, and the particular members involved. They predicted, for example, that change will have fewer consequences when peripheral rather than central members are involved. McGrath and his colleagues also emphasized the importance of the magnitude and direction of membership change (e.g., addition vs. subtraction of members), hypothesizing, for example, that the effects of change increase with the number of members who participate in it. Finally, they discussed the impact of the temporal patterning of membership change (e.g., frequency, regularity, predictability), predicting, for example, that groups with a history of repeated and predictable change will develop procedures for managing the disruptive effects of turnover.

SHARED COGNITION AND COMMUNICATION

Implicit in both Levine et al.'s and McGrath et al.'s analyses of the impact of membership change is the assumption that turnover affects performance to the extent that it influences (a) the amount, quality, and distribution of task- and team-relevant knowledge, skills, and attitudes within the team (see Cannon-Bowers, Tannenbaum, Salas, & Volpe, 1995) and (b) team members' ability to coordinate their actions in the service of attaining collective goals. In recent years, there has been increasing interest in the knowledge component of team effectiveness, particularly in the role that *shared cognition* plays (Salas & Cannon-Bowers, 2001). Shared cognition is often conceptualized in terms of shared mental models, which are assumed to influence team performance through their impact on members' ability to engage in coordinated actions (Fiore, Salas, & Cannon-Bowers, 2001). Shared mental models involve knowledge about the team's task, individual members' responsibilities, and potential situations the team may encounter. Interest in shared cognition in general and shared mental models in particular has been stimulated by two major developments. The first is increased awareness of the fact that human cognition is an interpersonal, as well as an intrapersonal, phenomenon (e.g., Levine, Resnick, & Higgins, 1993; Nye & Brower, 1996; Resnick, Levine, & Teasley, 1991). The second is increased desire to understand and enhance team performance (e.g., Mathieu, Heffner, Goodwin, Salas, & Cannon-Bowers, 2000; Stout, Cannon-Bowers, Salas, & Milanovich, 1999). Though shared cognition is currently eliciting a good deal of theoretical and empirical attention (e.g., Levine & Higgins, 2001; Salas & Cannon-Bowers, 2001; Tindale, Meisenhelder, Dykema-Engblade, & Hogg, 2001), many questions remain about how it should be defined and measured, what factors affect its development, and when it is most likely to influence team performance (e.g., Cannon-Bowers & Salas, 2001; Kraiger & Wenzel, 1997; Mohammed & Dumville, 2001; Rentsch & Klimoski, 2001).

Although, as Cannon-Bowers and Salas (2001) noted, the term *shared cognition* can have multiple meanings, it is typically measured by calculating the level of agreement between team members' mental representations of some relevant issue, such as task requirements, team process, or member expertise, with the assumption that higher agreement indicates more shared cognition (e.g., Levesque, Wilson, & Wholey, 2001; Mathieu et al., 2000; Stout et al., 1999). Though useful for many purposes, such indices have two potential problems. If obtained after task performance, they may reflect the kinds of memory distortions associated with most retrospective measures. If obtained during task performance, they may force team members to reflect on their mental activities at times and in ways that are "unnatural," thereby providing misleading information about the cognitions that typically accompany joint work. An alternative approach involves assessing team members' behaviors as they work together and then using these behaviors as markers, or indices, of their shared cognition (cf. Moreland, 1999; Weick & Roberts, 1993). This approach is consistent with the argument that, in many situations, it is neither possible nor conceptually useful to separate social interaction and cognition. In such cases, rather than being the cause or consequence of cognition, interaction *constitutes* cognition (Levine et al., 1993).

Communication between team members is a rich source of information about their shared cognition. A number of studies have demonstrated relationships between various communication indices (e.g., amount, sequence, type) and team performance (e.g., Bowers, Jentsch, Salas, & Braun, 1998; Hollenbeck et al., 1995; Tschan, 1995). Moreover, recent work has established links among communication, shared cognition, and team performance (e.g., Marks, Zaccaro, & Mathieu, 2000; Mathieu et al., 2000; Stout et al., 1999). Communication may be particularly useful in clarifying how shared cognition changes over time. Although team members may have shared cognition prior to interacting with one another, because of experience on other teams (Rentsch & Klimoski, 2001) or preprocess coordination (Fiore et al., 2001; Wittenbaum, Vaughan, & Stasser, 1998), such cognition typically occurs as a result of collaborative work. So far, little attention has been paid to temporal changes in the structure and content of shared cognition (for exceptions, see Levesque et al., 2001; Mathieu et al., 2000; Moreland, 1999). Given that shared cognition probably involves a set of temporally related processes and subprocesses (e.g., Gibson, 2001; Hinsz, Tindale, & Vollrath, 1997), it would seem useful to conduct longitudinal studies that investigate the dynamic properties of shared cognition, as indexed by communication between team members.

AN EXPERIMENTAL STUDY OF MEMBERSHIP CHANGE

As suggested above, personnel turnover can influence both team performance and team members' shared cognition. To investigate the relationships among turnover, performance, and shared cognition, we conducted a study in which teams had to adapt to newcomers who varied in task-relevant ability and status. Three-person teams (composed of two specialists and a commander) worked on an air surveillance task over 2 days. On both days, specialists monitored changing plane information (e.g., airspeed, altitude) and transmitted it to the commander, who integrated this information and assigned threat values to the planes. Team members had an opportunity to communicate during the task and received feedback on their performance afterward. At the beginning of Day 2, personnel turnover was manipulated by (a) replacing one of the specialists with a specialist from another team, (b) replacing the commander with a commander from another team, or (c) leaving the team's composition intact. Newcomers' task-relevant ability was assessed from how they and their team performed on Day 1.

Given that the team's task was highly structured and members had substantial experience performing their specialized roles on Day 1, we did not expect turnover per se to have major effects on team performance (cf. Argote et al., 1995; Arrow & McGrath, 1995; Devadas & Argote, 1995). Nevertheless, we anticipated that the characteristics of the newcomers, namely their task-relevant ability and status, might be important. Specifically, we predicted that (a) newcomers with higher task ability would have more positive impact on team performance than would those with lower ability (cf. Argote et al., 1997; Levine et al., 2003; Naylor & Briggs, 1965; Trow, 1960) and (b) higher status newcomers (commanders) would have more impact, for better or worse, than would lower status newcomers (specialists; cf. Arrow &

McGrath, 1995; Levine et al., 2003; Milanovich, Driskell, Stout, & Salas, 1998).

In regard to shared cognition, we expected that team members would initially use communication to develop a consensus about how to perform their task (Stout et al., 1999). Moreover, we expected that, under certain conditions, team members would later use communication to reconsider and, if necessary, alter this consensus. Two such conditions were investigated: team performance and personnel turnover. We hypothesized that, during the course of the experiment, team members' communication regarding their task strategy would increase following (a) the receipt of negative feedback about their performance and (b) the entry of a new member. These predictions were based on the assumptions that both poor performance and personnel turnover are disruptive events in the life of the group, which can threaten team members' confidence in the adequacy of their shared cognition. If so, this threat should stimulate members to communicate to restore confidence in their original shared cognition or to develop a better one. This reasoning is consistent with the suggestion that team failure and personnel turnover often cause groups to switch from tacit coordination (which is typically unspoken) to explicit coordination (which is typically spoken; Wittenbaum et al., 1998).

Method

Participants were 90 male undergraduate students recruited through campus advertisements. Randomly selected groups of 3 participants were brought to the laboratory, seated in adjacent booths containing personal computers, and told that they would work on an air-surveillance task. The task was presented using a simulation program (Network-Based Air Traffic Control, or NetATC), which ran on personal computers linked via a local area network to a file server using Novell Netware.[2] NetATC was designed to embody many of the challenges that real-world teams face, including the need to (a) solve problems requiring substantial communication and coordination; (b) process dynamic information that is distributed unequally across team members; (c) rely on computer systems for information acquisition and transmission; (d) operate in stressful environments characterized by time pressure and performance-contingent payoffs; and (e) adapt to role, status, and power differences within the team.

After learning that the experiment would be divided into several 15-minute shifts and that they could earn bonus money ($1 to $2 per shift) based on their team's performance, participants received 1 hour of training on NetATC. During training, participants learned how to monitor nine char-

_____

[2]The design of NetATC was influenced by the TIDE[2] program (Hollenbeck et al., 1997) but differs from it in a number of ways.

acteristics of planes flying through a simulated airspace: airspeed (in miles per hour); altitude (in feet); angle (the degree of the plane's ascent or descent); corridor (the plane's position relative to its authorized flight path— inside, on the edge, outside); direction (the size of the course adjustment needed for the plane to fly directly over the airbase, in degrees); identify friend or foe (IFF; friend, civilian, enemy); radar (weather, none, weapon); range (distance from the airbase, in miles); and size (large, medium, small). In addition, participants were told how the raw values of each characteristic were translated into threat levels, which the commander used in calculating the threat value for each plane (e.g., > 30,000 feet = low threat; 15,000–30,000 feet = medium threat; < 15,000 feet = high threat). Finally, participants learned how to send and receive messages using NetATC. Following this general training, the commander received individual training in how to use a threat formula to calculate a threat value for each plane, based on information about the plane's characteristics.[3] He also learned how to translate that value into a threat level (ranging from 1 to 7), which he entered into his computer and which appeared on all team members' screens.

The team then completed a 15-minute practice shift, followed by the first work session. This session began with a 5-minute face-to-face discussion, which was audiotaped. The team then performed four 15-minute shifts (Shifts 1, 2, 3, and 4), in which they monitored and made threat assignments for two planes. In all shifts, Specialist A monitored altitude, range, corridor, and size for all planes; Specialist B monitored airspeed, angle, direction, and radar; and the commander monitored IFF. Following each shift, the NetATC program calculated team performance (on a scale from 0 to 100) and displayed it on members' screens. In addition, team members were given an opportunity to communicate by e-mail before the next shift began. Approximately 1 week later, participants returned for the second work session (Shifts 5, 6, 7, and 8). Participants followed the same procedure as on Day 1, with two exceptions. First, 20 of the 30 teams experienced membership change. In 10 teams (commander change), the person who played the role of commander on Day 1 was replaced by someone who previously played the same role on a different team. In another 10 teams (specialist change), the person who played the role of Specialist A on Day 1 was replaced by someone who previously played the same role on a different team. Thus, in both turnover conditions, the newcomer on Day 2 had the same amount and type of experience as the individual he was replacing. In the remaining 10 teams (no change), membership remained stable on Days 1 and 2. In addition, the team task was harder on Day 2 than on Day 1, because there were more planes to monitor (four vs. two) and threat changes occurred more rapidly. Following

---

[3]The formula was: threat = [(altitude + range) × corridor + (airspeed + angle) × direction + (size + radar)] × IFF. Note that three plane characteristics—corridor, direction, and IFF—are particularly important, as they act as multipliers for other values.

the fourth shift, participants were debriefed and paid $25, plus whatever bonus money they had earned.

In addition to calculating team performance after each shift, NetATC stored and time-stamped all the computer-based actions of each team member during the shift. These actions included information acquisition (e.g., how frequently particular plane characteristics were monitored), the content and flow of communication in the team (e.g., which plane information was sent to the commander, how quickly members sent and read messages), and the commander's threat assignments (e.g., how quickly initial assignments were made).

Results

Team Environment Prior to Turnover

Before assessing the impact of membership change on team performance and shared cognition, we wanted to understand the state of the team before turnover occurred. To do this, we assessed three types of data.

Initial Discussions. In examining the pre-Shift 1 discussions of a sample of teams ($n = 16$), we found that team members engaged in what has been called preplanning or preprocess coordination (Fiore et al., 2001; Wittenbaum et al., 1998). During discussions, team members exchanged ideas about how to coordinate their actions to maximize collective performance (e.g., send direction and corridor information first, send threat levels rather than raw values, send information only when it changes, and assign threat to planes immediately). It appears, then, that team members used these discussions to develop a shared understanding of the demands of the air surveillance task and their responses to these demands. This shared understanding can be viewed as a kind of "common ground," which is a critical component of effective communication (Krauss & Fussell, 1991).

Team Performance. Next we examined how team performance changed across the four shifts on Day 1. It should be noted that (a) Shifts 1 and 3 were equal in difficulty, as were Shifts 2 and 4, and (b) Shifts 1 and 3 were easier than Shifts 2 and 4, because plane characteristics changed more rapidly in the latter shifts. A one-way repeated-measures analysis of variance conducted on performance across the four shifts revealed a significant cubic trend ($p < .01$), which showed evidence of learning.[4] That is, within each pair of shifts matched in difficulty, accuracy increased over time (Shift 1: $M = 69.40$ vs. Shift 3: $M = 72.53$, $p < .06$; Shift 2: $M = 61.80$ vs. Shift 4: $M = 66.33$, $p < .05$).

---

[4]Because the membership change manipulation was not introduced until Day 2, we did not expect Day 1 performance differences between teams that would later receive different levels of this manipulation. To test this assumption, we used (future) membership change condition (commander change, specialist change, no change) as an independent variable in analyses of Day 1 data. As expected, this variable did not have a significant impact, and hence the Day 1 analyses reported here treat the 30 teams as equivalent.

Behaviors Underlying Performance. Finally, to understand what accounted for team performance on Day 1, we examined the behaviors that team members emitted while monitoring planes and making threat assignments. Recall that the NetATC program stored all the computer-based actions of the commander and the two specialists. Over the 5-hour course of the experiment, our 30 teams generated almost 118,000 actions (e.g., looking up plane information, communicating this information, assigning threat values). Our goal was to use this information to provide a parsimonious account of team performance.

Although we did not have an explicit theory of team performance in the NetATC task, we had some hunches about what actions by specialists and commanders would facilitate accurate and timely threat assignments.[5] Using the database containing team members' computer-based actions, we derived several behavioral indices that we thought might affect team performance and then assessed their utility as predictors of performance in multiple regression analyses. On the basis of these analyses, we were able to derive an equation, using just four predictors, that accounted for approximately half the variance in overall team performance on Day 1 ($R^2 = .49$, $p < .01$). These predictors were commander's IFF latency, commander's threat latency, specialists' critical look-ups, and specialists' message latency. Commander's IFF latency refers to the amount of time that elapsed between a plane entering the airspace and the first IFF look-up by the commander (log transformed). Commander's threat latency refers to the amount of time that elapsed between a plane entering the airspace and the first threat assignment by the commander (log transformed). Specialists' critical look-ups refers to the ratio of look-ups involving "critical" characteristics of enemy planes (direction, corridor) to the total number of look-ups made by the two specialists (arcsine transformed). And specialists' message latency refers to the specialists' latency in reading messages sent by teammates (log transformed). (To create predictors for specialists, we combined data for the two specialists in each team.) As the regression equation indicates (Performance = $77.69 - .27X_1 - .30X_2 + .37X_3 - .17X_4$), teams performed better when commander's IFF latency (X_1), commander's threat latency (X_2), and specialists' message latency (X_4) were low and when specialists' critical look-ups (X_3) was high.

We also examined the predictive utility of the equation for each of the four shifts separately. We found that the equation did a poor job of predicting performance in Shift 1 ($R^2 = .14$, *ns*) but a good job in Shift 2 ($R^2 = .46$, $p < .01$), Shift 3 ($R^2 = .35$, $p < .05$), and Shift 4 ($R^2 = .64$, $p < .01$). These data suggest that team members learned quickly which behaviors were important to task performance and continued to exhibit these behaviors as time went on.

---

[5]See Tschan, Semmer, Nagele, and Gurtner (2000) for a detailed task analysis of NetATC.

Having established baseline information about our teams on Day 1, we were ready to assess the impact of turnover on Day 2. To do this, we looked at the three types of data just discussed, as well as communication data.

Initial Discussions. We first examined the pre-Shift 5 discussions of the same teams we had considered earlier, which were distributed about equally across the three membership change conditions. These discussions were very similar to those on Day 1 in terms of content (e.g., send direction and corridor first, assign threat values immediately). It is interesting to note that somewhat fewer suggestions were made on Day 2, which probably reflects the fact that most team members were already "on the same wave length" as a function of their prior task experience. In addition, there was a tendency for groups in the commander change and specialist change conditions to offer more suggestions than those in the no-change condition, which suggests that team members were more motivated to reiterate (or create) a shared understanding when a new person was present.

Team Performance: Overall Effects. We did not expect personnel turnover per se to have a dramatic impact on team performance on Day 2, because the team's task was highly structured and members had substantial experience performing their specialized roles on Day 1. Consistent with the task structure assumption, the regression findings reported above indicated that a particular set of behaviors by commanders and specialists was associated with effective performance across teams and shifts on Day 1.

To examine the overall consequences of turnover on team performance on Day 2, we conducted a Condition (commander change, specialist change, no change) × Shift (5, 6, 7, 8) repeated-measures analysis of variance on team performance scores. On Day 2, Shifts 5 and 7 were equal in difficulty, as were Shifts 6 and 8, and Shifts 5 and 7 were easier than Shifts 6 and 8 because plane characteristics changed more rapidly in the latter shifts. Neither the condition main effect nor the Condition × Shift interaction attained significance, indicating that membership change per se did not influence team performance. It appears that, by the time turnover occurred, members playing a given role on the same team or different teams were functionally interchangeable. Questionnaire data obtained on Day 2 lent support to this interpretation. After learning that their team would gain a new member but before they began working on the task, participants in the two turnover conditions were asked how well they expected their team to perform on the remaining shifts. Participants in the control condition were asked the same thing before they began working on the task. In all three conditions, participants expected their team to perform well in an absolute sense (commander change: M = 5.67; specialist change: M = 5.66; no change: M = 5.52, on a 7-point scale). A one-way analysis of variance conducted on responses to this question failed to yield a significant condition effect.

However, the analysis of variance did reveal significant linear ($p < .05$) and cubic ($p < .01$) trends in performance across shifts. As on Day 1, teams showed evidence of learning. That is, within each pair of shifts matched in difficulty, accuracy increased over time (Shift 5: M = 75.13 vs. Shift 7: M = 78.17, $p < .05$; Shift 6: M = 72.93 vs. Shift 8: M = 77.07, $p < .01$). It is also instructive to compare team performance across the 2 days. Overall accuracy increased from Day 1 (M = 67.52) to Day 2 (M = 75.83) ($p < .01$), indicating that team performance had not reached asymptote when turnover occurred. This increased accuracy across days is particularly interesting given that the surveillance task was harder on Day 2 than on Day 1.

Behaviors Underlying Performance. Next we assessed whether the regression equation that had done a good job of predicting team performance on Day 1 was also useful on Day 2. When applied to overall Day 2 performance, the equation (Performance = $94.03 - .08X_1 - .64X_2 + .18X_3 - .06X_4$) yielded an R^2 of .52 ($p < .01$), which was quite comparable with Day 1. Moreover, when applied to performance in the four shifts separately, the equation did a good job in all cases (Shift 5: $R^2 = .37$, $p < .05$; Shift 6: $R^2 = .70$, $p < .01$; Shift 7: $R^2 = .39$, $p < .05$; Shift 8: $R^2 = .58$, $p < .01$).

Team Performance: Ability and Status Effects. Although we did not expect that turnover per se would influence team performance, we did predict that newcomers' characteristics (ability and status) might be important. Specifically, we expected that (a) newcomers with higher task ability would have a more positive effect on team performance than would those with lower ability and (b) higher status newcomers (commanders) would have more impact, for better or worse, than would lower status newcomers (specialists).

We developed two indices of newcomer ability, one indirect and the other direct. The *indirect* index was based on how well the newcomer's "sending" team had performed on Day 1. We reasoned that newcomers who had worked on higher performing teams were probably more skillful than those who had worked on lower performing teams. Therefore, we used the performance of the newcomer's sending team on Day 1 as a proxy for his ability. The *direct* index of newcomer ability was based on his task-relevant behavior on Day 1, specifically his emission of role-appropriate behaviors included in the regression equation described earlier (IFF latency and threat latency for commanders; critical look-ups and message latency for specialists). We reasoned that newcomers who were highly proficient in using these critical behaviors were more skillful than those who were less proficient. In testing hypotheses about the impact of newcomer characteristics on team performance on Day 2, it was important to remove the variance due to the "receiving" team's ability. We did this by using partial correlations that controlled for the receiving team's performance on Day 1.

To assess the impact of newcomers' ability and status on team performance, we first computed two partial correlations (one for the commander change condition and one for the specialist change condition) between the indirect index of newcomers' ability (i.e., their sending team's performance on Day 1) and their receiving team's performance on Day 2. The relationship between newcomers' ability and team performance was positive in both cases. However, it was larger when membership change involved a new commander ($r = .79$, $p < .05$) than a new specialist ($r = .53$, ns). These results suggest that, compared with newcomers who had worked on lower performing teams on Day 1, those who had worked on higher performing teams had more positive impact on the teams they joined on Day 2. In addition, high-status newcomers had more influence than low-status newcomers.

Next, we computed four partial correlations (two for the commander change condition; two for the specialist change condition) between the direct indices of newcomers' ability (i.e., their critical task behaviors on Day 1) and their receiving team's performance on Day 2. When membership change involved a new specialist, neither correlation was significant (critical lookups: $r = .29$, ns; message latency: $r = .31$, ns). In contrast, when membership change involved a new commander, both correlations were significant (IFF latency: $r = -.65$, $p < .05$; threat latency: $r = -.67$, $p < .05$). These results indicate that newcomers with high ability and high status were particularly useful to the teams they entered.

Communication. We expected that, besides using communication to develop an initial consensus (i.e., shared cognition) about how to perform their task, team members would later use communication to reconsider and, if necessary, alter this consensus. In particular, we hypothesized that the receipt of negative performance feedback and the entry of a new member would motivate team members to communicate about their task strategy.

Recall that, on both days of the experiment, team members had an opportunity to communicate by e-mail between shifts (i.e., after Shifts 1, 2, and 3 on Day 1; after Shifts 5, 6, and 7 on Day 2).[6] The 895 messages sent during these periods were classified into one of four categories. Strategy-relevant messages (62%) included task-relevant queries, statements of problems with the team's current strategy, and suggestions for improving this strategy (e.g., "keep monitoring planes, but send plane information to the commander only when it changes" and "abbreviate the names of plane characteristics"). Motivational messages (16%) included compliments and encouragements (e.g., "good job, we'll hit 100 next time" and "let's go for max on this one"). Task-irrelevant messages (18%) included such statements as "I'd love to see her face if we all got a zero" and "we should be getting paid more, let's go on strike." Finally, acknowledgment messages (4%) included short replies indicating that a message had been received (e.g., "I got it" and "That's fine"). Intercoder reliability in classifying messages was high (91% agreement).

---

[6]Team members also communicated during the shifts, using free-input messages. Because the vast majority of these messages involved transmission of plane information, we restricted our attention to communication that occurred between shifts.

We restricted our analysis to the strategy-relevant and motivational messages because they were most germane to the issue of shared cognition. To determine the impact of team performance on communication, we examined the relationship between performance in a given shift and the volume of messages sent immediately following the shift. Regarding strategy-relevant messages, we found a consistent *negative* relationship between team performance in a given shift and the number of messages sent afterward (Shift 1: $r = -.53$, $p < .01$; Shift 2: $r = -.37$, $p < .05$; Shift 3: $r = -.38$, $p < .05$; Shift 5: $r = -.38$, $p < .05$; Shift 6: $r = -.43$, $p < .05$; Shift 7: $r = -.37$, $p < .05$). These results suggest that, as predicted, lower performance stimulated team members to communicate about their task strategy. Regarding motivational messages, we found (with one exception) a *positive* relationship between team performance in a given shift and the number of messages sent afterward (Shift 1: $r = .07$, ns; Shift 2: $r = .47$, $p < .01$; Shift 3: $r = .44$, $p < .05$; Shift 5: $r = .34$, $p < .07$; Shift 6: $r = .42$, $p < .05$; Shift 7: $r = .35$, $p < .07$). These results suggest that higher performance stimulated team members to congratulate themselves for past performance and energize themselves for future performance.

While these data suggest that performance in a given shift influenced communication following that shift, an alternative pattern of causality was also possible. That is, communication prior to a given shift may have influenced performance in that shift. To assess this possibility, we correlated the volume of both strategy-relevant and motivational messages sent before a given shift with performance in that shift. We found no significant relationships between communication and performance on either Day 1 or Day 2 (rs ranged from $-.25$ to $.20$).

Finally, we examined how personnel turnover affected the number of strategy-relevant and motivational messages sent after Shifts 5, 6, and 7, independent of team performance in those shifts. Using simultaneous multiple regression analyses, we predicted the number of strategy-relevant and motivational messages sent after Shifts 5, 6, and 7 using (a) two dummy variables representing experimental condition (commander change vs. no change; specialist change vs. no change) and (b) team performance in the relevant shift. Results indicated that personnel turnover and strategy-relevant messages were not associated during the first communication period (after Shift 5) but were associated during the later two periods (after Shifts 6 and 7). That is, after Shift 6, more strategy-relevant messages were sent in both the commander change and specialist change conditions than in the no-change condition ($\beta = .44$, $p < .05$, for commander change vs. no change; $\beta = .52$, $p < .01$, for specialist change vs. no change). A similar, though somewhat weaker, trend was found after Shift 7 ($\beta = .36$, $p < .07$, for commander change vs. no change; $\beta = .40$, $p < .06$, for specialist change vs. no change). These results suggest that, as predicted, membership change stimulated team members to communicate about their task strategy. In contrast, there was little evidence that turnover influenced motivational messages (a significant relationship was obtained only in the commander change vs. no-change comparison after Shift 6, $\beta = .39$, $p < .06$).

CONCLUSIONS AND IMPLICATIONS

In regard to team performance, we found that both newcomer ability and newcomer status made a difference in how teams adapted to personnel change. Following turnover, teams performed better when newcomers had high rather than low ability, and this effect was stronger when newcomers had high rather than low status. Although previous research has shown that newcomer ability affects team performance (Argote et al., 1997; Naylor & Briggs, 1965; Trow, 1960), the present study is the first to demonstrate the joint impact of ability and status.

In regard to shared cognition, our data suggested that both team performance and personnel turnover influenced strategy-relevant communication among team members. In all six cases (Shifts 1, 2, 3, 5, 6, and 7), there was a negative correlation between team performance during a shift and the number of strategy-relevant messages sent following that shift. Moreover, in two of three cases (Shifts 6 and 7), more strategy-relevant messages were sent when personnel turnover had previously occurred than when it had not. These findings suggest that both disappointing performance and personnel turnover increased team members' motivation to reiterate or revise their shared cognition about how to perform the NetATC task, which in turn stimulated strategy-relevant communication.

Though not predicted, our data also suggested that team performance influenced motivational communication among members. In five of six cases (Shifts 2, 3, 5, 6, and 7), there was a positive correlation between team performance during a shift and the number of motivational messages sent following that shift. These findings are interesting for at least two reasons. First, they reveal an important feature of the relationship between team performance and member communication, namely that performance can have different effects on different dimensions of communication. In the present study, lower performance was associated with *more* strategy-relevant communication, but *less* motivational communication, than was higher performance. Second, these findings are consistent with the notion that, besides affecting team performance and process, communication and shared cognition are relevant to "motivational outcomes such as cohesion, trust, morale, collective efficacy and satisfaction with the team" (Cannon-Bowers & Salas, 2001, p. 200).

It is intriguing that motivational communication was positively, rather than negatively, correlated with team performance. How much of this effect was due to "depressed" motivational communication in lower performing teams versus "elevated" motivational communication in higher performing teams is an open question. For example, members of lower performing teams may have worried that their colleagues would react negatively to exhortations to work harder and hence sent a relatively small number of motivational messages. In contrast, members of higher performing teams may have assumed that their colleagues would react positively to such exhortations and hence sent a relatively large number of motivational messages. Finally, it is worth noting that, unlike team performance, personnel turnover did not affect motivational communication. This is perhaps not surprising, given that turnover may have few motivational implications when both new and old members have substantial experience on the team task.

As our earlier discussion indicated, a good deal of attention has been devoted to the question of how membership change affects team performance. In contrast, much less attention has been given to the related question of how such change affects team members' shared cognition. In answering this latter question, it is important to keep in mind that shared cognition can be conceptualized as both a process and a product of social interaction (see chaps. 5, 6, and 7, this volume). Our study, which assessed the impact of membership change on communication, dealt with the process of shared cognition. Although much remains to be learned about this topic, research is also needed on how personnel turnover influences the content (or product) of shared cognition. Several potentially important determinants of this influence are suggested by Levine et al.'s (2003) analysis of newcomer innovation in work teams. Extrapolating from this analysis, one might predict that newcomers will be more successful in shaping a team's shared cognition when they use effective influence techniques, such as maintaining a consistent position, earning idiosyncrasy credits before presenting their ideas, and demonstrating expertise and trustworthiness. In addition, newcomers are likely to be more influential in some kinds of teams than in others—for example, in teams that are open to new members, contain fewer people than they need to perform effectively, are in early stages of development, and are performing poorly.

It is important to recall that team members in the present study were instructed to discuss the task at the beginning of both Day 1 and Day 2. On both occasions, they used the discussion period to exchange ideas for maximizing team performance (preprocess coordination). It is likely that these discussions improved subsequent performance, although, in the absence of no-discussion control groups, we cannot substantiate this hypothesis using our data. Prior research has shown that, without pressure to engage in preplanning, teams often fail to discuss strategy before beginning work (Hackman & Morris, 1975). However, when such preplanning is mandated, it improves team performance on tasks that require coordination and sharing between members (Hackman & Morris, 1975). To the extent that newcomer entry stimulates strategy discussion in natural teams, this entry may lead to the development of new shared mental models that improve team performance (cf. Gersick & Hackman, 1990).

Various kinds of newcomers can be identified (Arrow & McGrath, 1995), and their ability to influence a team's shared cognition may be affected by aspects of their past (e.g., whether they were previously members of similar teams), their present (e.g., whether they are replacing former team members), and their future (e.g., whether they will soon leave the team). For example, newcomers who recently belonged to a similar team (transfers) often have expertise on the team task, which should enhance their ability to exert influence. The situation is different for newcomers who do not have such experience and are taking the place of former members (replacements). Their ability to influence the team's shared cognition may depend on current members' perceptions of the people they are replacing. Thus, replacements following poor performers may be viewed as more competent than they really are and hence exert a good deal of influence, whereas replacements following good performers may be viewed as less competent than they really are and hence exert little influence. Finally, newcomers who are expected to remain on the team for only a short period (visitors) may be seen as having low commitment to the team, which in turn should reduce their ability to exert influence (cf. Gruenfeld et al., 2000).

In discussing how a team's shared cognition can be affected by the *entry* of new members, we touched on an issue that we have not explicitly addressed so far, namely how shared cognition can be affected by the *exit* of current members. Such exit can have various consequences, depending on the nature of the team's shared cognition and the characteristics of those who leave and those who stay behind. For example, if team members hold similar or identical knowledge, then the exit of even a large number of people may have little effect on shared cognition. In contrast, if team members hold different knowledge (i.e., if knowledge is distributed across members), then the exit of even a single person can disrupt shared cognition. Moreover, the degree of this disruption is likely to (a) increase as a function of the importance of the ex-member's knowledge for team performance and (b) decrease as a function of current members' ability to replace the lost knowledge (e.g., by acquiring it on their own, by recruiting new members who possess it). Finally, it should be noted that the departure of current members can sometimes enhance, rather than degrade, the team's shared cognition. This occurs when those who leave the team hold knowledge that is incompatible with that held by those who stay. Such incompatibility can undermine team members' confidence in their shared cognition and stimulate interpersonal conflict (cf. Levine & Higgins, 2001; Levine & Thompson, 1996).

Given the inevitability of membership change in teams, prior studies demonstrating the impact of such change on performance, and the data and arguments presented here linking personnel turnover to shared cognition, it is clear that team research would benefit from systematic attention to the relationships among membership change, shared cognition, and performance. We hope that the present chapter provides a useful starting point for such work.

REFERENCES

Abelson, M. A., & Baysinger, B. D. (1984). Optimal and dysfunctional turnover: Toward an organizational level model. *Academy of Management Review, 9*, 331–341.

Argote, L., Epple, D., Rao, R. D., & Murphy, K. (1997). *The acquisition and depreciation of knowledge in a manufacturing organization: Turnover and plant productivity.* Unpublished manuscript, Carnegie Mellon University.

Argote, L., Insko, C. A., Yovetich, N., & Romero, A. A. (1995). Group learning curves: The effects of turnover and task complexity on group performance. *Journal of Applied Social Psychology, 25*, 512–529.

Argote, L., & Kane, A. (2003). Learning from direct and indirect experience in organizations: The effects of experience content, timing, and distribution. In P. Paulus & B. Nijstad (Eds.), *Group creativity: Innovation through collaboration* (pp. 277–303). New York: Oxford University Press.

Arrow, H., & McGrath, J. E. (1993). Membership matters: How member change and continuity affect small group structure, process, and performance. *Small Group Research, 24*, 334–361.

Arrow, H., & McGrath, J. E. (1995). Membership dynamics in groups at work: A theoretical framework. In B. M. Staw & L. L. Cummings (Eds.), *Research in organizational behavior* (Vol. 17, pp. 373–411). Greenwich, CT: JAI Press.

Arrow, H., McGrath, J. E., & Berdahl, J. L. (2000). *Small groups as complex systems: Formation, coordination, development, and adaptation.* Thousand Oaks, CA: Sage.

Bowers, C. A., Jentsch, F., Salas, E., & Braun, C. C. (1998). Analyzing communication sequences for team training needs assessment. *Human Factors, 40*, 672–679.

Cannon-Bowers, J. A., & Salas, E. (2001). Reflections on shared cognition. *Journal of Organizational Behavior, 22*, 195–202.

Cannon-Bowers, J. A., Tannenbaum, S. I., Salas, E., & Volpe, C. E. (1995). Defining competencies and establishing team training requirements. In R. A. Guzzo & E. Salas (Eds.), *Team effectiveness and decision making in organizations* (pp. 333–380). San Francisco: Jossey-Bass.

Carley, K. (1992). Organizational learning and personnel turnover. *Organization Science, 3*, 20–46.

Devadas, R., & Argote, L. (1995, May). *Collective learning and forgetting: The effects of turnover and group structure.* Paper presented at the meeting of the Midwestern Psychological Association, Chicago.

Fiore, S. M., Salas, E., & Cannon-Bowers, J. A. (2001). Group dynamics and shared mental model development. In M. London (Ed.), *How people evaluate others in organizations* (pp. 309–336). Mahwah, NJ: Erlbaum.

Gersick, C. J., & Hackman, J. R. (1990). Habitual routines in task-performing groups. *Organizational Behavior and Human Decision Processes, 47*, 65–97.

Gibson, C. R. (2001). From knowledge accumulation to accommodation: Cycles of collective cognition in work groups. *Journal of Organizational Behavior, 22*, 121–134.

Glaser, R., & Klaus, D. J. (1966). A reinforcement analysis of group performance. *Psychological Monographs: General and Applied, 80*(13, Whole No. 621), 1–23.

Goodman, P. S., & Leyden, D. P. (1991). Familiarity and group productivity. *Journal of Applied Psychology, 76*, 578–586.

Gruenfeld, D. H., Martorana, P. V., & Fan, E. T. (2000). What do groups learn from their worldliest members? Direct and indirect influence in dynamic teams. *Organizational Behavior and Human Decision Processes, 82*, 45–59.

Guzzo, R. A., & Salas, E. (Eds.). (1995). *Team effectiveness and decision making in organizations.* San Francisco: Jossey-Bass.

Hackman, J. R. (1998). Why teams don't work. In R. S. Tindale, L. Heath, J. Edwards, E. Posavac, F. B. Bryant, Y. Suarez-Balcazar, et al. (Eds.), *Theory and research on small groups* (pp. 245–267). New York: Plenum.

Hackman, J. R., & Morris, C. G. (1975). Group tasks, group interaction process, and group performance effectiveness: A review and proposed integration. In L. Berkowitz (Ed.), *Advances in experimental social psychology* (Vol. 8, pp. 45–99). New York: Academic Press.

Hinsz, V. B., Tindale, R. S., & Vollrath, D. A. (1997). The emerging conceptualization of groups as information processors. *Psychological Bulletin, 121*, 43–64.

Hollenbeck, J. R., Ilgen, D. R., Sego, D. J., Hedlund, J., Major, D. A., & Phillips, J. (1995). Multilevel theory of team decision making: Decision performance in teams incorporating distributed expertise. *Journal of Applied Psychology, 80*, 292–316.

Hollenbeck, J. R., Sego, D. J., Ilgen, D. R., Major, D. A., Hedlund, J., & Phillips, J. (1997). Team decision-making accuracy under difficult conditions: Construct validation of potential manipulations using the TIDE[2] simulation. In M. T. Brannick, E. Salas, & C. Prince (Eds.), *Team performance assessment and measurement: Theory, methods, and applications* (pp. 111–136). Mahwah, NJ: Erlbaum.

Ilgen, D. R. (1999). Teams embedded in organizations: Some implications. *American Psychologist, 54*, 129–139.

Insko, C. A., Gilmore, R., Moehle, D., Lipsitz, A., Drenan, S., & Thibaut, J. W. (1982). Seniority in the generational transition of laboratory groups: The effects of social familiarity and task experience. *Journal of Experimental Social Psychology, 18*, 557–580.

Insko, C. A., Thibaut, J. W., Moehle, D., Wilson, M., Diamond, W. D., Gilmore, R., et al. (1980). Social evolution and the emergence of leadership. *Journal of Personality and Social Psychology, 39*, 431–448.

Jacobs, R. C., & Campbell, D. T. (1961). The perpetuation of an arbitrary tradition through several generations of a laboratory microculture. *Journal of Abnormal and Social Psychology, 62*, 649–658.

Kenny, D. A., Hallmark, B. W., & Sullivan, P. (1993). The analysis of designs in which individuals are in more than one group. *British Journal of Social Psychology, 32*, 173–190.

Kim, P. H. (1997). When what you know can hurt you: A study of experiential effects on group discussion and performance. *Organizational Behavior and Human Decision Processes, 69*, 165–177.

Kraiger, K., & Wenzel, L. H. (1997). Conceptual development and empirical evaluation of measures of shared mental models as indicators of team effectiveness. In M. T. Brannick, E. Salas, & C. Prince (Eds.), *Team performance assessment and measurement: Theory, methods, and applications* (pp. 63–84). Mahwah, NJ: Erlbaum.

Krauss, R. M., & Fussell, S. R. (1991). Constructing shared communicative environments. In L. B. Resnick, J. M. Levine, & S. D. Teasley (Eds.), *Perspectives on socially shared cognition* (pp. 172–200). Washington, DC: American Psychological Association.

Levesque, L. L., Wilson, J. M., & Wholey, D. R. (2001). Cognitive divergence and shared mental models in software development project teams. *Journal of Organizational Behavior, 22*, 135–144.

Levine, J. M., Choi, H. S., & Moreland, R. L. (2003). Newcomer innovation in work teams. In P. Paulus & B. Nijstad (Eds.), *Group creativity: Innovation through collaboration* (pp. 202–224). New York: Oxford University Press.

Levine, J. M., & Higgins, E. T. (2001). Shared reality and social influence in groups and organizations. In F. Butera & G. Mugny (Eds.), *Social influence in social reality: Promoting individual and social change* (pp. 33–52). Bern, Switzerland: Hogrefe & Huber.

Levine, J. M., & Moreland, R. L. (1985). Innovation and socialization in small groups. In S. Moscovici, G. Mugny, & E. Van Avermaet (Eds.), *Perspectives on minority influence* (pp. 143–169). Cambridge, England: Cambridge University Press.

Levine, J. M., & Moreland, R. L. (1994). Group socialization: Theory and research. In W. Strocbe & M. Hewstone (Eds.), *European review of social psychology* (Vol. 5, pp. 305–336). Chichester, England: Wiley.

Levine, J. M., & Moreland, R. L. (1998). Small groups. In D. T. Gilbert, S. T. Fiske, & G. Lindzey (Eds.), *The handbook of social psychology* (4th ed., Vol. 2, pp. 415–469). Boston: McGraw-Hill.

Levine, J. M., & Moreland, R. L. (1999). Knowledge transmission in work groups: Helping newcomers to succeed. In L. L. Thompson, J. M. Levine, & D. M. Messick (Eds.), *Shared cognition in organizations: The management of knowledge* (pp. 267–296). Mahwah, NJ: Erlbaum.

Levine, J. M., Moreland, R. L., & Choi, H. S. (2001). Group socialization and newcomer innovation. In M. A. Hogg & R. S. Tindale (Eds.), *Blackwell handbook of social psychology: Group processes* (pp. 86–106). Oxford, England: Blackwell.

Levine, J. M., Resnick, L. B., & Higgins, E. T. (1993). Social foundations of cognition. *Annual Review of Psychology, 44*, 585–612.

Levine, J. M., & Thompson, L. (1996). Conflict in groups. In E. T. Higgins & A. W. Kruglanski (Eds.), *Social psychology: Handbook of basic principles* (pp. 745–776). New York: Guilford Press.

MacNeil, M. K., & Sherif, M. (1976). Norm change over subject generations as a function of arbitrariness of prescribed norms. *Journal of Personality and Social Psychology, 34*, 762–773.

Marks, M. A., Zaccaro, S. J., & Mathieu, J. E. (2000). Performance implications of leader briefings and team-interaction training for team adaptation to novel environments. *Journal of Applied Psychology, 85*, 971–986.

Mathieu, J. E., Heffner, T. S., Goodwin, G. F., Salas, E., & Cannon-Bowers, J. A. (2000). The influence of shared mental models on team process and performance. *Journal of Applied Psychology, 85*, 273–283.

McGrath, J. E., & O'Connor, K. M. (1996). Temporal issues in work groups. In M. A. West (Ed.), *Handbook of work group psychology* (pp. 25–52). Chichester, England: Wiley.

Milanovich, D. M., Driskell, J. E., Stout, R. J., & Salas, E. (1998). Status and cockpit dynamics: A review and empirical study. *Group Dynamics: Theory, Research, and Practice, 2*, 155–167.

Milliken, F. J., Bartel, C. A., & Kurtzberg, T. R. (2003). Diversity and creativity in work groups: A dynamic perspective on the affective and cognitive processes that link diversity and performance. In P. Paulus & B. Nijstad (Eds.), *Group creativity: Innovation through collaboration* (pp. 32–62). New York: Oxford University Press.

Mohammed, S., & Dumville, B. C. (2001). Team mental models in a team knowledge framework: Expanding theory and measurement across disciplinary boundaries. *Journal of Organizational Behavior, 22*, 89–106.

Moreland, R. L. (1999). Transactive memory: Learning who knows what in work groups and organizations. In L. L. Thompson, J. M. Levine, & D. M. Messick (Eds.), *Shared cognition in organizations: The management of knowledge* (pp. 3–31). Mahwah, NJ: Erlbaum.

Moreland, R. L., Argote, L., & Krishnan, R. (1998). Training people to work in groups. In R. S. Tindale, L. Heath, J. Edwards, E. Posavac, F. B. Bryant, Y. Suarez-Balcazar, et al. (Eds.), *Theory and research on small groups* (pp. 37–60). New York: Plenum.

Moreland, R. L., & Levine, J. M. (1989). Newcomers and oldtimers in small groups. In P. Paulus (Ed.), *Psychology of group influence* (2nd ed., pp. 143–186). Hillsdale, NJ: Erlbaum.

Moreland, R. L., Levine, J. M., & Wingert, M. L. (1996). Creating the ideal group: Composition effects at work. In E. H. Witte & J. H. Davis (Eds.), *Understanding group behavior: Vol. 2. Small group processes and interpersonal relations* (pp. 11–35). Hillsdale, NJ: Erlbaum.

Naylor, J. C., & Briggs, G. E. (1965). Team-training effectiveness under various conditions. *Journal of Applied Psychology, 49*, 223–229.

Nye, J. L., & Brower, A. M. (1996). *What's social about social cognition?* Thousand Oaks, CA: Sage.

Rentsch, J. R., & Klimoski, R. J. (2001). Why do "great minds" think alike?: Antecedents of team member schema agreement. *Journal of Organizational Behavior, 22*, 107–120.

Resnick, L. B., Levine, J. M., & Teasley, S. D. (Eds.). (1991). *Perspectives on socially shared cognition.* Washington, DC: American Psychological Association.

Rogelberg, S. G., Barnes-Farrell, J. L., & Lowe, C. A. (1992). The stepladder technique: An alternative group structure facilitating effective group decision making. *Journal of Applied Psychology, 77*, 730–737.

Salas, E., Bowers, C. A., & Edens, E. (2001). *Improving teamwork in organizations: Applications of resource management training.* Mahwah, NJ: Erlbaum.

Salas, E., & Cannon-Bowers, J. A. (2001). Special issue preface. *Journal of Organizational Behavior, 22*, 87–88.

Salas, E., Dickinson, T. L., Converse, S. A., & Tannenbaum, S. I. (1992). Toward an understanding of team performance and training. In R. W. Swezey & E. Salas (Eds.), *Teams: Their training and performance* (pp. 3–29). Norwood, NJ: Ablex.

Steiner, I. D. (1972). *Group process and productivity.* New York: Academic Press.

Stout, R. J., Cannon-Bowers, J. A., Salas, E., & Milanovich, D. A. (1999). Planning, shared mental models, and coordinated performance: An empirical link is established. *Human Factors, 41*, 61–71.

Sundstrom, E. D. (1999). *Supporting work team effectiveness: Best management practices for fostering high performance.* San Francisco: Jossey-Bass.

Tindale, R. S., Meisenhelder, H. M., Dykema-Engblade, A. A., & Hogg, M. A. (2001). Shared cognition in small groups. In M. A. Hogg & R. S. Tindale (Eds.), *Blackwell handbook of social psychology: Group processes* (pp. 1–30). Malden, MA: Blackwell.

Trow, D. B. (1960). Membership succession and team performance. *Human Relations, 13*, 259–269.

Tschan, F. (1995). Communication enhances small group performance if it conforms to task requirements: The concept of ideal communication cycles. *Basic and Applied Social Psychology, 17*, 371–393.

Tschan, F., Semmer, N. K., Nagele, C., & Gurtner, A. (2000). Task adaptive behavior and performance in groups. *Group Processes and Intergroup Relations, 3*, 367–386.

Turner, M. E. (Ed.). (2001). *Groups at work: Theory and research.* Mahwah, NJ: Erlbaum.

Virany, B., Tushman, M. L., & Romanelli, E. (1992). Executive succession and organization outcomes in turbulent environments: An organizational learning approach. *Organization Science, 3*, 72–91.

Weick, K. E., & Roberts, K. H. (1993). Collective mind in organizations: Heedful interrelating on flight decks. *Administrative Science Quarterly, 38*, 357–381.

Wittenbaum, G. M., Vaughan, S. I., & Stasser, G. (1998). Coordination in task-performing groups. In R. S. Tindale, L. Heath, J. Edwards, E. Posavac, F. B. Bryant, Y. Suarez-Balcazar, et al. (Eds.), *Theory and research on small groups* (pp. 177–204). New York: Plenum.

Ziller, R. C., Behringer, R. D., & Goodchilds, J. D. (1962). Group creativity under conditions of success or failure and variations in group stability. *Journal of Applied Psychology, 46,* 43–49.

9

THE IMPORTANCE OF AWARENESS FOR TEAM COGNITION IN DISTRIBUTED COLLABORATION

CARL GUTWIN AND SAUL GREENBERG

Although the phrase *team cognition* suggests something that happens inside people's heads, teams are very much situated in the real world, and there are a number of activities that have to happen out in that world for teams to be able to think and work together. This is not just spoken communication. Depending on the circumstances, effective team cognition includes activities such as using environmental cues to establish a common ground of understanding, seeing who is around and what they are doing, monitoring the state of artifacts in a shared work setting, noticing other people's gestures and what they are referring to, and so on (Clark, 1996; Hutchins, 1996).

In this chapter, we argue that *awareness* of other group members is a critical building block in the construct of team cognition, and consequently that *computational support for awareness* in groupware systems is crucial for supporting team cognition in distributed groups. Our main message is that

We are grateful to Microsoft Research, Intel Corporation, the Alberta Software and Engineering Research Consortium, the National Sciences and Engineering Research Council of Canada, and Smart Technologies for providing funding, some equipment, and encouragement at various phases of this work.

for people to sustain effective team cognition when working over a shared visual workspace, our groupware systems must give team members a sense of *workspace awareness*. We first describe the collaborative situations we address in this chapter, and then we introduce workspace awareness and discuss why it is a problem in conventional groupware systems.

COLLABORATIVE SITUATIONS

In this chapter, we consider only a subset of collaborative situations. These constrain collaboration to the environment that people work within, the type of systems they use to support distributed collaboration, the tasks that people do, and the type of groups.

- *Environment: shared workspaces.* Many teams often work over a shared visual workspace: a bounded space where people can see, generate, and manipulate artifacts related to their activities. We concentrate on flat, medium-sized surfaces (e.g., a large table) upon which objects can be placed and manipulated, and around which a small group of people can collaborate.
- *Systems: real-time distributed groupware.* Real-time distributed groupware systems allow teams to work together at the same time, but from different places (e.g., Ellis, Gibbs, & Rein, 1991). Here, we are interested only in groupware that provide an electronic equivalent of shared workspace.
- *Tasks: generation and execution.* Primary task types in shared workspaces are generation and execution activities (McGrath, 1984) in which people create new artifacts, navigate through a space of objects, or manipulate existing artifacts.
- *Groups: small groups and mixed-focus collaboration.* Small groups of between two and five people primarily carry out tasks in these medium-sized workspaces. These groups often engage in mixed-focus collaboration, in which people shift frequently between individual and shared activities during a work session (e.g., Dourish & Bellotti, 1992; Salvador, Scholtz, & Larson, 1996).

Within these boundaries, a rich variety of small-group collaboration is possible. Typical real-life examples might include two people arranging, ordering, and sorting slides on a light table; a research group generating ideas on a whiteboard; managers of a project planning a task timeline; or a group laying out a page for typesetting.

WORKSPACE AWARENESS AND
THE FAILINGS OF GROUPWARE

Team cognition happens fairly naturally when people work face-to-face over shared physical workspaces. While we recognize that certain task domains may require people to follow an explicit process, people's actions as they perform rudimentary workspace operations are typically graceful and are executed with little conscious effort. An effective team maintains and updates a shared mental model (e.g., Cannon-Bowers, Salas, & Converse, 1993) of its members' actions and task work; this happens naturally as each member tracks the evolution of the product developed within the workspace.

All this works so well in face-to-face settings because people easily maintain a sense of workspace awareness. We define *workspace awareness* as "the up-to-the-moment understanding of another person's interaction with the shared workspace" (Gutwin & Greenberg, 2002, p. 417). We elaborate on this definition in later sections, but for now we say that workspace awareness is limited to those activities happening within the temporal and physical bounds of the task that the group is carrying out over a visual workspace. This includes awareness of people, how they interact with the workspace, and the events happening within the workspace.

Workspace awareness is something people take for granted in the everyday world. Because acquiring awareness information is so simple, people rarely consider it as an intentional activity. As a consequence, the role of awareness is often overlooked when analyzing team behavior. In turn, this has meant that groupware systems developed for distributed teams working over some type of shared visual surface—electronic whiteboards, documents, drawings, blueprints—often neglect to include support for workspace awareness. This has contributed to their notable lack of success. Unlike the widespread use of communications systems such as e-mail and instant messaging, systems supporting a shared visual surface have not gained a broad following. This is surprising given that teams regularly work over shared workspaces in face-to-face settings.

The problem is that maintaining this awareness has proved difficult in current real-time distributed systems in which information resources are poor and interaction mechanisms are foreign. Without good awareness, the ease and naturalness of collaboration is lost, making remote collaboration awkward, inefficient, and clumsy compared with face-to-face work. Thus, effective team cognition is compromised by the technology.

There are three main reasons why most groupware does not support workspace awareness. First, the input and output devices used in groupware systems generate only a fraction of the perceptual information that is available in a face-to-face workspace. Second, a user's interaction with a computational workspace generates much less information than actions in a physical workspace. Third, groupware systems often do not present even the limited awareness information that is available to the system.

As an example, consider the basic shared whiteboard in Figure 9.1 (Roseman & Greenberg, 1996). As each person draws, their actions are communicated to the other machine, so both participants' workspaces contain the same objects. At this moment in their task, the participants have scrolled

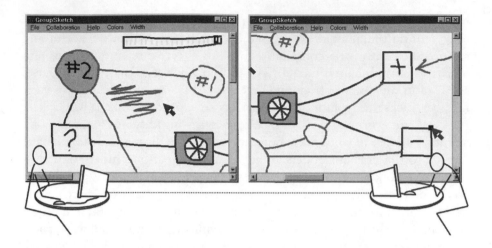

Figure 9.1. Sketch, a shared whiteboard.

their viewports to different parts of the workspace, and only a portion of their views overlap.

Systems such as this one show almost none of the awareness information that would be available to a co-located group working with a physical whiteboard. People's hands and bodies are reduced to simple telepointers, there is no sound, and only a small piece of the entire drawing can be seen by a single person at one time. When different people scroll to different parts of the workspace (e.g., for pursuing individual activity), any information about where the other person is working or what they are doing is lost and can only be gathered through verbal communication. This system-imposed tunnel vision is equivalent to wearing blinders while working together.

Without this awareness, collaboration between team members in real time becomes awkward. It is difficult or impossible for the two participants to discuss particular objects, provide timely assistance, monitor the other person's activities, or anticipate that person's actions. Lack of information about others means that many of the little things that contribute to smooth and natural collaboration are missing from the interaction.

CHAPTER OVERVIEW

In the remainder of this chapter, we argue that groupware designs and groupware systems must support workspace awareness. To do this, we first articulate the characteristics of workspace awareness typical in the everyday world, including what information people require and the mechanisms they typically use to get it. This will help designers know what information must be captured, transmitted, and presented to all team members. Next, we introduce several interface techniques for actually capturing and presenting awareness information in our electronic workspaces. Finally, we validate the effectiveness of one interface technique by summarizing our experimental evaluations of it.

AWARENESS AND WORKSPACE AWARENESS

Awareness is knowledge created through interaction between an agent and its environment—in simple terms, "knowing what is going on" (Endsley, 1995). Awareness has four basic characteristics (Adams, Tenney, & Pew, 1995; Endsley, 1995; Norman, 1993):

1. Awareness is knowledge about the state of a particular environment.
2. Environments change over time, so awareness must be kept up to date.
3. People maintain their awareness by interacting with the environment.
4. Awareness is usually a secondary goal—that is, the overall goal is not simply to maintain awareness but to complete some task in the environment.

Several types of awareness have been investigated in previous research. These include conversational awareness (e.g., Clark, 1996), casual awareness of others in work groups (e.g., Borning & Travers, 1991), and situation awareness (e.g., Gilson, 1995, McNeese, Salas, & Endsley, 2001). In particular, past work on *situation assessment* and *situation awareness* provides a wealth of theory and practice for our concept of workspace awareness. Specifically, situation assessment describes the human processes of gathering information (e.g., attention, pattern recognition, communication), whereas situation awareness is the end product resulting from effective situation assessment. Workspace awareness transforms and extends these ideas to the setting of a distributed visual workspace.

As mentioned in the introduction of this chapter, we define workspace awareness as the up-to-the-moment understanding of another person's interaction with the shared workspace. This definition bounds the concept in three ways. First, workspace awareness is an understanding of people in the workspace rather than just of the workspace itself. Second, workspace awareness is limited to events happening inside the workspace. Third, the physical nature of the workspace itself influences team cognition (which includes how people communicate and why they maintain workspace awareness): The combination of a working surface and the artifacts within it make the shared workspace both an external representation of the team's joint activity and its external memory (Clark, 1996; Hutchins, 1990; Norman, 1993). These con-

TABLE 9.1
Elements of Workspace Awareness

Category	Element	Specific questions
Who	Presence	Is anyone in the workspace?
	Identity	Who is participating? Who is that?
	Authorship	Who is doing that?
What	Action	What are they doing?
	Intention	What goal is that action part of?
	Artifact	What object are they working on?
Where	Location	Where are they working?
	Gaze	Where are they looking?
	View	How much can they see?
	Reach	How far can they reach?

straints make workspace awareness a specialized kind of situation awareness, in which the situation comprises the other team members interacting with the workspace. The next sections describe in more detail a framework for workspace awareness. This framework articulates the elements of workspace awareness, the mechanisms by which it is maintained, and its uses in team cognition.

WORKSPACE AWARENESS FRAMEWORK

Part 1: What Information Makes Up Workspace Awareness?

The first part of the framework divides the concept of workspace awareness into several elements of knowledge that answer basic "who, what, and where" questions about other team members and their activities. The elements reflect the fact that when we work with others in a physical shared space, we know who we are working with, what they are doing, and where they are working. Table 9.1 shows these elements and lists the questions that each element can answer. Note that the elements relate to awareness of present activities; Gutwin and Greenberg (2002) discussed additional elements that relate to the past.

"Who" awareness includes presence, identity, and authorship (Table 9.1, top). Awareness of presence and identity is simply the knowledge that there are others in the workspace and who they are, and authorship involves the mapping between an action and the person carrying it out. "What" awareness covers actions, intentions, and artifacts (Table 9.1, middle). Awareness of actions and intentions is the understanding of what another person is doing, either in detail or at a general level. Awareness of artifact means knowledge about what object a person is working on. "Where" awareness covers location, gaze, view, and reach (Table 9.1, bottom). Location, gaze, and view relate to where the person is working, where they are looking, and what they can see. Awareness of reach involves understanding the area of the workspace where a person can change artifacts, because sometimes a person's reach can exceed their view.

Although these elements appear to be merely commonsense factors associated with one's interaction with the environment, we suggest that they are the building blocks of team cognition, and we further suggest that they form the foundation for robust, coordinated, and efficient team work in computer-supported cooperative work (CSCW). Before discussing the uses of workspace awareness, however, we first turn to the ways in which it is gathered in real-world settings.

Part 2: How Is Workspace Awareness Information Gathered?

There are three main sources of workspace awareness information in face-to-face collaboration and three corresponding mechanisms that people use to gather it. People obtain information that is produced by people's bodies in the workspace, from workspace artifacts, and from conversations and gestures. The mechanisms that they use to gather it are called consequential communication, feedthrough, and intentional communication.

Conversation, Gesture, and Intentional Communication

A primary source of information that is ubiquitous in collaboration is conversation and gesture, and their mechanism is intentional communication (e.g., Birdwhistell, 1952; Clark, 1996; Heath & Luff, 1992). Verbal conversations are the prevalent form of communication in most groups, and there are three ways in which awareness information can be picked up from verbal exchanges. First, people may explicitly talk about awareness elements with their partners and simply state where they are working and what they are doing. Explicit communication may also involve gestures and other visual actions (e.g., Short, Williams, & Christie, 1976).

Second, people can gather awareness information by overhearing others' conversations. Although a conversation between two people may not explicitly include a third person, it is understood that the exchange is public information that others can pick up. For example, Hutchins (1990) described how navigation teams on Navy ships talk on an open circuit, allowing everyone to hear each other's conversations, greatly adding to the team's resiliency in changing environments.

Third, people can pick up others' verbal shadowing, the running commentary that people commonly produce alongside their actions, spoken to no one in particular. Heath, Jirotka, Luff, and Hindmarsh (1995) called this behavior *outlouds* and suggested that they play a strong role in informing others about one's activities.

Bodies and Consequential Communication

Other important sources of awareness information in real-world collaboration are the other team members' bodies in the workspace. Because most activities that people do in a workspace are done through some visible bodily action, the position, posture, and movement of heads, arms, eyes, and hands "becomes an essential part of the flow of information fundamental for creating and sustaining teamwork" (Segal, 1994, p. 24). Watching other people work is therefore a principal mechanism for gathering awareness information.

The mechanism of seeing and hearing other people active in the workspace is called *consequential communication*: information transfer that emerges as a consequence of a person's activity within an environment (Segal, 1994). This kind of bodily communication is not intentional in the way that explicit gestures are: The producer of the information does not intentionally undertake actions to inform the other person, and the perceiver merely "picks up" what is available. Nevertheless, consequential communication provides a great deal of information.

Artifacts and Feedthrough

The artifacts in the workspace are a third source of awareness information (e.g., Dix, Finlay, Abowd, & Beale, 1993; Gaver, 1991). By their positions, orientations, and movement, artifacts can show the state of people's interaction with them. Artifacts also contribute to the acoustic environment, making characteristic sounds when they are created, destroyed, or manipulated. Tools in particular have signature sounds, such as the snip of scissors or the scratch of a pencil.

The mechanism of determining a person's interactions through the sights and sounds of artifacts is called *feedthrough* (Dix et al., 1993). When artifacts are manipulated, they give off information, and what would normally be feedback to the person performing the action can also inform others who are watching or listening. When both the artifact and the actor can be seen, feedthrough is strongly coupled with consequential communication; at other times (such as in a groupware system) there may be a spatial or temporal separation between the artifact and the actor, leaving feedthrough as the only vehicle for information.

Part 3: How Do Teams Use Workspace Awareness?

Workspace awareness is used for many things in collaboration. Awareness can reduce effort, increase efficiency, and reduce errors for the activities of collaboration. This section describes three representative examples of activities that are aided by workspace awareness: management of coupling, simplification of verbal communication, and coordination of actions in the shared workspace.

Management of Coupling

When people collaborate in a physical space, they shift seamlessly and effortlessly back and forth between individual and shared work (e.g., Dourish

& Bellotti, 1992; Gaver, 1991). Salvador, Scholtz, and Larson (1996) called the degree to which people are working together *coupling*. Some of the reasons that people move from loose to tight coupling are that they see an opportunity to collaborate, that they need to discuss or decide something, that they need to plan the next activity, or that their current task requires another person's involvement. Awareness of others' activities is crucial for smooth changes in coupling, both by helping people decide who they need to work with and by helping people decide when to make the transitions. This is verified in actual observations: For example, Heath et al. (1995) detailed how dealers in a financial office manage coupling by carefully monitoring their colleagues' activities.

Whether in an office or in a two-dimensional workspace, people try to keep track of others' activities when they are working in a loosely coupled manner, for the express purpose of determining appropriate times to initiate closer coupling. Without workspace awareness information, people will miss opportunities to collaborate or may interrupt the other person inappropriately.

Simplification of Communication

Workspace awareness allows people to use the workspace and the artifacts in it to simplify their verbal communication, making team interaction more efficient. The type of communication we are interested in here is discussion involving task artifacts, which is a major part of the verbal activity in a shared workspace. In these conversations, the workspace can be used as a "conversational prop" (Brinck & Gomez, 1992)—an external representation of the task that allows efficient nonverbal communication (Clark, 1996; Hutchins, 1990). Workspace awareness is important here because interpreting the visual signals depends on knowledge of where in the workspace they occur, what objects they relate to, and what the sender is doing. We illustrate the principle through three examples: deictic reference, visual evidence, and gaze awareness.

Deictic References. The practice of pointing or gesturing to indicate a noun used in conversation is called deictic reference and is ubiquitous in shared workspaces (e.g., Seely Brown, Collins, & Duguid, 1989; Segal, 1995; Tang, 1991; Tatar, Foster, & Bobrow, 1991). Often, transcripts of verbal activity in a shared-workspace task cannot be correctly interpreted without a videotape of the workspace itself, because so many of the utterances contain words like "this one," "that one," "here," and "there" (e.g., Segal, 1994). Deictic references allow communication to be much more efficient, primarily because constructing these indexical terms without being able to point and gesture is very difficult.

Visual Evidence. When people converse, they require evidence that their utterances have been understood. In verbal communication, a common form of this evidence is back-channel feedback. In shared workspaces, visual actions can also provide evidence of understanding or misunderstanding. Clark (1996, p. 326) provided an example from an everyday setting, in which Ben is getting Charlotte to center a candlestick in a display: "Okay, now, push it farther—farther—a little more—right there. Good." Charlotte moves the candlestick after each of Ben's utterances, providing visual evidence that she has understood his instructions and has carried them out to the best of her interpretation.

Gaze awareness is knowing where another is looking and directing their attention (Ishii & Kobayashi, 1992). It serves as visual evidence (to confirm that one is looking at the right place) and even as a deictic reference (as eye gaze can function as an implicit pointing act). It helps people monitor what others are doing. For example, if several people's gaze are directed at the same place, one can assume either that they are working together or that one person is monitoring another person's actions.

The role of workspace awareness in deixis (i.e., when one's pointing or gesturing action disambiguates conversational references, such as when one says "this one" while pointing to an object), visual evidence, and gaze awareness means that the elements of awareness are part of conversational common ground in shared spaces (Clark, 1996). This implies that not only do you have to be aware of me to interpret my visual communication, but that I have to know what you are aware of me as well, so that I can safely make use of the workspace in my communication.

Coordination of Actions

Coordinating actions in a collaborative activity means making them happen in the right order and at the right time to complete the task without conflicting with others in the group. Coordination can be accomplished in two ways in a shared workspace: "one is by explicit communication about how the work is to be performed . . . another is less explicit, mediated by the shared material used in the work process" (Robinson, 1991). This second way is more efficient and much smoother but requires that people maintain workspace awareness.

Awareness aids coordination, ranging from fine-grained continuous coordination on a tightly coupled task to coarse-grained occasional coordination on a loosely coupled task. Awareness eases coordination because it informs participants about the temporal and spatial boundaries of others' actions, and because it helps them fit the next action into the stream. Workspace awareness is particularly evident in continuous action wherein people are working with the same objects. For example, CSCW researchers have noted that concurrency locks—in which the system monitors when one person selects an object and blocks others from using it—are less important or even unnecessary when participants have adequate information about what objects others are currently using (Greenberg & Marwood, 1994). Another example is the way that people manage to avoid bumping into each other's hands in a confined space. Workspace awareness allows people to track and predict others' movements so as to coordinate access to the physical space or objects within it. Tang (1989) saw this kind of coordination when observing how small design groups managed their interaction over a tabletop: "the many 'coordinated dances' observed among the hands of the collaborators in the workspace . . . indicate a keen peripheral awareness of the other participants" (p. 95). Many of the coordination characteristics that we think of in successful teams ("working like a well-oiled machine," "singing off the same page") mean, at least in artifact-based shared workspaces, that the team is maintaining and using workspace awareness knowledge to track, predict, and mesh with the other members.

Summary of the Framework

We defined workspace awareness as the up-to-the-moment understanding of another person's interaction with the shared workspace, and we introduced a three-part workspace awareness framework. In the first part of our framework, the who, what, and where information elements are a starting point for thinking about the awareness requirements of particular task situations and provide a vocabulary for describing and comparing awareness support in groupware applications. The second part of the framework indicates how workspace awareness information is given off and gathered via intentional and consequential communication, as well as artifact state via feedthrough. The third part suggests that people actually use workspace awareness to manage their coupling and action coordination as they shift back and forth between individual and shared work. Now that we have discussed what workspace awareness is and how it works in collaboration, in the next section we turn to the issue of how it can be implemented in a groupware system to support distributed teams.

SUPPORTING AWARENESS IN DISTRIBUTED GROUPWARE

The framework describes workspace awareness as it happens in face-to-face environments. When teams are distributed, however, it becomes much more difficult to maintain awareness of others, because groupware systems provide only a fraction of the information available in a physical workspace. In particular, two of the main awareness-gathering mechanisms—consequential communication and feedthrough—are greatly compromised in most systems.

In this section, we outline computational techniques that can be used to support workspace awareness in distributed groupware. We cover three main topics. First, we describe how *embodiments* can provide people with a representation in the workspace and provide a means for consequential communication. Second, we discuss the idea of *expressive artifacts*—workspace objects that maximize the amount of feedthrough information that is provided for the group's benefit. Third, we present *visibility techniques* that address the visibility problem in groupware, in which the narrow field of view prevents people from seeing others' awareness information that is situated in the workspace. We also give examples of these concepts to show how we can operationalize awareness support in our technology, which in turn supports effective distributed team cognition.

Embodiments

An embodiment is a visible representation that stands in for a person's body in a computational workspace. Embodiments are generally thought of as a way to provide a basic sense of presence in a virtual world, but they can also be a vehicle for both consequential and gestural communication. Although the limits of conventional input devices constrain an embodiment's expressiveness, they can still convey a great deal of awareness information. There are three main types of embodiments used in distributed groupware: telepointers, avatars, and video images.

Telepointers

Telepointers are the simplest form of embodiment and show the location of each team member's mouse cursor. Telepointers are effective at conveying awareness information, because the mouse cursor is the primary means by which people carry out actions in computational workspaces. In addition to simple cursor location, telepointers provide implicit information about presence, identity, activity, and even the specifics of an action.

In addition to the basic representation, telepointers can also be augmented to provide other awareness information (Greenberg, Gutwin, & Roseman, 1996). In the GroupSketch multiuser sketchpad, for example, telepointers are labeled with the name of their owner to show identity, change their shape to indicate what tool each person is using, and are oriented to different angles to distinguish one from the next (Greenberg & Bohnet, 1991).

Avatars

Avatars are embodiments that represent people with stylized pictorial representations of actual bodies. They are primarily used in collaborative virtual environments where the world is shown in three dimensions (Benford, Bowers, Fahlen, Greenhalgh, & Snowdon, 1995). Avatars provide a more humanlike body on which identity information and some kinds of gesture are more easily interpreted. The better avatars provide an embodiment that looks more or less like a person, have a recognizable face, and include an arm and hand to carry out any actions. Seeing the body in the workspace tells one where the distant avatar is located. Seeing the position of the face shows where it is looking. Seeing the hand shows where it is pointing (Fraser, Benford, Hindmarsh, & Heath, 1999).

Although avatars are an obvious choice in certain environments, the richer sense of presence that they provide does come at a cost: that the whole workspace be presented in a 3D or perspective view. Therefore, this technique must be weighed against the requirements for individual workspace interaction.

Video Images

Although video techniques go beyond the standard technical setup of most groupware systems, it is worth noting that several research systems have provided particularly effective video embodiments. These systems combine video images of team members with the representation of the computational workspace. What is particularly relevant is that the images are usually captured directly, and ideally one's body is in the "correct" place relative to the workspace. This is important for correctly interpreting deictic references and gaze awareness information.

Video techniques provide a far more realistic and expressive embodiment than anything described above. There are several different ways that video can be used. First, with large display devices, silhouettes or shadows of people's bodies can be represented on the workspace (Tang & Minneman, 1991). Second, full-fidelity video of arms and hands can provide detailed information about actions and movements (Tang & Minneman, 1990). This allows a full range of motion (and two hands if needed) for gesturing over the artifacts in the workspace. Third, full-fidelity video of the entire upper body can show arms, hands, and faces (Ishii & Kobayashi, 1992), providing gaze awareness information and allowing eye contact. For example, Ishii's ClearBoard System (Ishii & Kobayashi, 1992) gives the impression of working with a remote collaborator through a pane of glass.

Expressive Artifacts

Information produced by workspace artifacts—feedthrough—is one of the primary ways that people maintain workspace awareness. However, in computational workspaces, the interaction idioms and techniques used for manipulating artifacts often obscure people's actions, reducing feedthrough and compromising awareness. Unlike the physical world, interaction with computational environments is not limited to direct manipulation. *Symbolic manipulation* techniques are commands that let users specify actions in powerful and flexible ways. They are shortcuts using buttons, toolbars, and key commands that emphasize rapid invocation and execution. While often a good idea in single-user systems, symbolic manipulation produces minimal feedback (and thus minimal feedthrough), reducing people's ability to maintain awareness. This leads to three drawbacks for team members trying to stay aware of one another. First, symbolic actions have little or no visible representation in the workspace; actions are therefore harder to see in the workspace and are more likely to go unnoticed. Second, many symbolic actions are performed in similar ways so they are difficult to distinguish from one another. Third, symbolic actions can happen almost instantaneously, allowing little time for others to see and interpret them.

These problems can be addressed by transforming the minimal information provided by these actions to a more visible form as feedthrough. This approach makes artifacts more expressive: As Segal (1995) suggested, "compensate for consequential information that is lost . . . by providing enhanced feedback from the system indicating what specific actions each operator is performing" (p. 411). Below, we discuss two approaches—process feedthrough and action indicators—that make actions more obvious, distinguishable, and interpretable to others.

Process Feedthrough

Some symbolic commands are invoked through interface widgets such as buttons, menus, or dialog boxes. The feedback provided from these command objects is never seen by other members of a distributed team: First, it is considered to be part of the application rather than part of the workspace, and second, it is considered to be distracting to other users. Feedback from these interfaces, however, can help the group to determine what actions people are composing. When other people receive this information, it becomes *process feedthrough*.

As a simple example of process feedthrough, consider a button in the interface of a groupware application. When a person's cursor moves over the button, it becomes highlighted on all users' screens; when a person presses the button, it is shown being pressed on all screens. While the highlight and the press give people a chance to interpret the action and determine what the other person is doing, it is very brief and easily missed. An alternative is to augment this natural feedthrough to make the action more visible. In Figure 9.2a, for example, the feedthrough of Carl's button press (left) is emphasized for Saul (right) by the remote button making a clicking sound and by adding a graphic that lingers longer than the actual press (Greenberg, Gutwin, & Roseman, 1996).

While buttons normally show too little feedthrough, menus may show too much—they carry a greater risk of distracting others or even obscuring their work. We can achieve better balance by muting the feedthrough. For example, Saul's menu in Figure 9.2b (right) displays only a portion of the feedback information that is visible to Carl, the local user (left).

Providing process feedthrough shows how actions are being composed and invoked but does not make the action itself more noticeable. When actions are hard to see, they can be augmented with artificial indicators, discussed next.

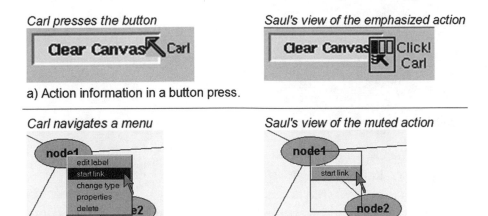

Carl presses the button

Clear Canvas Carl

Saul's view of the emphasized action

Clear Canvas Click! Carl

a) Action information in a button press.

Carl navigates a menu

node1
edit label
start link
change type
properties
delete
e2

Saul's view of the muted action

node1
start link
node2

b) A pop-up menu, as it is seen locally (left) and remotely (right).

Figure 9.2. Examples of process feedthrough.

Action Indicators and Animations

Symbolic actions happen quickly and abruptly, making them hard to see and hard to interpret. For example, when someone presses the "delete" key to remove a selected object, the operation is nearly instantaneous. When actions are invisible, our approach is to create an artificial signal for them; these signals (called *action indicators*) can be given a more perceivable workspace representation.

For example, an otherwise instantaneous delete operation can be made more obvious in several ways. One solution is to draw a text notification near the object on remote screens before removing the object, giving the rest of the group information and time to interpret its sudden disappearance. A more sophisticated solution, however, is to have the artifact itself visibly animate the otherwise invisible action, making it more perceptible. Figure 9.3 shows an example, in which the object labeled "node2" is deleted within a groupware concept map editor. The node does not simply disappear but swells up for a moment (Frame 2) before gradually fading away (Frames 3 and 4). Through this "supernova" effect, the effects of the delete action have been drawn out and made more noticeable.

A final indication technique uses sound cues. Sound has the advantage of being perceptible even when the object is off-screen and can be combined with the visual approaches described earlier. Different sounds can indicate different types of action and can even convey characteristics and progress of the action (e.g., Gaver, 1991). For example, the system in Figure 9.3 plays a descending "whoosh" sound that fades away along with the visual representation of the deleted node.

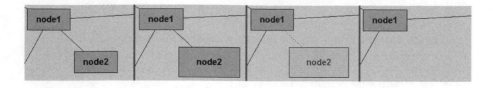

Figure 9.3. "Supernova" animation of a delete action.

Visibility Techniques

Embodiments and expressive artifacts go a long way to restoring some of the workspace awareness information that is missing in a computational shared workspace. However, they are by nature situated in the workspace; that is, the information is produced at the workspace location where the action is taking place. This provides a valuable context for interpreting the information, but it also means that if a person is viewing a different part of the workspace, they will miss the information entirely. This is the visibility problem, and it occurs in groupware when the workspace is larger than the screen and when people can move their views independently.

There are a number of possible solutions to the visibility problem. The one we concentrate on here is the idea of providing multiple views of the workspace to give people different perspectives and greater visibility. In the following sections, we discuss three visibility displays: the radar view, the over-the-shoulder view, and the cursor's-eye view. Other possibilities described elsewhere include a variety of techniques that distort the workspace so that areas where others are working are larger than the areas that have no activity (Greenberg, Gutwin, & Cockburn, 1996).

Figure 9.4 illustrates and contrasts the various techniques. Figure 9.4a gives a bird's eye overview of the entire workspace, where two people, Carl and Saul, are working within it. Each can only see a portion of the workspace, as indicated by the bounding boxes. Figure 9.4b gives an example of what Saul may see. Most of his window shows a detailed view where he sees a portion of the workspace at full size. The smaller add-on window at the upper left serves as a placeholder for awareness information, where it could take on one of the three forms shown in Figures 9.4c–e.

Radar Views

Radar views are overview representations that show the entire workspace in miniature. They are usually presented as small windows inset into the main view. Although they do not take up much room, they provide a high-level perspective on artifacts and events in unseen areas of the workspace. For example, Figure 9.4b shows a radar view of a concept map workspace embedded as an inset window atop the detailed view; it is shown larger in

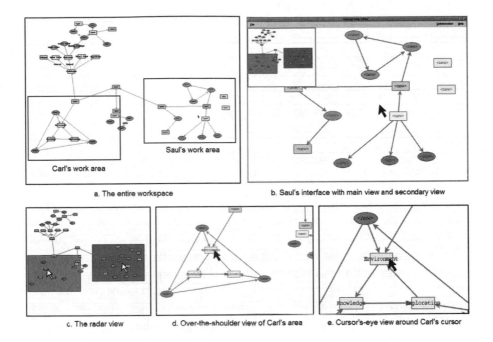

a. The entire workspace

b. Saul's interface with main view and secondary view

c. The radar view

d. Over-the-shoulder view of Carl's area

e. Cursor's-eye view around Carl's cursor

Figure 9.4. Secondary views of the workspace for increased visibility.

Figure 9.4c. In the radar view, we see that two people's telepointers and main-view extents have been added to the basic overview. Augmentation such as this adds secondary embodiments to the display and can therefore show who is in the space, where they are working (at two levels of detail), and what they are doing. However, because objects are shown at much lower resolution than in a normal view, radar views are best at helping people maintain high-level awareness of presence, locations, and general activities.

Over-the-Shoulder Views

The over-the-shoulder view shows a reduced version of another person's main view (Figure 9.4d), which is still larger than what would be seen in the radar view. The inspiration for this view is the idea of looking over at another person's work area in a face-to-face setting. This typically allows one to see what objects a coworker has in front of them, to see what they can see, and to look more closely at something that may have been noticed in peripheral vision. However, unlike the single radar view, separate over-the-shoulder views are needed to represent every participant.

Cursor's-Eye Views

A "cursor's-eye" view shows a small area directly around another person's mouse cursor (Figure 9.4e). Although its extents are limited, the cursor's-eye view shows objects and actions in full size and full detail. This view is useful when the precise details of another person's work are required. However, this view does not show the entire scene and, as with over-the-shoulder views, a separate view is required for each person.

EFFECTS OF AWARENESS SUPPORT ON GROUPWARE USABILITY

Of all of the awareness techniques and displays, the radar view is the one that we have found in practice to be the most useful in groupware applications (Gutwin, Roseman, & Greenberg, 1996). To understand how the radar view affects group work in a measurable way, we conducted an experiment to test the effects of awareness support on groupware usability (Gutwin, 1997; Gutwin & Greenberg, 1999). We hypothesized that increased support for workspace awareness would improve the usability of groupware. In our study, we compared how distance-separated people performed various construction tasks using two awareness interfaces to a groupware pipeline construction system. The tasks embodied several essential activities that we believe are common to many workspace tasks. In particular,

- In the Follow task, one person goes to specific predefined locations to do some work on the pipeline. The other person, who does not know about these locations ahead of time, has to follow that person to those locations and do additional work to support the activities of the first person.
- In the Copy task, participants were asked to construct two identical structures. One person, the leader, had a picture of what was to be built. The other person, the copier, did not have the picture and so had to copy the leader's actions.
- In the Direct task, one participant was asked to verbally guide the other through six detailed construction tasks. The director had a map showing what was to be added and where but was not allowed to move around in the workspace.

The two groupware conditions differed only in the awareness information presented in the secondary awareness interfaces: the basic overview versus a radar view (Figure 9.5). Both were visible as insets on the main application (not shown, but similar to Figure 9.4b). The radar view and the overview differed in three ways, as compared in Figure 9.5.

1. *Update granularity.* The radar showed workspace objects as they moved, whereas the overview was only updated after the move was complete.
2. *Viewport visibility.* The radar showed both people's viewports (the area of the workspace visible in each person's main view), whereas the overview showed only the local user's viewport.

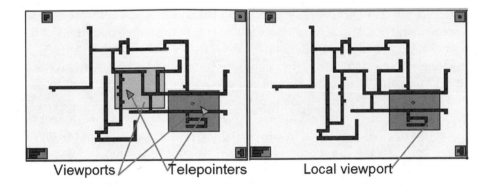

Viewports   Telepointers   Local viewport

Figure 9.5. Radar view (left) and overview (right).

3. *Telepointer visibility.* The radar showed miniature telepointers for both users, whereas the overview did not show any telepointers.

A variety of results were obtained (see Gutwin & Greenberg, 1999, for details). When using the radar view, groups finished the Follow and Direct tasks significantly faster (about 3 minutes with the radar and about 4.5 with the overview). Also, groups using the radar view spoke significantly fewer words in the Follow task (about 100 words with the radar view and about 225 with the overview). No differences were found in perceived effort for any of the tasks, and no differences were found on any measure for the Copy task. After all tasks were completed and pairs had used both interfaces, participants were asked which system the participant preferred overall. All of the 38 people who responded chose the radar view over the basic overview.

The primary reasons for the radar view's success is that visual awareness information makes it easier to communicate useful information without talking; and awareness information gives people confirmation about the other person's activities. Thus, our data support the aspect of our awareness framework highlighting the criticality of both visual and conversational common ground in facilitating coordination. For example, we saw that the radar condition provided visual indication of the other person's location and activity by showing view rectangles and telepointers. This information helped people complete the Follow and Direct tasks more quickly. In the Follow task, for example, followers could simply watch where the leader's view rectangle went on the screen and then go there themselves; in contrast, the overview condition forced people to construct complicated verbal directions to tell the other person where to go. The radar view transformed the task from a verbal one to a visual one, making it simpler and more efficient. This transformation also explains why groups used significantly fewer words in the Follow task when they used the radar view.

We also saw that the radar view provided continuous feedthrough about location and object position, which allowed groups to complete the Follow and Direct tasks more quickly. In particular, this feedback gave people visual evidence of understanding (Brennan, 1990), which was more effective and less error-prone than verbal evidence. This difference was particularly apparent in the Direct task, in which the director guides the actor's movement by giving her an instruction. With each instruction, the director requires evidence that he has succeeded in conveying the correct meaning to the actor, and that the actor has successfully moved where she is supposed to go. In addition, the director often cannot give the next instruction until he knows that the actor has successfully completed the current one. The information differences between the radar view and the overview provided directors with different kinds of evidence, and afforded different means—verbal versus visual—for establishing that instructions had been understood and carried out. In the overview, actors had to verbally acknowledge that they had completed the direction (e.g., "OK, I'm there"); this confirmation, however, is given at the end of the action, and if the action has been in error, considerable effort has been wasted while the actor went the wrong way. In contrast, the radar view showed up-to-the-moment object movement and viewport location. In the Direct task, these representations could be used as immediate visual evidence of the actor's understanding and intentions. If the actor started moving the wrong way, the director would see the misunderstanding immediately and could interrupt the actor to correct the action. In addition, the availability of continuous evidence made it possible for people to give continuous instructions. This is a strategy with far fewer verbal turns, and where the actor acknowledges implicitly through his or her actions. Clark (1996) summarized the difference between verbal and visual acknowledgment for ongoing "installment" utterances like instructions: "in installment utterances, speakers seek acknowledgments of understanding (e.g., 'yeah') after each installment and formulate the next installment contingent on that acknowledgment. With visual evidence, [the speaker] gets confirmation or disconfirmation while he is producing the current installment" (p. 326).

In summary, evidence of understanding and action in the radar was accurate, easy to get, and timely. The director was able to determine more quickly whether the instruction was going to succeed and could reduce the cost of errors. These results add weight to the overall hypothesis that awareness support improves groupware usability.

Summary of Awareness Support

We believe these various computational techniques—embodiments, expressive artifacts, and visibility techniques—have promise for distributed

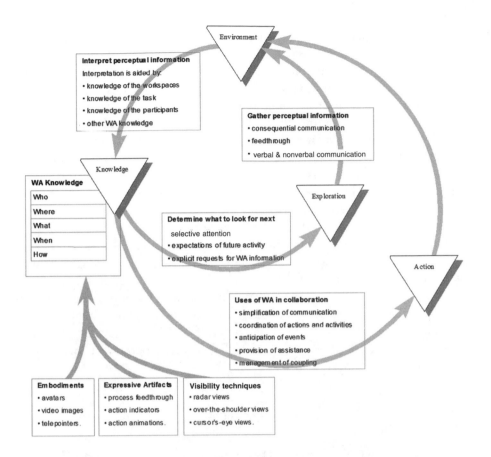

Figure 9.6. Workspace awareness framework and techniques.

team cognition because they operationalize workspaces awareness support in technology. Of all of the awareness techniques and displays, the radar view is the one that we have found to be the most useful in groupware applications. Our investigations comparing awareness techniques show that the basic over-view itself is valuable when the workspace is larger than the screen, and that the feedthrough and consequential communication provided in the radar view allow people to maintain workspace awareness even when their collaborators are out of view (Gutwin, Roseman, & Greenberg, 1996).

CONCLUSIONS

Our main message is that for people to sustain effective team cognition when working over a shared visual workspace, groupware systems must give team members a sense of workspace awareness. In this chapter, we have explored several issues that must be considered before this message can be implemented effectively. These issues are illustrated in the diagram of Figure 9.6.

First, designers need a better understanding of what exactly is meant by workspace awareness. This is the role of our workspace awareness framework, in which we described what information makes up workspace awareness, how workspace awareness information is gathered, and how teams use it. Second, developers need a repository of computational interaction techniques that support workspace awareness if they are to codify it within actual systems. We described several such techniques, including various forms of embodiments that give off bodily expressions, expressive artifacts for showing feedthrough, and three visibility techniques for displaying awareness information when people are looking at different parts of a workspace. Third, we need to show that these techniques are effective. As an example, we summarized a study that we have done that looks at the fine-grained effects of several awareness techniques and that validates where they are useful.

Unlike the everyday world in which awareness just "happens" as teams work within it, designers of distributed shared workspace groupware must explicitly program in features to gather awareness information, to transmit that information down the communication channel, and to display it effectively on the screen. This will only happen if we give designers a good understanding of workspace awareness and a proven repertory of interaction techniques that support it.

REFERENCES

Adams, M., Tenney, Y., & Pew, R. (1995). Situation awareness and the cognitive management of complex systems. *Human Factors, 37*, 85–104.

Benford, S., Bowers, J., Fahlen, L., Greenhalgh, C., & Snowdon, D. (1995). User embodiment in collaborative virtual environments. In *Proceedings of the Conference on Human Factors in Computing Systems* (pp. 242–249). New York: ACM.

Birdwhistell, R. L. (1952). *Introduction to kinesics: An annotation system for analysis of body motion and gesture.* Louisville, KY: University of Kentucky Press.

Borning, A., & Travers, M. (1991). Two approaches to casual interaction over computer and video networks. In *Proceedings of the Conference on Human Factors in Computing Systems* (pp. 13–19). New York: ACM.

Brennan, S. (1990). *Seeking and providing evidence for mutual understanding.* Unpublished doctoral dissertation, Stanford University.

Brinck, T., & Gomez, L. M. (1992). A collaborative medium for the support of conversational props. In *Proceedings of the ACM Conference on Computer Supported Cooperative Work* (pp. 171–178). New York: ACM.

Cannon-Bowers, J., Salas, E., & Converse, S. (1993). Shared mental models in expert decisionmaking teams. In N. J. Castellan, Jr. (Ed.), *Current issues in individual and group decision making* (pp. 221–246). Hillsdale, NJ: Erlbaum.

Clark, H. (1996). *Using language.* Cambridge, England: Cambridge University Press.

Dix, A., Finlay, J., Abowd, G., & Beale, R. (1993). *Human–computer interaction*. New York: Prentice Hall.

Dourish, P., & Bellotti, V. (1992). Awareness and coordination in shared workspaces. In *Proceedings of the Conference on Computer-Supported Cooperative Work* (pp. 107–114). New York: ACM.

Ellis, C., Gibbs, S., & Rein, G. (1991). Groupware: Some issues and experiences. *Communications of the ACM, 34*(1), 38–58.

Endsley, M. (1995). Toward a theory of situation awareness in dynamic systems. *Human Factors, 37*(1), 32–64.

Fraser, M., Benford, S., Hindmarsh, J., & Heath, C. (1999). Supporting awareness and interaction through collaborative virtual interfaces. In *Proceeding of ACM UIST99* (pp. 27–36). New York: ACM.

Gaver, W. (1991). Sound support for collaboration. In L. Bannon, M. Robinson, & K. Schmidt, (Eds.), *Proceedings of the Second European Conference on Computer Supported Cooperative Work* (pp. 293–308). Amsterdam: Klewer.

Gilson, R. D. (1995). Introduction to the special issue on situation awareness. *Human Factors, 37*(1), 3–4.

Greenberg, S., & Bohnet, R. (1991). GroupSketch: A multi-user sketchpad for geographically-distributed small groups. In *Proceedings of Graphics Interface* (pp. 207–215). San Francisco: Morgan Kaufmann.

Greenberg, S., Gutwin, C., & Cockburn, A. (1996). Using distortion-oriented displays to support workspace awareness. In A. Sasse, R. J. Cunningham, & R. Winder (Eds.), *People and Computers XI: Proceedings of the HCI '96* (pp. 299–314). New York: Springer-Verlag.

Greenberg, S., Gutwin, C., & Roseman, M. (1996). Semantic telepointers for groupware. In *Proceedings of the OzCHI '96 Sixth Australian Conference on Computer–Human Interaction* (pp. 54–61). Los Alamitos, CA: IEEE Computer Society.

Greenberg, S., & Marwood, D. (1994). Real time groupware as a distributed system: Concurrency control and its effect on the interface. In *Proceedings of the Conference on Computer-Supported Cooperative Work* (pp. 207–217). New York: ACM.

Gutwin, C. (1997). *Workspace awareness in real-time distributed groupware*. Unpublished doctoral dissertation, University of Calgary, Calgary, Alberta, Canada.

Gutwin, C., & Greenberg, S. (1999). Effects of awareness support on groupware usability. *ACM Transactions on CHI, 6*, 243–281.

Gutwin, C., & Greenberg, S. (2002). Descriptive framework of workspace awareness for real-time groupware. *Computer Supported Cooperative Work, 11*(3–4), 411–446.

Gutwin, C., Roseman, M., & Greenberg, S. (1996). A usability study of awareness widgets in a shared workspace groupware system. In *Proceedings of ACM CSCW '96 Conference on Supported Cooperative Work* (pp. 258–267). New York: ACM.

Heath, C., Jirotka, M., Luff, P., & Hindmarsh, J. (1995). Unpacking collaboration: The interactional organisation of trading in a city dealing room. *Computer Supported Cooperative Work, 3*, 147–165.

Heath, C., & Luff, P. (1992). Collaboration and control: Crisis management and multimedia technology in London Underground line control rooms. *Computer-Supported Cooperative Work, 1,* 69–94.

Hutchins, E. (1990). The technology of team navigation. In J. Galegher, R. Kraut, & C. Egido (Eds.), *Intellectual teamwork: Social and technological foundations of cooperative work* (pp. 191–220). Hillsdale, NJ: Erlbaum.

Hutchins, E. (1996). *Cognition in the wild.* Cambridge, MA: MIT Press.

Ishii, H., & Kobayashi, M. (1992). ClearBoard: A seamless medium for shared drawing and conversation with eye contact. In *Proceedings of the Conference on Human Factors in Computing Systems* (pp. 525–532). New York: ACM.

McGrath, J. (1984). *Groups: Interaction and performance.* Englewood Cliffs, NJ: Prentice Hall.

McNeese, M., Salas, E., & Endsley, M. (2001). *New trends in cooperative activities: Understanding system dynamics in complex environments.* San Diego, CA: Human Factors and Ergonomics Society Press.

Norman, D. (1993). *Things that make us smart.* Reading, MA: Addison-Wesley.

Robinson, M. (1991). Computer-supported cooperative work: Cases and concepts. In *Proceedings of Groupware '91* (pp. 59–75). Utrecht, Netherlands: Software Engineering Research Centre.

Roseman, M., & Greenberg, S. (1996). Building real-time groupware with GroupKit, a groupware toolkit. *Transactions on Computer–Human Interaction, 3*(1), 66–106.

Salvador, T., Scholtz, J., & Larson, J. (1996). The Denver model for groupware design. *SIGCHI Bulletin, 28*(1), 52–58.

Seely Brown, J., Collins, A., & Duguid, P. (1989, January–February). Situated cognition and the culture of learning. *Educational Researcher,* 32–42.

Segal, L. (1994). *Effects of checklist interface on non-verbal crew communications* (NASA Ames Research Center, Report No. 177639). Moffett Field, CA: NASA.

Segal, L. (1995). Designing team workstations: The choreography of teamwork. In P. Hancock, J. Flach, J. Caird, & K. Vicente (Eds.), *Local applications of the ecological approach to human–machine systems* (pp. 392–415). Hillsdale, NJ: Erlbaum.

Short, J., Williams, E., & Christie, B. (1976). Communication modes and task performance. In R. M. Baecker (Ed.), *Readings in groupware and computer supported cooperative work: Assisting human–human collaboration* (pp. 169–176). Mountain View, CA: Morgan-Kaufmann.

Tang, J. (1989). *Listing, drawing, and gesturing in design: A study of the use of shared workspaces by design teams.* Unpublished doctoral dissertation, Stanford University.

Tang, J. (1991). Findings from observational studies of collaborative work. *International Journal of Man–Machine Studies, 34,* 143–160.

Tang, J. C., & Minneman, S. L. (1990). Videodraw: A video interface for collaborative drawing. In *Proceedings of ACM SIGCHI Conference on Human Factors in Computing Systems* (pp. 313–320). New York: ACM.

Tang, J. C., & Minneman, S. L. (1991). VideoWhiteboard: Video shadows to support remote collaboration. In *Proceedings of ACM SIGCHI Conference on Human Factors in Computing Systems* (pp. 315–322). New York: ACM.

Tatar, D., Foster, G., & Bobrow, D. (1991). Design for conversation: Lessons from cognoter. *International Journal of Man–Machine Studies, 34*, 185–210.

10

INTEGRATING INTELLIGENT AGENTS INTO HUMAN TEAMS

KATIA SYCARA AND MICHAEL LEWIS

As the role of teams becomes more important in organizations, developing and maintaining high-performance teams has been the goal of several researchers (Beyerlein, Johnson, & Beyerlein, 2001; Cannon-Bowers & Salas, 1998b; Decker, Sycara, & Williamson, 1997; Hess, Entin, Hess, Hutchins, Kemple, Kleinman, Hocevar, & Serfaty, 2000; McNeese, Salas, & Endsley, 2001; Salas, Bowers, & Edens, 2001). One major question is how to turn a team of experts into an expert team. Several strategies such as task-related cross-training (Cannon-Bowers & Salas, 1998a; Salas, Cannon-Bowers, & Johnston, 1997) have emerged. In addition to traditional behaviorally based methods for facilitating team development, advances in computer science and robotics are now allowing the introduction of artificial intelligence (i.e., intelligent agents) into teamwork in a variety of roles and functions. This advent of agent technologies raises two questions: (a) what kinds of assistance can be provided and (b) what kinds of assistance prove beneficial. The reported research attempts to answer these questions through technology demonstrations to document what is possible and behavioral experiments to identify what may be helpful.

The greatest impediment to assisting human users lies in communicating user intent to an agent and making the agent's results intelligible to the human. Today in almost all cases the limiting factor in human–agent interaction has become not computing cycles or connectivity (the machine side) but the user's ability or willingness to communicate his or her desires and sift, organize, and interpret the machine's response to satisfy them (the human side). The characteristics of increased flexibility and autonomy that make agents suitable to plan and execute tasks on behalf of human users also make monitoring and evaluating more difficult for the humans. For example, if you were to task an agent to book an inexpensive flight to Athens, Greece, with a departure on Tuesday, you should not be surprised to get back an itinerary with a 14-hour overnight layover in Memphis, another in Warsaw, and an arrival on Thursday. By the time you have enumerated your preferences in sufficient detail to have confidence in the agent's booking, you might as well have gone online and booked it yourself. Except in cases when an agent's task performance is completely correct and deterministic, uncertainties as to agent progress in performing the task, alerting the user to potential failures, or protecting the user from unauthorized agent actions may need to be addressed for even the simplest interactions.

The degree of difficulty of these challenges varies with an agent's role. There are three possible functions that software agents might have within human teams:

1. Support the individual team members in completion of their own tasks
2. Assume the role of a (more or less) equal team member by performing the reasoning and tasks of a human teammate
3. Support the team as a whole

The first function, to support the individual team members in completion of their own tasks, focuses on the specific tasks that an individual must accomplish as part of the team and the subdivision of tasks among the human and the agent (or agents) to ensure high-quality performance. In a scheduling task, for example, the agent might propose an initial schedule for the human to examine and suggest reordering based on knowledge about the team's goals not considered in the agent's computations. The agent could then prepare a new schedule incorporating the changes in priorities to be approved by the human and forwarded to the team. In this example, the agent and human share task responsibility, with the agent providing algorithmic scheduling capabilities and the human supplying more detailed knowledge of team goals. Aiding individual tasks can improve team performance both by improving the individual's performance, in this case a better schedule, and by freeing the human's cognitive resources for teamwork.

With the second function, serving as a teammate, issues associated with communication and coordination among team members become relevant as well (Cannon-Bowers & Salas, 1998a; Fiore, Salas, Cuevas, & Bowers 2003; Grosz & Kraus, 1996; Lenox, Roberts, & Lewis, 1997; Tambe & Zhang, 1998). A software agent in this role must not only perform its assigned task but also use communications and modeling to share information and goals and maintain its intelligibility to other team members. If the scheduling agent were promoted to team member status, for example, it would need a much more sophisticated model of the team's goals and interdependencies among its teammates' tasks to make the same adjustments to job priorities. Filling the role of a human teammate is extremely challenging for software agents because they are idiot savants, capable of complex computations but requiring intensive artificial intelligence programming to replicate the sorts of commonplace reasoning and ad hoc assistance one would expect of a human in the same role.

The third function is to support the team as a whole by facilitating communication, allocation of tasks, coordination among the human agents, and focus of attention. Issues here deal with how to support interactions among team members using agents (Lenox et al., 1998) and what kind of software agent architecture and processing allows agents to monitor team activity, as well as access and distribute information and the results of their reasoning to human team members that need them. Specifically, the focus is on how software agents could be used to support and promote teamwork along the dimensions identified by Cannon-Bowers and Salas (1998a). Surprisingly, the task of supporting teamwork explicitly appears more amenable to agent assistance than that of incorporating teamwork into the performance of individual tasks. As part of the communications infrastructure, a software agent can initiate searches for supporting and related information or facilitate passing information to appropriate teammates without the sophistication of modeling needed to fill a human role.

Tasks confronted by human teams often require individual specializations, separated locations, and differing responsibilities. No single agent could provide all the forms of assistance diverse members of a team might need. A system comprised of multiple, functionally specific agents, however, can configure itself as needed to deliver the right support to the team and its members tailored to the team's particular task and situation. For multiple agents to provide effective flexible assistance, however, requires developing a sophisticated multiagent infrastructure with explicit mechanisms for communication and coordination.

We have developed the Reusable Environment for Task Structured Intelligent Network Agents (RETSINA) multiagent infrastructure (Decker, Sycara, & Williamson, 1997; Sycara, Decker, Pannu, Williamson, & Zeng, 1996; Sycara, Paolucci, Giampapa, & van Velsen, 2001) that provides a domain-independent, componentized framework to (a) allow heterogeneous multiple agents to coordinate in a variety of ways (Sycara & Zeng, 1996), (b) enable a single agent to be part of a multiagent infrastructure, and (c) allow effective human–agent interaction. To this end, RETSINA provides facilities for reuse and combination of different existing low-level infrastructure components (Shehory & Sycara, 2000) and also defines and implements a sophisticated individual agent architecture that provides higher level agent services, such as planning and execution of various tasks. In addition to agents that request and provide services, RETSINA includes a category of agents called *middle agents* (Decker, Pannu, Sycara, & Williamson, 1997; Wong & Sycara, 2000). When a human or agent needs to find an agent with a given capability to delegate a task to it, a request is sent to a middle agent. The middle agent serves as an intermediary by matching the request to the set of agent capability advertisement in its database and providing contact information to the requester (Sycara, Klusch, Widoff, & Lu, 1999).

In this chapter we report on our research addressing the challenges of integrating agent technology in support of human teams. Our research approach consisted of (a) identification of a validated model of human teamwork in high-performance teams to guide identification of situations in which agents could provide value-added assistance as well as identification of abilities that an agent should have to provide the needed assistance; (b) development and extension of our previous work on the RETSINA infrastructure to demonstrate agent-based team aiding in different complex, time-stressed scenarios, such as joint mission planning and noncombatant evacuation; and (c) evaluation of agent team aiding in controlled laboratory experiments on simpler but still useful problems, namely a target identification task and a path-planning task.

First, we present an overview of teamwork models, various teamwork challenges, and various teamwork dimensions that we used to base our identification of agent-based team-aiding strategies. We then briefly discuss the RETSINA infrastructure and provide an illustrative demonstration scenario, pointing out the different kinds of assistance the agents can provide. A controlled experiment we conducted using the TANDEM synthetic radar task to investigate agent support for teamwork is described, as well as experiments using the MokSAF route planning simulation to investigate agent impacts on a deliberative team-planning task. We end the chapter with our conclusions and a discussion of future work.

MODELS OF TEAMWORK

Our approach to human teamwork is based on the Air Warfare Team Observation (ATOM) model proposed by Smith-Jentsch, Zeisig, Acton, and McPherson (1998). Using a principal-components factor analysis, researchers investigating team process and performance in Navy teams identified four dimensions crucial to effective teamwork (see Exhibit 10.1). We have used these dimensions (a) to guide our exploration of where agent technology

EXHIBIT 10.1
NAWC/TSD ATOM teamwork dimensions

Information Exchange	Communication
• Seeking information from all available sources • Passing information to the appropriate persons before being asked • Providing "big picture" situation updates	• Using proper phraseology • Providing complete internal and external reports • Avoiding excess chatter • Ensuring communications are audible and ungarbled
Supporting Behavior	Team Initiative/Leadership
• Correcting team errors • Providing and requesting backup or assistance when needed	• Providing guidance or suggestions to team members • Stating clear team and individual priorities

may provide value-added assistance, (b) in our implementation of agent architecture and agent interactions with the human team members in our demonstration scenarios, and (c) to generate hypotheses and choose variables to manipulate and measure in our human experimental studies.

The ATOM model postulates that, besides their individual competence in domain-specific tasks, team members in high-performance teams must have domain-independent team expertise that is comprised of the different categories of Exhibit 10.1. The performance of teams, especially in tightly coupled tasks, is believed to be highly dependent on these interpersonal skills.

In our research we investigated human–agent interaction in situations in which an agent is an assistant helping a particular team member perform a task, such as an agent that highlights high-priority targets on a screen. The impacts of agent assistance of this sort were evaluated for both simple agents that aggregated and presented information and a more sophisticated route planning agent. Another possibility we investigated was to perform tasks for the team as a whole (many-to-one) such as monitoring communications to identify and record references to common targets. Our experiment with a synthetic radar task compared this sort of team aiding with agent assistance at individual tasks.

Besides the controlled laboratory experimentation, we explored the three types of assistance that agents can provide to human teams in a series of feasibility demonstrations that use our RETSINA multiagent infrastructure software system in complex multiagent scenarios involving hybrid human–agent teams. Using teams of RETSINA agents, we have created a wide variety of applications in areas ranging from financial portfolio management to aircraft maintenance. A key advantage to such multiagent systems is their ability to access, assemble, and filter large amounts of digital information from diverse sources. For domains such as the modern battlefield in which massive amounts of information are already in digitized form, agents could prove to be valuable teammates for humans who have difficulty in accessing and interpreting the electronic data.

To aid human teams using teams of agents requires good models of teamwork for each. For agents, the teamwork model must account for shared information such as goals or plans, models of themselves and other agents, and communications policies and protocols. For human teams, the model must fit empirical data as well. The model we adopt for agent teamwork is based on theories of joint intentions (Cohen & Levesque, 1990) and shared plans (Grosz & Kraus, 1996). *Joint intentions* theory revolves around the problem of maintaining shared goals. Agents communicate to inform one another of their commitment to a goal (forming the team), goal achievement (more effort not needed), or decommitment (goal found to be unachievable). *Shared plan* theory extends coordination to a common high-level team model that allows agents to understand requirements for plans that might achieve a team goal. This allows team members to match their own capabilities to roles in the plans. Joint intentions theory solves problems such as multiagent foraging wherein team members can act relatively independently in pursuing the team's goal. Shared plans allow teammates to support one another directly. A robot with tracks, for example, might carry a wheeled fire-fighting robot across rubble to the location of a fire.

Much as traditional team research has grappled with issues surrounding coordination among human teams and the benefits of anticipating and interpreting situations (e.g., Entin & Serfaty, 1999; Fiore, Salas, & Cannon-Bowers, 2001; Foushee, 1984; Orasanu & Salas, 1993; Stout, Cannon-Bowers, Salas, & Milanovich, 1999), our models attempt to provide a framework through which agents are able to plan and coordinate around a shared task understanding. As such, for software agents to be effective teammates (for other agents or humans), there must be models of the teammate performance at differing levels of specificity. It is easy for an agent or robot to recognize its own impasses because it has direct access to its own goals and plans. To monitor another's performance, however, requires modeling the other's goals, plans, and actions with sufficient fidelity to differentiate among rescinded, suspended, resequenced, and failed plans. Plan recognition at this level, especially recognizing the goals or plans of a human teammate, is an open problem. Because of all the difficulties inherent in imperfect plan recognition, our approach has been to use modeling as a basis for providing anticipatory assistance by agents to human team members without requiring precise plan recognition. In this form of agent-based team aiding, illustrated in the technological demonstrations (see later), the agents use models of the human team members' tasks to base intent inferencing so they can proactively seek, organize, and cache information likely to be needed in the near future.

Our technology demonstrations are intended to explore the limits to agent-based team aiding. The first of these demonstrations, Jocasta, showcased the abilities of RETSINA agents in a joint mission planning scenario to provide proactive assistance. In the subsequent agent storm demonstration, agents autonomously coordinated their team-oriented roles and actions while executing a mission in the Modular Semi-Automated Forces (ModSAF) simulation environment. The third demonstration, the Noncombatant Evacuation Operations (NEO), illustrates many of the potential uses of intelligent agents in human teams and the importance of developing these capabilities. Software agents were shown able to anticipate the information needs of their human team members, prepare and communicate task information, engage in planning and replanning in response to changes in situation or the capabilities of other team members, and effectively support team member mobility. In this chapter, we report in some detail on the agent-based team assistance in the NEO demonstration.

SUPPORTING HUMAN TEAMS IN NONCOMBATANT EVACUATION OPERATIONS

RETSINA agents have been used to support teams in different military simulations including joint mission planning. In this chapter, we report on our experience in developing a demonstration of RETSINA agents supporting a human team in a NEO scenario. This demonstration illustrates the use of agent technology for cooperatively planning and executing a hypothetical evacuation of U.S. civilians from a Middle Eastern city, let us call it Kabul, in an escalating terrorism crisis. In the scenario, agents are used to help the human team evaluate a crisis situation, form an evacuation plan, follow an evolving context, monitor activity, and dynamically replan.

The scenario unfolds as follows. The year is 2010 and the location is Kabul, Afghanistan. A conference is taking place there. Many of the conference participants are U.S. citizens. A revolutionary group, called the Gazers, starts massive protests, including protests against the United States and detonation of small incendiary bombs. The U.S. Ambassador in Afghanistan forms a team with a representative of U.S. Transportation Command in St. Louis, Missouri, and with the Joint Forces Commander (JFC) who is located in a U.S. base in Germany. The three human team members must make decisions as the situation escalates. There are a number of software agents that support the human team. We describe the most important ones. First, there are three Voice Agents that are interface-type agents. They receive the voice input from the human team's members and through speech-to-text translation store the messages. Another type of interface agent, the Messenger Agents, subsequently translate the human input into software-understandable code. This code indicates the goals of the human team members that the rest of the software agent system tries to plan for and fulfill. These human goals, of course, may change, as the situation evolves in the world. The Voice

Agents and the Messenger Agents are RETSINA agents and therefore possess planning and communication capabilities. They communicate both with the human team members and also with one another through their RETSINA communication modules. The Voice Agents and the Messenger Agents aid the team as a whole because they

- keep track of the communications of the human team members
- keep track of the evolving goals of the human team members, new goals, which goals have been satisfied, and which ones are still pending
- keep track of which agent has been tasked to perform one or more particular tasks in fulfillment of different goals
- keep track of the current world state

Besides the Voice Agents and Messenger Agents, there are a variety of other agents that play the role of teammates. There is the Webmate Agent (Chen & Sycara, 1998) that can search in the Web to find multimedia information, including video clips and textual articles that contain information relevant to a particular input query. There are two Weather Agents that can provide weather information for different parts of the world. There are two Airline Reservation Agents, a Route Planning Agent that can plan routes taking into consideration constraints of nontraversibility of routes, and a Visual Recognition Agent that can recognize events in the world, such as road blocks or explosions. There is CAMPS, a military asset deployment agent that can make schedules for the deployment of military aircraft. In addition, there are two kinds of middle agents, a Matchmaker and a Facilitator, who facilitate the discovery and matching of agents that provide certain services (e.g., weather information) with agents that request these services (e.g., the Route Planning Agent may want to find an agent that can provide weather information).

As the human team members communicate, plan, and collaborate, the agents that aid the team as a whole, namely the Voice Agents and the Messenger Agents, keep track of the human team members' communications and goals. They then decompose these goals into subgoals that must be planned for and fulfilled. In the course of this decomposition, the Messenger Agents, through the services of the Matchmaker and Facilitator middle agents, find the appropriate agents to fulfill the current subgoals. For example, when the Ambassador hears that the terrorist group has exploded bombs in the city, he communicates to the JFC and the Air Operations Officer that they should be starting to look for civilian transport for the 50 U.S. citizens who are participating in the conference. The Ambassador's Messenger Agent understands this communication as a goal to be fulfilled, communicates this to the other Messengers, and starts looking for agents that could fulfill this goal. An inquiry of the Matchmaker middle agent lets the Messenger know that there are two Airlines Reservation Agents that can fulfill the goal of getting schedules and availability of flights from Kabul to the United States. The Messenger chooses one of the Airlines Reservation Agents, contacts it, and inquires about availability of seats for flights to the United States. The Air Reservation Agent returns a schedule of departing flights to the United States. The Ambassador's Messenger Agent displays a message on the Ambassador's screen, saying that the flight schedule is ready for him to view whenever he wants to. In this way, the anticipatory assistance of the Messenger Agent and Air Reservations Agent is unobtrusive. In other words, the results of the information gathering are not imposed on the Ambassador, with the possible risk of interrupting a highly critical and time-stressed communication, but the Ambassador is simply notified so he can view the results whenever it is convenient for him. In addition, if the Ambassador wishes, he can share the flight schedules with the other human team members. To do this, the Ambassador presses a button on his display, which notifies the Ambassador's Messenger Agent that it is wished for the display to be shared. The Ambassador's Messenger then communicates with the Messenger Agents of the Air Operations Officer and the JFC transmitting the flight schedules to them so they can notify the respective human team members and allow them to display the flight schedules on their respective screens.

The above example step in the NEO demonstration illustrates a number of innovations in agent-based team support as implemented in the RETSINA system. First, coordination of the Messenger Agents, the Matchmaker middle agent, and the Air Reservation Agent allows *anticipatory/proactive information* delivery. As soon as the Ambassador expresses a desire/goal that is relevant to the task of the human team, the appropriate agents are discovered and tasked without any further explicit tasking by the Ambassador. This ability implements in the agents the monitoring and cooperative behavior of humans that has been identified as one of the hallmark characteristics of human high-performance teams. Second, RETSINA agents can also be invoked explicitly by a human team member, thus exhibiting information-gathering and problem-solving abilities. Third, it is not necessary for the Messenger Agent to know explicitly the name or location in the infosphere of Air Reservation Agents; the Messenger can find such agents through inquiry to the middle agents about the desired agent functionality (yellow pages inquiry) rather than agent name. In a dynamic environment, where agents come and go unpredictably, it is not possible to know the exact name of an agent that provides particular services, hence service discovery by capability is the effective way to go. Fourth, after the Air Reservation Agent returns the flight schedules, the Messenger does not display them immediately on the Ambassador's browser but rather notifies the Ambassador as unobtrusively as possible, so the Ambassador can view the schedules at his convenience. This kind of human–agent collaboration is done for the following reasons: (a) The Ambassador may be engaged in other high-priority activities that involve viewing of other results, hence he may not want to be inter-rupted; and (b) the Ambassador's goal of finding airline flights for the evacu-ees may have changed during the time that it takes the Air Reservations Agent to find the flight schedule information; such goal changes may result from changes in the situation. Fifth, getting the flight schedules is coordi-nated by the Messenger of the human team member that initiated this goal, in our example, the Ambassador. This is done so as to control the collabora-tion of the Messenger Agents and avoid redundant work with possibly con-fused results. Sixth, the results of the activity of the software agents are ini-tially shown to the goal originator, in this example, the Ambassador. It is up to the human goal originator to choose to share the results with the other members of the human team. This is done so as to control the information flow and display of the results for computational efficiency but also to save cognitive load for the human team members (in case it is not necessary for all human team members to view the results of agent computations). Figure 10.1 illustrates the interrelationships among the functions of the RETSINA agents, the cognitive processes of human team members, and the team be-haviors both support.

During the NEO demonstration, additional agent team aiding examples of interest include the following:

- When the need for a route to the airport is mentioned, the Route Planning Agent (RPA) is tasked by the Messenger Agent of the Ambassador. Given its access to a multimodal map and knowledge of other contingencies, the RPA plans a route to the airport. It sends this plan to the Ambassador's Messenger, which then displays a multimodal map with a planned evacua-tion route.

- Through a Phone Agent, a site evacuation specialist in the field informs the system that the environment has changed: A road-block interferes with the originally planned route to the air-port. This information is propagated from the Voice Agent to the Ambassador's Messenger, which passes the message along to the RPA. The RPA returns a revised route to the Ambassa-dor and subsequently to the rest of the human team members through their Messengers.

- The Visual Recognition Agent discerns that a bomb has ex-ploded at the airport. It notifies all Messenger Agents. In this example, the Visual Recognition Agent provides situation as-sessment, situation monitoring, and alerting of team members. All of these abilities have been identified as characteristics of high-performance human teams.

- Given the new information about the bomb explosion provided by the Visual Recognition Agent's alert, the JFC recommends

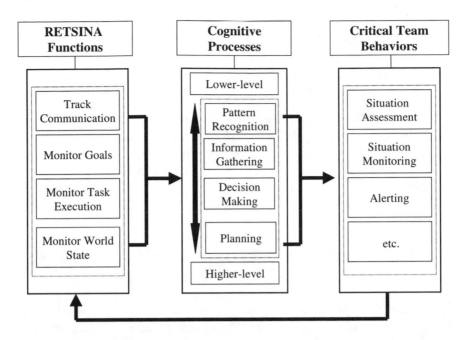

RETSINA Functions	Cognitive Processes	Critical Team Behaviors
Track Communication	Lower-level	Situation Assessment
Monitor Goals	Pattern Recognition	Situation Monitoring
Monitor Task Execution	Information Gathering	Alerting
Monitor World State	Decision Making	etc.
	Planning	
	Higher-level	

Figure 10.1. Reusable Environment for Task Structured Intelligent Network Agents (RETSINA) functions and the cognitive processes they support.

abandonment of the goal of evacuating the people through civilian flights and expresses the goal of deploying military airlift. The JFC's Messenger tasks the CAMPS Agent to create and validate a feasible military airlift schedule in cooperation with other agents that have information about the current location and availability of U.S. military assets in the region. Meanwhile, the RPA is tasked to create a route for the U.S. military airport in the host country that is closest to Kabul.

The above examples from the NEO system demonstration illustrate the types of human–agent interaction and agent-based team aiding that the RETSINA system provides. These aiding strategies include the following:

1. *Aiding an individual human team member* in information gathering or planning tasks.
2. *Acting as team members themselves.* In this capacity, RETSINA agents (a) provide proactive and reactive information and planning support, (b) perform information gathering and planning tasks to promote the team goals, and (c) perform task decomposition and task allocation to other members of the agent team so as to efficiently contribute to the team goals.
3. *Aiding the human team as a whole.* In this capacity, RETSINA agents (a) provide situation assessment; (b) monitor and alert

team members to important situation changes; (c) communicate their results in unambiguous, multimodal, and nonintrusive ways; and (d) discover (through middle agents) suitable additional team members and information sources that can aid the team.

Unlike most examples of human teams in which the team members are statically known a priori, RETSINA does not make any such closed world assumptions but *allows dropping, adding, and discovering new teammates dynamically*. This functionality reflects the requirements of real situations (especially military situations in which teammates may become incapacitated and others must be found to take up their roles).

EXPERIMENTS IN AGENT-SUPPORTED HUMAN TEAMWORK: TARGET IDENTIFICATION EXPERIMENTS

The RETSINA technology demonstrations have substantiated the feasibility of deploying networks of intelligent agents capable of individual initiative and coordination as well as tasking by humans. The very complexity and sophistication of these demonstrations, however, make it difficult to evaluate basic factors affecting human ability and willingness to work with agent teammates. In a parallel series of experiments with human subjects, we investigated the factors that theories of teamwork suggest might affect people's ability to work with software agents.

In the first experiment, agents' tasks were simplified to aggregation of data and record keeping to examine the relative effectiveness of aiding "domain-independent" teamwork tasks. In a second series of experiments, agents were limited to supporting individuals but called on to help in a more complex deliberative team-planning task.

The TANDEM Simulation Environment

The first experiment used a moderate fidelity simulation (TANDEM) of a target identification task, jointly developed at the Naval Air Warfare Center-Training Systems Division and the University of Central Florida and modified for these experiments. The TANDEM simulation was developed under the Tactical Decision Making Under Stress (TADMUS) program of the U.S. Office of Naval Research and simulates cognitive characteristics of tasks performed in the command information center of an Aegis missile cruiser. Figure 10.2a. shows a typical TANDEM display. Information about the hooked target (highlighted asterisk) is obtained from the pull-down menus A, B, and C.

The cognitive aspects of the Aegis command and control tasks that are captured include time stress, memory loading, data aggregation for decision

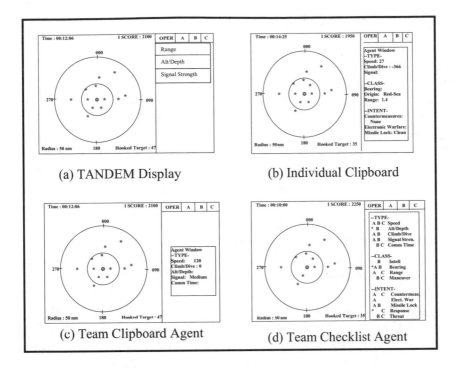

(a) TANDEM Display   (b) Individual Clipboard

(c) Team Clipboard Agent   (d) Team Checklist Agent

Figure 10.2. TANDEM components with and without agent aiding.

making, and the need to rely on and cooperate with other team members (team mode) to successfully perform the task. The more highly skilled tasks of the individual team members that involved extracting and interpreting information from radar, sonar, and intelligence displays are not modeled in the simulation. Instead of interpreting displayed signals to acquire diagnostic information about targets, TANDEM participants access this information manually from menus. In accessing new information, old information is cleared from the display, creating the memory load of simultaneously maintaining up to five parameter values and their interpretation.

In the TANDEM task participants must identify and take action on a large number of targets (high workload) and are awarded points for correctly identifying the targets (type, intent, and threat) and taking the correct action (clear or shoot). A maximum of 100 points is awarded per target for correct identification and correct action. Users "hook" a target on their screen by left-clicking on the target or selecting "hook" from a menu and specifying a target's unique contact number. Only after a target is hooked can users access information relative to that target. In team configuration, TANDEM consists of three networked PCs each providing access through menus to five parameters relative to a "hooked" target. Their tasks involve identifying the type of contact (submarine, surface, or aircraft), its classification (military or civilian), and its intent (peaceful or hostile). Each of these decisions is made at a different control station and depends on five distinct parameter values, only three of which are available at that station. Participants therefore must communicate among themselves to exchange parameter values to classify the target. If the team finds a target to be hostile it is shot, otherwise it is cleared and the team moves on to another target. Just as TANDEM simulates cognitive aspects of the Aegis missile command and control task, it provides a context to simulate the gathering, aggregation, and presentation of communications, command, control, and intelligence information by intelligent agents. To investigate impacts on human–human coordination, one can tailor presentations of aggregated information to support different aspects of the participants' cognitive tasks.

Supporting Individuals Versus Teams

One of our experiments using the TANDEM simulation examined different ways of deploying machine agents to support multiperson teams: (a) supporting the individual (within a team context) by keeping track of the information he or she has collected and helping the individual with his or her task and with passing information to teammates (Individual Clipboard, Figure 10.2b); (b) supporting communication among team members by automatically passing information to the relevant person, which should reduce communication errors and facilitate individual classification (Team Clipboard Agent, Figure 10.2c); and (c) supporting task prioritization and coordination by providing a shared checklist of which team member had access to which data (Team Checklist Agent, Figure 10.2d). We hypothesized that the Individual Agent should aid the individual task and aid communication among team members. This agent shows all data items available to an individual team member (in this case, Alpha) and fills in the values for the data items as the individual selects them from the menu. The values under the TYPE heading assist the individual with his or her task while the other team members may need to request the remaining values. The Team Clipboard Agent should also aid the individual task and aid team communication to a greater degree than the Individual Agent. This agent aggregates values from all members of the team to help the individual with his or her task. It automatically passes values as they are selected from a menu to the appropriate team member. Thus, when altitude/depth is selected from someone else's menu, it is passed to an individual team member (Alpha) who can use it to make the type identification. We hypothesized that this agent should reduce verbal communication among team members and reduce communication errors. The third agent, Team Checklist Agent, should aid team coordination. This agent shows who has access to what data. For example, all three team members (Alpha, Bravo, Charlie) have access to speed, but only Bravo has access to "intelligence." The final condition is a control in which we observed team performance without the aid of any machine agent. This is the standard TANDEM task described in Smith-Jentsch, Johnston, and Payne (1998). The goal of the study is to examine the impact of the aiding alternatives on communication patterns, data-gathering strategies, reliance (i.e., use of) on the agents, and performance.

Method

Teams of 3 participants were recruited for this study. Each team was assigned to one of four conditions: (a) control, (b) individual agent, (c) team clipboard agent, or (d) team checklist agent. TANDEM was used with 3-person teams, each member with a different identification task to perform (air/surface/submarine, military/civilian, and peaceful/hostile). One person was assigned to Alpha, one to Bravo, and one to Charlie. Alpha, Bravo, and Charlie had different items on their menus and different tasks during the trials. Alpha identified the type of target (air, surface, or submarine); Bravo determined whether the target was civilian or military; and Charlie determined whether the target was peaceful or hostile. In addition, Charlie acted as the leader by indicating the type, classification, and intent of each target to the system and taking the final action (shoot or clear).

There were five pieces of information for each identification task, three of which must agree to make a positive identification. These pieces of information were distributed among the 3 team members. Each team member saw different data items on the menus and had three data items required for his or her identification task and several other items that the other team members might need to complete their tasks. Thus, the participants needed to communicate with one another to perform their tasks for roughly two thirds of the targets. All five pieces of information might agree for a particular target; however, in many cases, the ambiguity of the data was manipulated such that only three pieces agreed.

Materials

Targets were divided into three groups: (a) easy—all three pertinent items on the individual's menu agree; (b) medium—only two items on the menu agree, a team member must ask one or both teammates for data; and (c) hard—two items on the menu agree but do not provide the correct solution. For example, Alpha's task was to identify the type of target. If the target was easy, all three items on Alpha's menu indicated the same type (e.g., air). If the target was of medium difficulty, one or two values would indicate air and the other might indicate submarine. If the target was hard, two of Alpha's menu items might indicate air, but the remaining three items—one from Alpha's menu and two from the other team members' menus—might indicate surface. Thus, the target would be a surface vessel. Participants had no way of knowing the difficulty level of the targets.

Participants

Forty teams of 3 participants each were recruited for this study (10 teams in each of the four conditions). Participants were recruited as intact teams, consisting of friends or acquaintances. Six teams were eventually dropped because of problems with data collection, and one team in the individual checklist condition was dropped because of poor (29%) accuracy in target identification.

Procedure

Each team participated in a 90-minute session that began with a 15-minute training session in which the TANDEM software and team goals were explained. The team was told to identify as many targets as possible, as accurately as possible during the 15-minute trial. After the training session, the team participated in three 15-minute trials. At the conclusion, participants were asked to complete a brief questionnaire.

Several forms of data were collected during the trials: (a) performance data from TANDEM logs, including the type and number of targets hooked and classified, the percentage of targets correctly identified, and the number of times the agents were consulted; (b) communication data encoded from observers or audio tapes, including the number of requests for data (e.g., does anyone have initial range?), the number of responses (e.g., range is 5.6 nm), the number of target identifications (e.g., it's civilian), and the number of confirmations (e.g., target is sub, civilian); (c) observer data, including ratings on team communication, situation assessment, leadership, and supporting behaviors; and (d) questionnaires completed by the participants before they left.

Results

An analysis of variance (ANOVA) on the number of correctly processed targets showed a main effect for type of agent, $F(3, 29) = 3.961$, $p = .018$ (control mean = 10.29, SD = 5.4; individual clipboard mean = 12.52, SD = 5.88; team checklist mean = 15.96, SD = 5.26; team clipboard mean = 16.67, SD = 6.06). A similar effect was noted for correctly processed hard targets, $F(3, 29) = 4.518$, $p = .01$ (control mean = 2.83, SD = 2.08; individual clipboard mean = 3.67, SD = 2.57; team checklist mean = 5.04, SD = 2.33; team clipboard mean = 5.29, SD = 2.33). For hard targets post hoc tests found both of the team aiding displays (team checklist, $p = .008$; team clipboard, $p = .004$) differed from the control condition, and the team clipboard was found to differ from the individual clipboard ($p = .04$) as well. This ranking is illustrated in Figure 10.3 with the individual clipboard falling between the control and team conditions.

In this study aiding teamwork directly (team clipboard/checklist) appeared more effective than supporting team members at their individual tasks

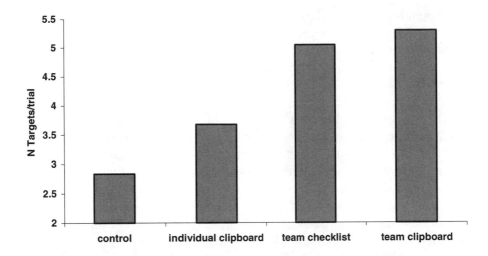

Figure 10.3. Performance differences due to team aiding.

despite the reductions in memory load and ready accessibility to parameters for sharing provided by the individual clipboard. The potential for coordinating human–human interactions through agent systems seems a particularly promising approach because of the high payoff and the reusable and largely domain-independent character of the team-supporting tasks.

Our TANDEM experiments have demonstrated the value of agents for fast-paced high-workload tasks. Not surprisingly, we found that agent aiding was most effective when it addressed the most demanding aspects of the teams' task; efficiently requesting and exchanging data were the crucial, resource-consuming activities. The agents that supported these activities directly were more effective than the clipboard agent that acted to reduce memory load, a less critical factor in this experiment. The use of agents to support teamwork activities such as information exchange, communication, and monitoring appears especially promising because these activities are crucial across a variety of domains and might be addressed through development of a common agent infrastructure and interaction techniques.

EXPERIMENTS IN AGENT-SUPPORTED HUMAN TEAMWORK: USING THE INFOSPHERE TO MAKE PLANS

Typically, human decision makers, particularly military commanders, face time pressures and an environment in which changes may occur in the task, division of labor, and allocation of resources. Information such as terrain characteristics, location and capabilities of enemy forces, direct objectives, and doctrinal constraints must all play a part in the commander's decisions. Software agents have privileged access to the masses of information in the digital infosphere and can plan, criticize, and predict consequences from this sea of information with greater accuracy and finer granularity than a human commander could. Information within this infosphere can be used for data fusion and "what-if" simulations or be visualized to provide situation awareness. There is also, however, information that may not be explicitly represented electronically and is therefore inaccessible to software agents. Such information includes intangible or multiple objectives involving morale, the political impact of actions (or inaction), intangible constraints, and the symbolic importance of different actions or objectives. Before agents can consider information that is outside their infosphere, this information must be reexpressed in agent-accessible terms. Military commanders, like other professional decision makers, have vast experiential information that is not easily quantifiable. Commanders must deal with idiosyncratic and situation-specific factors such as nonquantified information, complex or vaguely specified mission objectives, and dynamically changing situations (e.g., incomplete/changing/ new information, obstacles, and enemy actions). To cooperate with software agents in planning tasks, commanders must find ways to translate these intangible constraints into tangible ones their agents can understand. The issue therefore becomes how should software agents interact with human teams to assist with problems that may be vague, ill-specified, and have multiattribute goals.

MokSAF: A Team-Planning Environment

We have developed a computer-based simulation called *MokSAF* to evaluate how humans can interact and obtain assistance from agents within a team environment. MokSAF is a simplified version of a virtual battlefield simulation called *ModSAF* (Modular Semi-Automated Forces). MokSAF allows two or more commanders to interact with one another to plan routes over a particular terrain. Each commander is tasked with planning a route from a starting point to a rendezvous point by a certain time. The individual commanders must then evaluate their plans from a team perspective and iteratively modify these plans until an acceptable team solution is developed.

One of the interface agents used within the MokSAF environment is illustrated in Figure 10.4. This agent presents a terrain map, a toolbar, and details of the team plan. The terrains displayed on the map include soil (plain areas), roads (solid lines), freeways (thicker lines), buildings (black dots), rivers, and forests. The rendezvous point is represented as a red circle and the start point as a yellow circle on the terrain map. As participants create routes with the help of a route planning agent (see below), the routes are shown in bright green. The second route shown is from another MokSAF commander who has agreed to share his planned route. The partially transparent rect-

Start Point (Commander)

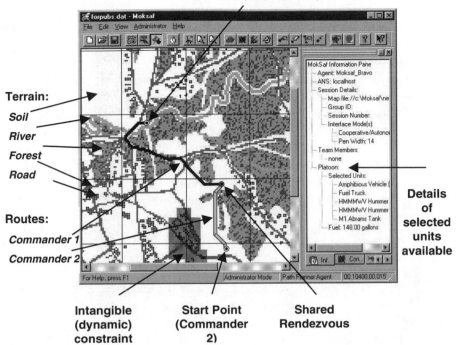

Terrain:
Soil
River
Forest
Road

Routes:
Commander 1
Commander 2

Details of selected units available

Intangible (dynamic) constraint   **Start Point (Commander 2)**   **Shared Rendezvous**

Figure 10.4. MokSAF display.

angles represent intangible constraints that the user has drawn on the terrain map. These indicate which areas should be avoided when determining a route.

Route Planning Agents

Three different *route planning agents* (RPA) have been developed to interact with the human team members in the planning task (Payne, Sycara, & Lewis, 2000). The first agent, the Autonomous RPA, performs much of the task itself. This agent acts like a "black box." The agent creates the route using its knowledge of the physical terrain and an artificial intelligence planning algorithm that seeks to find the shortest path. The agent is only aware of physical constraints, which are defined by the terrain map and the platoon composition, and intangible constraints, which are graphically specified by the commanders.

The second agent, the Cooperative RPA, analyzes routes through a corridor drawn by the human team members, selects the optimal route, and helps them to refine their plans. In this mode, the human and agent work jointly to solve the problem (e.g., plan a route to a rendezvous point). The workload should be distributed such that each component is matched to its strengths. Thus, the commander, who has a privileged understanding of the intangible constraints and utilities associated with the mission, can direct the route around these constraints as desired. However, the commander may not have detailed knowledge about the terrain, and so the agent can indicate where the path is suboptimal due to violations of local physical constraints such as traversing swamp or wooded areas.

The third condition, the Naïve RPA (or control), provides minimal assistance to the human commanders in their task of drawing and refining routes. Using this RPA, the commander draws a route that the agent then critiques for constraint violations such as impassible terrain or insufficient fuel. The commander is allowed to iteratively alter his failed route until a plan is found that passes muster. All three RPAs are intended to be used for iterative cooperative refinement of routes, and the task of coordinating with other commanders requires continuous replanning as the team searches for its own best solution.

Method

The MokSAF experiments examine a deliberative, iterative, and flexible planning task. There are three commanders (Alpha, Bravo, and Charlie), each with a different starting point but the same rendezvous point. Each commander selects units for his or her platoon from a list of available units. This list currently contains M60A3 tanks, M109A2 artillery units, M1 Abrams tanks, AAV-7 amphibious assault vehicles, HMMWVs (i.e., hummers), ambulances, combat engineer units, fuel trucks, and dismounted infantry. This list can be easily modified to add or delete unit types. With the help of an RPA, each commander plans a route from his or her starting point to the rendezvous point for the specified forces.

Once a commander is satisfied with the individual plan, he or she can share it with the other commanders and resolve any conflicts. Conflicts could arise due to several issues, including shared routes and resources or the inability of a commander to reach the rendezvous point at the specified time. The commanders also must coordinate regarding the number and types of vehicles they can take to the rendezvous because their mission specifies the number and composition of forces needed at the rendezvous point. Commanders were additionally instructed not to plan routes that took them on the same paths as any other commander, which required them to coordinate routes to avoid shared paths.

Participants

Twenty five teams consisting of 3 persons were recruited (10 teams used the Autonomous RPA, 10 teams used the Cooperative RPA, and 5 teams used the Naïve RPA) from the University of Pittsburgh and Carnegie Mellon University communities. Participants were recruited as intact teams, consisting of friends or acquaintances. Each team member began at a different starting point, but all had the same rendezvous point. Teammates communicated with one another using electronic messaging to complete their tasks successfully. Results are reported for the 23 teams for which there are complete data.

Procedure

Each team participated in a 90-minute session that began with a 30-minute training session in which the MokSAF environment and team mission were explained. The team was told to find the best paths between the start and rendezvous points, to avoid certain areas or go by other areas, to meet the mission objectives for numbers and types of units in their platoon, and to avoid crossing paths with the other commanders. After the training session, the team participated in two 15-minute trials. Each trial used the same terrain but different start and rendezvous points and different platoon requirements. At the conclusion, participants were asked to complete a brief questionnaire. We measured individual and team performance at the planning task and analyzed communications among the team members.

Results

Data were examined from two critical points in the session: the time that individuals first shared their individual routes (first share) and at the end of the 15-minute session (final). Overall, we found that the two aided conditions, Autonomous RPA and Cooperative RPA, achieved lower cost paths, earlier rendezvous, and lower fuel usage.

These results held true both for the team as a whole and for individual participants. It was expected that path lengths between the first time a route was shared and at the end of a trial would vary because of issues related to conflict resolution among the teammates. As shown in Figure 10.5, participants in the aided conditions managed to maintain the quality of their plans despite the modifications and replanning needed to coordinate with other team members. An ANOVA for total path length found a main effect for type of agent, $F(2, 20) = 67.975, p < .001$ (naïve mean = 552.5, $SD = 41.45$; autonomous mean = 282.6, $SD = 52.06$; cooperative mean = 260.22, $SD = 31.25$), and post hoc tests using Tukey's honestly significant difference statistic showed both the cooperative and autonomous groups differed significantly ($p < .001$) from the naïve control condition. A main effect was also found for total route times, $F(2, 20) = 3.519, p = .049$ (naïve mean = 2617, $SD = 358$; autonomous mean = 2,170, $SD = 275$; cooperative mean = 2,192, $SD = 215$). As Figure 10.6 shows, the conditions retain a cooperative, autonomous, naïve ordering although post hoc tests show the only significant difference ($p = .04$) to be between the cooperative and naïve agents. Although the RPA agents did not support teamwork directly, their assistance for the individual planning task allowed the commanders to find new routes

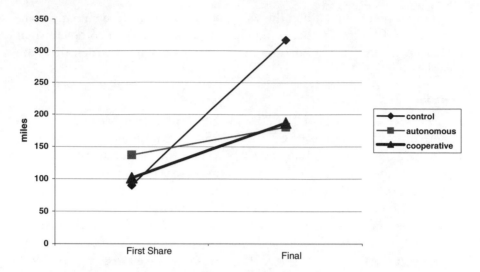

Figure 10.5. Team aiding and resultant path lengths.

as short as the ones they abandoned. Unaided commanders, in contrast, were forced to resort to longer paths to accommodate the requirements of coordinating with their team.

Teams participated in three sessions. The first session was training. The second session involved a more challenging task to correctly find an appropriate route from the starting point to the rendezvous point for all three commanders. They appeared to spend most of their time on this individual task and very little time on the team task of coordinating the selection of vehicles and meeting at the rendezvous point. On this more difficult Session 2 task, teams using the Cooperative RPA most closely approximated reference performance on the interdependent team task of selecting units. Although the main effect for vehicle selection (sum of over- and underrepresented unit types) only approaches significance, $F(2, 20) = 3.078$, $p = .068$ (naïve mean = 12.75, $SD = 6.99$; autonomous mean = 9.1, $SD = 2.56$; cooperative mean = 6.78, $SD = 3.87$), as Figure 10.7 shows, the difference appears substantial.

Discussion

Aided conditions were universally superior to the control in path length and fuel usage. Differences among the aided conditions arose due to differing levels of control over the precise path and more subtle differences in cognitive loading that allowed Cooperative RPA participants extra opportunity to consider team obligations.

In its current form, the aided conditions, Autonomous RPA and Cooperative RPA have been shown to provide a better interface for both indi-

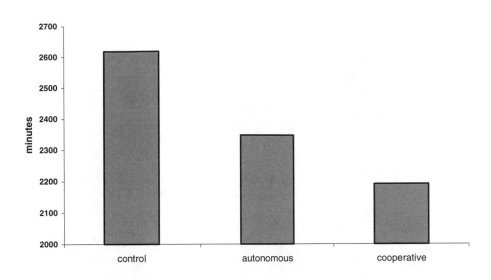

Figure 10.6. Travel time differences due to team aiding.

vidual route planning and team-based replanning. Despite this clear superiority over the unaided condition (Naïve RPA), participants in the Autonomous RPA group frequently expressed frustration with the indirection required to arrange constraints in the ways needed to steer the agent's behavior and often remarked that they wished they could "just draw the route by hand."

Comments on the Naïve RPA focused more closely on the minutiae of interaction. In its current form, the user "draws" a route on the Interface Agent by specifying a sequence of points at the resolution of the terrain database. To do this, the user clicks to specify an initial or intermediate point in the path and then clicks again at a second point. A sequence of points is then drawn in a straight line between these locations. A route is built up incrementally by piecing together a long sequence of such segments. Although tools are provided for deleting unwanted points and moving control points, the process of manually constructing a long route is both tedious and error-prone. While the Cooperative RPA automatically avoids local obstacles such as trees and closely follows curves in roads due to their less costly terrain weights, a user constructing a manual route is constantly fighting unseen obstacles that void his or her path or line segments that stray a point or two off a road into high-penalty terrain. The anticipated advantages of heuristic planning and cooperation among human users were largely lost due to the necessity of focusing on local rather than global features of routes in the Naïve RPA condition. Rather than zooming in and out on the map to see the start and rendezvous points before beginning to draw, our participants were forced to work from the first at the highest magnification to draw locally correct segments. The resulting problems of maintaining appropriate

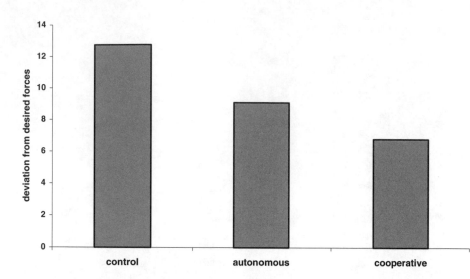

Figure 10.7. Effect of team on vehicle selection.

directions across scrolling segments of a map are not dissimilar to hiking with a compass. Although you can generally move in approximately the right direction, you are unable to take advantage of features of the terrain you might exploit if a more global view were available.

While the Naïve RPA gratuitously forced the human to deal with physical constraints to which it already had direct access, the Autonomous RPA also diverted the user from the conceptual task of choosing and coordinating routes to that of representing intangible constraints. We believe this conceptual incongruity between the route planning and representation tasks left Autonomous RPA participants unprimed for route planning related communications and coordination. Although the quality (path length/fuel usage) of routes between these two groups was very similar, Cooperative RPA teams were better able to coordinate the composition of their forces and deal with deconflicting routes. These results emphasize the importance of designing human–agent interactions that promote direct interaction with the problem domain rather than focusing on information needs of the automation.

CONCLUSIONS

This chapter draws together two complementary lines of research: the development of complex multiagent systems for aiding teams and factors that affect their acceptance and usefulness. As the amount of digital information available on the battlefield, to emergency response teams, and in people's daily lives grows exponentially, intelligent assistance to filter, organize, and make sense of these seas of information is becoming a necessity. Whether this delegated information processing is done in an ad hoc fashion or reflects efficient design in allocation of function and exercise of control will depend on extending our scientific understanding of the problems of interaction among human–agent teams.

The ATOM model of teamwork suggests that teams could be aided along four general dimensions: accessing information, communicating, monitoring, and planning.[1] Researchers in the information agent area have conventionally focused on information access, whereas those in the personal associate tradition (Banks & Lizza, 1991) have concentrated on monitoring (and intervention). Our research suggests that there may be fruitful applications of agent technology to communications and planning as well.

The TANDEM experiments illustrate the extent to which assistance in information exchange can have a major impact particularly in real-time high-workload tasks. As we come to rely more and more on ad hoc interlocking teams made possible by the increasing interconnection and digitalization of the battlefield, there will be fewer opportunities for team training and co-adaptation shown to be essential to high-performance teams. For newly formed teams, such as our TANDEM participants, assistance in selecting and directing communications provided major benefits. The agent's role of identifying salient changes in the tactical picture as humans uncovered them and relaying these updates to the appropriate teammates is a new role for software agents. Rather than acting as personal agents assisting the information recipients by seeking this information (pull) or a personal agent assisting the information provider in finding information, the agent supports distribution (push) of their products. As networked communications become increasingly interconnected and ubiquitous as envisioned for the Air Force's Joint Battlespace Infosphere (Holzhauer et al., 2001), automation of these tasks of updating and distributing new information will be crucial to maintaining an electronic tactical picture. We believe that software agents must play a central role (Sycara & Lewis, 2002) both in incorporating new information into an evolving picture and in providing a gateway for humans to augment, annotate, and enrich this tactical picture.

The closely related dimension of *communication* that characterizes the interpretability of communicated messages becomes a matter of good information presentation (agent-to-human) and design of effective interaction techniques (human-to-agent). Our Mobile Communications Among Heterogeneous Agents (Mocha; see http://www.ri.cmu.edu/projects/project_425.html) project addresses the agent-to-human problem by tailoring information presentation to the available device and user's context. The planning dimension enters this mix through anticipatory information retrieval

---

[1]The ATOM descriptors of "leadership" and "initiative" do not yet fit the team roles allowed agents. Current activities in this category center on recognizing failures in plans and missed planning opportunities (critiquing).

and intelligent caching featured in the Jocasta technology demonstration. Human-to-agent communication was investigated in our route planning experiments. Our findings highlight the importance of designing interactions that focus attention on the human's goals and problem domain rather than the agent's information needs. This need to tailor human–agent interactions to tasks and domain suggests that intelligent agents are likely to add to rather than detract from efforts needed in human–computer interface design. As software agents become more common in human teams, we expect monitoring, correction, and intervention to become more acceptable, but they are likely to be the last capabilities to be introduced into successful systems.

Already, much intelligence and general information can be gathered from the Internet whether for military operations or surgical ones. The most crucial real-time data, however, remains trapped in stovepipe systems and stand-alone monitors and alarms. For software agents to truly contribute to human teams, the common information available to other team members must be made available to them as well. As the movement toward integrating real-time data and other organizational data gains ground, the usefulness of agents will increase even more rapidly. An especially promising strategy may be to use agents such as our Interoperator (Giampapa, Paolucci, & Sycara, 2000) to assist in flexible interconnection of legacy systems.

Agent assistance will be particularly critical to military teams as their operations become more agile and situation specific. As unfamiliar forces are brought together for one-time missions, the infosphere they establish between their networked information systems will become a primary mechanism for coordination. In this uncertain environment, supporting teamwork becomes crucial. Our results suggest that software agents are well suited for this task. Because the domain independence of teamwork agents would allow them to be rapidly deployed across a broad range of tasks and settings, teamwork appears to be a particularly high payoff area for further agent research.

REFERENCES

Banks, S., & Lizza, C. (1991). Pilot's associate: A cooperative, knowledge-based system application. *IEEE Intelligent Systems and Their Applications, 6*(3), 18–29.

Beyerlein, M. M., Johnson, D. A., & Beyerlein, S. T. (Eds.). (2001). *Virtual teams: Advances in interdisciplinary studies of work teams.* New York: Elsevier Science/ JAI Press.

Cannon-Bowers, J. A., & Salas, E. (1998a). Individual and team decision making under stress: Theoretical underpinnings. In J. A. Cannon-Bowers & E. Salas (Eds.), *Making decisions under stress: Implications for individual and team training* (pp. 17–38). Washington, DC: American Psychological Association.

Cannon-Bowers, J. A., & Salas, E. (Eds.). (1998b). *Making decisions under stress: Implications for individual and team training.* Washington, DC: American Psychological Association.

Chen, L., & Sycara, K. (1998). WebMate: A personal agent for browsing and searching. In K. P. Sycara & M. Wooldridge (Eds.), *Proceedings of the Second International Conference on Autonomous Agents* (pp. 132–139). New York: ACM.

Cohen, P. R., & Levesque, H. J. (1990). Intention is choice with commitment. *Artificial Intelligence, 42,* 213–261.

Decker, K., Pannu, A., Sycara, K., & Williamson, M. (1997). Designing behaviors for information agents. In *Proceedings of the First International Conference on Autonomous Agents* (pp. 132–139). New York: ACM.

Decker, K., Sycara, K., & Williamson, M. (1997). Middle-agents for the Internet. In *Proceedings of the 15th International Joint Conference on Artificial Intelligence* (pp. 578–584). San Francisco, CA: Morgan Kaufmann.

Entin, E. E., & Serfaty, D. (1999). Adaptive team coordination. *Human Factors, 41,* 312–325.

Fiore, S. M., Salas, E., & Cannon-Bowers, J. A. (2001). Group dynamics and shared mental model development. In M. London (Ed.), *How people evaluate others in organizations: Person perception and interpersonal judgment in industrial/organizational psychology* (pp. 309–336). Mahwah, NJ: Erlbaum.

Fiore, S. M., Salas, E., Cuevas, H. M., & Bowers, C. A. (2003). Distributed coordination space: Toward a theory of distributed team performance. *Theoretical Issues in Ergonomic Science, 4,* 340–364.

Foushee, H. C. (1984). Dyads and triads at 35,000 feet: Factors affecting group process and aircrew performance. *American Psychologist, 39,* 885–893.

Giampapa, J., Paolucci, M., & Sycara, K. (2000). Agent interoperation across multiagent boundaries. In *Proceedings of the Fourth International Conference on Autonomous Agents* (pp. 179–186). New York: ACM.

Grosz, B., & Kraus, S. (1996). Collaborative plans for complex group action. *Artificial Intelligence Journal, 86,* 269–357.

Hess, K. P., Entin, E. E., Hess, S. M., Hutchins, S. G., Kemple, W. G., Kleinman, D. L., et al. (2000). Building adaptive organizations: A bridge from basic research to operational exercises. In *Proceedings of the 2000 Command and Control Research and Technology Symposium.* DOD C4ISR Cooperative Research Program. Retrieved on November, 13, 2003 from http://www.dodccrp.org/Activities/Symposia/2002CCRTS/Proceedings/Tracks/Track_5.htm

Holzhauer, D., Combs, V., Linderman, M., Duncomb, J., Dyson, R., & Young, D. (2001, June). *Building an experimental Joint Battlespace Infosphere (YJBI-CB).* Paper presented at the Sixth International Command and Control Research and Technology Symposium, United States Naval Academy, Annapolis, MD.

Lenox, T., Lewis, M., Roth, E., Shern, R., Roberts, L., Rafalski, T., & Jacobson, J. (1998). Support of teamwork in human–agent teams. In *Proceedings of IEEE International Conference on Systems, Man, and Cybernetics* (pp. 1341–1346). Piscataway, NJ: IEEE.

Lenox, T., Roberts, L., & Lewis, M. (1997). Human–agent interaction in a target identification task. In *Proceedings of IEEE International Conference on Systems, Man, and Cybernetics* (pp. 2702–2706). Piscataway, NJ: IEEE.

McNeese, M., Salas, E., & Endsley, M. (Eds.). (2001). *New trends in collaborative activities: Understanding system dynamics in complex environments.* Santa Monica, CA: Human Factors and Ergonomics Society.

Orasanu, J., & Salas, E. (1993). Team decision making in complex environments. In G. Klein, J. Orasanu, R. Calderwood, & C. E. Zsambok (Eds.), *Decision making in action: Models and methods* (pp. 327–345). Norwood, NJ: Ablex.

Payne, T., Sycara, K., & Lewis, M. (2000). Varying the user interaction within multiagent systems. In *Proceedings of the Fourth International Conference on Autonomous Agents* (pp. 412–418). New York: ACM.

Salas, E., Bowers, C. A., & Edens, E. (Eds.). (2001). *Improving teamwork in organizations: Applications of resource management training.* Mahwah, NJ: Erlbaum.

Salas, E., Cannon-Bowers, J. A., & Johnston, J. H. (1997). How can you turn a team of experts into an expert team?: Emerging training strategies. In C. E. Zsambok & G. Klein (Eds.), *Naturalistic decision making. Expertise: Research and applications* (pp. 359–370). Hillsdale, NJ: Erlbaum.

Shehory, O., & Sycara, K. (2000). The RETSINA communicator. In *Proceedings of the Fourth International Conference on Autonomous Agents* (pp. 199–200). New York, NY: ACM.

Smith-Jentsch, K., Johnston, J. H., & Payne, S. (1998). Measuring team-related expertise in complex environments. In J. A. Cannon-Bowers & E. Salas (Eds.), *Decision making under stress: Implications for individual and team training* (pp. 61–87). Washington, DC: American Psychological Association.

Smith-Jentsch, K. A., Zeisig, R. L., Acton, B., & McPherson, J. (1998). Team dimensional training. In J. A. Cannon-Bowers & E. Salas (Eds.), *Decision making under stress: Implications for individual and team training* (pp. 271–312). Washington, DC: American Psychological Association.

Stout, R. J., Cannon-Bowers, J. A., Salas, E., & Milanovich, D.M. (1999). Planning, shared mental models, and coordinated performance: An empirical link is established. *Human Factors, 41,* 61–71.

Sycara, K., Decker, K., Pannu, A., Williamson, M., & Zeng, D. (1996). Distributed intelligent agents, IEEE expert. *Intelligent Systems and Their Applications, 2*(6), 36–46.

Sycara, K., Klusch, M., Widoff, S., & Lu, J. (1999). Dynamic service matchmaking among agents in open information environments. *SIGMOD Record (ACM Special Interests Group on Management of Data), 28,* 47–53.

Sycara, K., & Lewis, M. (2002). From data to actionable knowledge and decision. In *Proceedings of the Fifth International Conference on Information Fusion* (pp. 577–584). Sunnyvale, CA: International Society of Information Fusion.

Sycara, K., Paolucci, M., Giampapa, J., & van Velsen, M. (2001). The RETSINA MAS infrastructure. *Journal of Autonomous Agent and Multiagent Systems, 7,* 29–48.

Sycara, K., & Zeng, D. (1996). Coordination of multiple intelligent software agents. *International Journal of Intelligent and Cooperative Information Systems, 5,* 181–211.

Tambe, M., & Zhang, W. (1998). Towards flexible teamwork in persistent teams. In *Proceedings of the International Conference on Multi-Agent Systems* (pp. 277–284). Piscataway, NJ: IEEE.

Wong, H. C., & Sycara, K. (2000). A taxonomy of middle-agents for the Internet. In *Proceedings of the Fourth International Conference on Multi-Agent Systems* (p. 4). New York: ACM.

IV

CONCLUSIONS

11

WHY WE NEED *TEAM* COGNITION

STEPHEN M. FIORE AND EDUARDO SALAS

Contributors to this volume have addressed a number of issues and questions to provide an overview of the different approaches to team cognition. In this vein, authors have considered the team cognition construct as a process or a product of group interaction. In particular, team cognition can be related to the *process* of information encoding, storage, and retrieval, such that a group *product* emerges (Larson & Christensen, 1993). As this suggests, groups or teams can be considered to be information-processing units (Hinsz, Tindale, & Vollrath, 1997) in a manner analogous to early views of human cognition (e.g., Newell & Simon, 1972). Thus, team cognition can describe a process (e.g., the transmission of team-relevant knowledge) or a product (e.g., shared mental model).

When discussing the state of the shared cognition construct in their brief review of recent literature, Cannon-Bowers and Salas (2001) noted that there are three overarching benefits to this construct. First, it enables researchers to explain the complexity of the phenomena surrounding team process. Second, it may be of use in predicting team performance based on

The views herein are those of the authors and do not necessarily reflect those of their affiliated organizations. Writing this chapter was partially funded by Grant No. F49620-01-1-0214 from the Air Force Office of Scientific Research to Eduardo Salas, Stephen M. Fiore, and Clint A. Bowers. We thank Florian Jentsch for comments on an earlier version of this chapter.

the metrics used to explain team processes. Third, these may both be useful in the designing of interventions to help overcome process problems in teams. Fitting within this perspective, the contributors to this volume represent researchers who use this construct with one or more of these goals. Our objective with this chapter is not to summarize this work presented by our contributors. Rather we choose to discuss their work in the context of some of the broader themes and issues associated with the team cognition construct. Our hope is that this serves not to provide a conclusion to this volume but to stimulate additional thinking on where the field must go if we are to fully understand the complexity surrounding inter- and intraindividual cognition.

In concluding chapters of edited volumes, it is not uncommon to find at least some use of metaphors or analogies. It seems authors of such chapters believe that the complex and typically diverse contributions making up an edited volume require either analogies or metaphors to capture or reify the overarching issue(s). Indeed, analogies and metaphors often provide useful insights into the understanding of complex phenomena. We will not break from this tradition as we discuss our points using a number of analogies, some proximal and some distal, to the team cognition construct. Specifically, we first look at what may be the foundational goal of team cognition, but we do so from an analogous situation in neuroscience. We then examine how the contributors to this volume address this goal, and we close with some points on where the field stands and where it appears to be going.

A BINDING PROBLEM

Throughout this volume on *team cognition* we see continuing discussion of the need to understand *team coordination*. Although not always explicitly articulated as such, inherent in these discussions is that the manifestation of team cognition is the seamless execution of coordinated behaviors. Analogous views have existed in one form or another throughout the latter half of the 20th century. For example, in early research for the military Glaser (1958) noted how process variables such as anticipatory cuing and sequence predictability could facilitate team coordination. These early constructs described the degree to which patterns of behaviors are cued by fellow member actions and "warn" team members when and how to respond (Glaser, 1958). In his seminal work on group productivity, Steiner (1972) noted that coordination decrements resulted in teams often performing below their full potential, a phenomenon he termed *process loss*. These process losses occurred for any number of reasons, ranging from diminished motivation to distinct compositions to the interdependence of the task (Steiner, 1972). Although much research has been conducted to address this issue, coordination and attempts to reduce coordination decrement remain important issues. Based on the consistent appearance of this coordination goal, one could reasonably argue that team coordination is the de facto goal of team cognition. This is a deceptively simple point, but a point that gets to the core of understanding team cognition. Specifically, how does *team cognition* lead to *team coordination*; that is, how does the manifestation of cognition in teams eventually result in a coordinated entity in and of itself?

As mentioned, analogies are often helpful in illustrating complex issues and can sometimes provide useful insights into one's understanding (see Schooler, Fallshore, & Fiore, 1995). To understand the complexity of this relation between team cognition and team coordination, consider the following analogy from what has been one of the more perplexing issues in cognitive neuroscience. Here we compare the myriad team processes and products and the assumed coalescence of these, to what is known as the *binding problem* in theories of consciousness. Given that this volume emphasized team cognition, we felt it appropriate to argue that, from a conceptual standpoint, team coordination is analogous to the binding problem. Just as organization theorists attempt to determine how human, communication, and even computer systems cooperate to produce a coordinated entity (i.e., a team), neuroscientists attempt to understand how the variety of sensory channels monitored by the brain coalesce to produce conscious experience.

Consider an example of the binding problem with respect to the perception of a moving object. In such objects,

> the color, shape, and movement are located in one object, whereas the brain events supporting these different facets are apparently located in three different loci. Even if there is synchrony between the neurons in these three different areas, how does this synchrony generate the unified phenomenal object? (Smythies, 1999, p. 164; see also Treisman, 1996)

In trying to understand the complex relation among the input of individual team members, team processes, and team performance, we are asking an analogous question. How do the skills of the team members, the roles they must perform, and the communication strategies they use result in coordinated action?

The binding *problem* with respect to consciousness is sometimes answered by theorizing a binding *mechanism*, a neural mechanism that acts to fuse relevant information into a functional entity (von der Malsburg, 1995). A heavily researched theoretical account for a binding mechanism focuses on synchrony in neuronal firing, in which "binding is achieved by synchronized activity of cells responding to different properties of the same object" (Treisman, 1996, p. 174). When trying to understand team process, many of the contributors to this volume are implicitly theorizing that team cognition may be the mechanism that fuses the multiple inputs of a team into its own functional entity. Further, the notion of "synchronized" neural firing from theories of consciousness certainly resonates with the way we characterize coordinated team performance; that is, exceptional team performance is exemplified by the synchronized actions of the individual members. Thus, whereas neuroscientists attempt to ascertain what is the relation between the brain and consciousness, we attempt to address what is the relation between team cognition and team coordination.

In some of the early writings on what is now called team cognition, theoreticians boldly spoke of notions such as a *team mind* or *collective mind* (e.g., Thordsen & Klein, 1989; Weick & Roberts, 1993) and even made explicit linkages to notions of team consciousness. These analogies provided a helpful starting point to help us conceptualize the complex interaction of a team. What was then required was for the cognitive components, that is, the components being *bound* to produce the coordinated entity, to be specified in such a way that we could begin to both articulate and measure the factors driving team coordination. By framing the research this way, we can better illustrate how the theories, methods, and data discussed in this volume have led to a fuller understanding of team cognition and thus team coordination. For example, researchers in this volume apply terminology such as *awareness* or *metacognition*, constructs that have been applied to describe the phenomenology associated with consciousness (see Cohen & Schooler, 1997). Importantly, though, the researchers in this volume operationalize their constructs in such a way that validation by means of empirical tests is feasible. As such, criticisms levied against similar constructs in consciousness research (see Simon, 1997) are less tenable in the context of team cognition.

In short, cognitive neuroscience has made significant strides in understanding the variety of events potentially making up conscious experiences. Similarly, organizational psychology has made substantial progress in delineating the subfactors of effective teamwork. But, what is less well known in both disciplines is how these subcomponents are bound. When viewing team cognition as the binding mechanism that produces coordinated behavior, we can then discuss the operationalizations of the components of team cognition, and in the next section we consider contributions from this volume within the context of some of the broader themes occurring across chapters.

THE TEAM COGNITION PUZZLE

Continuing with our use of metaphors, understanding this relation between team cognition and team coordination and the differing approaches in this field is like fitting together pieces of a puzzle. The contributors to this volume each have pieces of the puzzle to understanding the relation between team cognition and team coordination. One might argue that the contributors are not working on the same puzzle, but that is debatable. Specifically, the puzzle itself is always team coordination, whether it be coordinating to solve a problem or to make a decision, and the pieces are the team cognition constructs leading to it, whether they be mental models, metacognition, or mutual awareness.

Within this volume there are two distinct themes with respect to the overarching views of team cognition and how contributors are operationalizing these constructs. The conceptualizations can be loosely categorized as fitting under a general theme of *awareness* or *communication*. More specifically, the contributors to this volume view team cognition as a form of awareness that binds the actions of the team or view team communication (both implicit and explicit) as the manner in which team cognition is developed or scaffolded such that coordination results.

This relation among awareness, communication, and team cognition fits well within our analogy to consciousness. The distinction between aware and not aware is often used to distinguish conscious from nonconscious processes in that being able to articulate (i.e., communicate) the nature of this awareness is sometimes a metric used to disentangle consciousness (see Cohen & Schooler, 1997). Some have argued that stringently linking awareness with the ability to articulate this awareness as a metric for consciousness is not necessarily an accurate portrayal of the phenomenology associated with consciousness. Specifically, Schooler and Fiore (1997) noted that content reportability and subjective awareness are not fully overlapping categories in that one is not always able to report something of which one is fully aware (e.g., Schooler, Fiore, & Brandimonte, 1997).

We can make a similar argument for team cognition in that the theorizing of Schooler and Fiore (1997) supports distinctions made between explicit and implicit team coordination. Researchers in team performance describe implicit team coordination not as occurring in the absence of conscious awareness but rather as occurring in the absence of explicit articulation (see Entin & Serfaty, 1999; Fiore, Salas, & Cannon-Bowers, 2001; Fiore, Salas, Cuevas, & Bowers, 2003). Because implicit coordination is often used to describe coordination without explicit communication, it is often used as a proxy measure for the level of shared awareness within a team (see, e.g., Entin & Serfaty, 1999). Thus, implicit coordination in the context of teams may indeed be something of which the team is *aware*, but not something they have articulated. We next use the two themes of awareness and communication in a brief discussion of the pieces to the team cognition puzzle presented in this volume. What is important to note across these contributions is the careful articulation of the operationalization of these constructs.

Theme One: Team Cognition as Shared Awareness

Within the broader theme of team cognition as awareness, Hinsz (chap. 3, this volume) discussed a particular form of awareness within the team task. He showed how adapting the construct of metacognition and considering it within the mental model framework assist not only in understanding team processes but also in providing an avenue with which to measure certain aspects of team cognition. By exploring the ways in which a group processes information associated with the group's beliefs, Hinsz illuminated the accuracies and inaccuracies associated with components of metacognitive awareness within a group. These findings are important particularly because they show how deconstruction of cognitive components associated with group process can highlight areas associated with process problems. To the degree that these are problems critical to team performance, they can be translated to team training interventions. Further, Hinsz's linking of the belief association matrix to the mental model construct provides an important method of quantification, what Hinsz described as a "model" of mental models. Such methods represent critical steps in our attempts to operationalize constructs associated with what could be amorphous notions of awareness.

By blending cognitive and social approaches, Rentsch and Woehr (chap. 2, this volume) illustrated a unique component to the theme of team cognition as awareness. First, their notion of awareness of teammates' knowledge, in addition to overlap in teammate knowledge, provides an important addition to conceptualizations of team cognition. Similar to theorizing on transactive memory systems (e.g., Liang, Moreland, & Argote, 1995; Moreland & Argote, 2003; Moreland & Myaskovsky, 2000), this component of awareness has to do with perceptions of "who knows what." By taking into account one's perspective on a teammate's knowledge, researchers may be better able to predict how sharedness relates to performance. Furthermore, Rentsch and Woehr's adaptation of social relations modeling to team member schemas uniquely approaches team cognition from the standpoint of person perception and shared cognition (see also Fiore et al., 2001). Second, these methods provide a fruitful avenue with which one can understand team process and performance. Akin to techniques adapted by Hinsz, the melding of these approaches lends strength to our understanding of teams by allowing more quantitative models and methods to measure the awareness component of team cognition.

The pioneering work of Gutwin and Greenberg (chap. 9, this volume) in the area of computer-supported collaborative work has been instrumental to our understanding of how it is that awareness is foundational to team cognition. Their systematic development of systems to support teamwork has led to an elegant articulation of some of the most critical issues surrounding team cognition in distributed work. An intriguing aspect of their framework involves the utility of the common-ground construct arising out of communications research and psycholinguistics (e.g., Fussell & Krauss, 1989). Gutwin and Greenberg used common ground from two converging points: visual and conversational. Their work shows how converging approaches to scaffold-distributed interaction facilitates awareness through social cognitive processes of visual and conversational (i.e., communications based) common ground. Further, the operationalization of system design factors that support "embodiments" and similar "expressive artifacts" most certainly provides the visual cues necessary to support team cognition. Indeed, these techniques can surmount limitations associated with distributed work arising from *team opacity*, the experience of increased ambiguity and artificiality associated with distributed interaction that can hinder mutual awareness (see Fiore et al., 2003).

Fiore and Schooler (chap. 7, this volume) similarly argued for the foundational nature of mutual awareness in driving team cognition and coordination. They noted that team cognition in the context of problem solving hinges on shared awareness of the problem that can be developed through facilitated communication. They illustrated the degree to which process mapping techniques scaffold shared problem models that drive effective process and performance. Fiore and Schooler noted that the process mapping technique forces the individual team members to articulate their conceptualization of the problem. This increases the level of awareness for a given problem and illustrates how communication in problem-solving teams drives the level of shared cognition experienced.

Theme Two: Team Cognition and Team Communication

Cooke, Salas, Kiekel, and Bell (chap. 5, this volume) argued how it is that team processes such as communication can produce effective team knowledge. Using the term *holistic knowledge*, they described how individual cognitive components are integrated through team processes such as communication to produce team cognition. This is essentially team cognition emerging as a result of team interaction "sharpening" individual cognition into a well-sculpted "whole" product. Furthermore, Cooke et al. illustrated how techniques used in cognitive psychology can be adapted to assist in capturing analogous processes in teams. Associative thought has long been analyzed in cognitive psychology using techniques devised to tap semantic linkages (e.g., in studies of priming and memory). Cooke et al. used variants of such methodologies to ascertain the degree to which team members similarly view team-related knowledge. Finally, they described exciting emerging techniques that may be able to capture cognition more dynamically. They showed how coding schemes can be developed to ascertain higher level cognition within a team (e.g., a team's overall understanding of a situation). In particular, they used communication protocols as a *window to team cognition* and argued that if "teams are to be the unit of analysis under our holistic definition, we will need to measure behaviors exhibited by the team as a whole." Protocol analyses have a long history in cognitive psychology (e.g., Chi, de Leeuw, Chiu, & Lavancher, 1994; Ericsson & Simon, 1993), but, by using techniques adapted from methodologies developed for assessing comprehension (e.g., latent semantic analysis; see Foltz, Kintsch, & Landauer, 1998), Cooke et al. paved the way for online assessment of communication and comprehension processes in team cognition. As such, these forms of systematic and rigorous methods of analyzing the team communications supporting team cognition represent important contributions to the field.

Within the broad theme of team cognition and team communication, Levine and Choi (chap. 8, this volume) illustrated how changes in team membership alter the nature of the discussion to include more strategy-relevant messages. They suggested that teams experiencing turnover as well as those performing more poorly are more likely to try to revise or reiterate what is, or what should be, the shared cognition as they attempt to ensure a mutual understanding of the task. Thus, teams try to alter the nature of their shared cognition when they are *aware* that their performance is suffering or when there may be a disruption to the level of sharedness (i.e., during membership change). Their analyses of team communication protocols illustrated how turnover affects this awareness; they further noted that understanding how the process of team cognition is altered is a critical and open area of research.

Relating communication to team cognition is at the core of the chapter by MacMillan, Entin, and Serfaty (chap. 4, this volume). They described how it is that communication can be altered by task and team structure factors and can affect level of awareness of the team members. What is noteworthy is that they attempted to scaffold team cognition through their structural manipulations such that communication is reduced while level of awareness is either facilitated or not negatively affected. Specifically, MacMillan et al. illustrated how the deleterious consequences of *communication overhead* can be attenuated with manipulations of organizational structure. They additionally highlighted the beneficial effects of mission planning whereby reflective activity prior to interaction facilitates coordination. These findings are analogous to studies of expert problem solving in which research documents that experts in a particular field spend a considerable amount of time representing a problem before attempting to solve it (e.g., Chi, Glaser, & Rees, 1982). Thus, teams given the opportunity to engage in preprocess coordination (see Fiore et al., 2003) illustrate how preparatory behaviors such as planning can facilitate later coordinative efforts. These activities increase mutual organizational awareness and assist by developing shared task representations.

Sycara and Lewis's (chap. 10, this volume) application of theories of team performance to intelligent agents research similarly fits within both of our thematic approaches to team cognition. One could argue that these agents support team member awareness such that team cognition is scaffolded at multiple levels. In these instances cognitive activity formerly managed by varying team roles is offloaded to intelligent agent technology. These agents are programmed to engage in both lower level (e.g., information gathering) and higher level (planning) information-processing activities so as to facilitate team-level awareness that supports coordination within a team. The agents, then, may decrease the communication demands formerly tied to particular team members (because these tasks are now automated). Like

MacMillan et al., then, Sycara and Lewis showed the apparent paradoxical effects of increases in awareness along with decreases in communication.

By identifying what are labeled implicit and explicit coordination mechanisms, Espinosa, Lerch, and Kraut (chap. 6, this volume) showed how a task-analytic approach can illuminate team cognition. Indeed, their work represents an important addition to the long history of psychological research into task factors, process, and performance (e.g., in cognitive psychology, Reitman, 1965; Simon, 1973; Voss & Post, 1988; in social psychology, McGrath, 1984; Steiner, 1972). Like Gutwin and Greenberg, Espinosa et al. took their investigation of how tasks affect group process and performance into the realm of distributed teams and added a new layer of context to this area. Their articulation of the importance of *task dependencies* and related antecedents shows how communication and subsequent coordination can be altered. Further, their distinctions for implicit and explicit coordination mechanisms help to formalize the connections among, for example, team communication, shared mental models, and group outputs and fit within our conceptualization of team cognition as a means of binding member inputs.

Summary

In this section we have discussed how contributors to this volume have used the team cognition construct to help readers understand how communication and awareness result in the coordinated actions of the individuals composing a team. Given our analogy to consciousness, it behooves us to levy the following query of the team cognition construct, a query often levied against the construct of consciousness. Specifically, is team cognition an epiphenomenon, in that it is merely an *additive* process/product associated with multiple members, or is it truly a *synergistic* process/product? Within consciousness studies, this question can be considered more rhetorical as it relates to attempts to theorize about such a complex issue. But, such a question may indeed be more appropriate for team cognition researchers in that considerable resources are brought to bear with the implementation of teams in organizations. That is, the consequences of understanding team cognition have a more immediate societal impact than the consequences of understanding consciousness. More specifically, the field must address the positive (i.e., synergistic) aspects of team cognition as well as the negative (i.e., inhibitory) aspects of team cognition. Organizational and social psychologists have been addressing the negative consequences of group interaction for a number of years (e.g., Hackman, 1998; Hastie, 1986; Janis, 1972; Stroebe & Diehl, 1994), and for the field to mature we must continually ask whether the byproducts of team cognition are always beneficial or whether there are times when they may be inhibitory. As such, from both the laboratory and from the field, we must better specify the functional and dysfunctional aspects of team cognition as we fit the pieces of this puzzle together.

Related to this, the field must better address to what degree team cognition is a process associated with interaction or whether it is a product resulting from interaction. This issue is reminiscent of problems surrounding the construct of situation awareness in military research in which the distinction is sometimes made between situation awareness and situation assessment (e.g., Salas, Cannon-Bowers, Fiore, & Stout, 2001). Situation *assessment* is the term used to describe the processes (e.g., attention, pattern recognition, communication) that are engaged to produce the end product of situation *awareness*. Approaches to this issue can vary whereby some frame their research around training situation assessment processes, whereas others measure outcomes by assessing situation awareness levels (see McNeese, Salas, & Endsley, 2001). Similarly, in team cognition, addressing this distinction depends on the level of analysis chosen by the researcher. Some frame their questions around consideration of a process of team cognition such as implicit strategies for coordination, whereas others consider team cognition to be a product resulting from this interaction (e.g., a shared mental model).

The preceding discussion shows how, metaphorically, team cognition can be like a field-dependence task, where it may be the figure or it may be the ground. What may be required to integrate approaches, then, is a multilevel theoretical approach. In such approaches researchers theorize about multiple levels of analysis (e.g., individuals, groups, and organizations) to better specify how they are conceptualizing construct(s) that can cut across levels (see Klein & Kozlowski, 2000). Theoretical models with a multilevel approach can take on differing forms, for example, a "cross-level model in which higher-level variables are hypothesized to moderate the relationship of two or more lower-level variables . . . [or] models focused . . . on the role of the individuals in shaping the organizational context" (Klein, Cannella, & Tosi, 1999, p. 246). By not taking a multilevel approach, some suggest that one could not only miss relationships but also inaccurately specify the relations they are attempting to address (see discussions in Klein & Kozlowski, 2000). A number of contributors to this volume have presented theories or frameworks that begin to meet some of the criteria for a multilevel theoretical model. The development of such models for team cognition may be an important step forward if they can specifically formulate an integration of cognitive processes and cognitive products within teams so that empirically testable principles can be derived.

TEAM COGNITION DEVELOPMENT

We began this volume by asking and answering the question "Why *team* cognition?" At the conclusion of this volume, we would like to revisit this question and more specifically ask (and answer), "Do we need the construct of *team cognition*?" As one might expect, we believe the answer to this question is yes, and we have discussed the value added by the team cognition construct. To add to this, we note that progress in science typically occurs when disciplines begin to adopt and adapt theoretical and empirically derived principles from tangential disciplines (see Dunbar, 1995, 1997). Further, the bond between disciplines is strengthened by the use of techniques that have consistently documented predictive utility in other domains. Perhaps we can more cogently state that the contribution the construct makes is as an organizing framework rather than an end to itself (see Cannon-Bowers & Salas, 2001). Team research has progressed in important ways because constructs coming out of cognitive psychology have been applied and adapted to aid our understanding of team process and performance. For example, the mental model construct has been used for over 10 years to drive a number of productive research efforts. Indeed its influence is still felt as a number of chapters in this volume rely on the mental model construct to elucidate team process and performance. Nonetheless, the message of this chapter is that the adoption is only useful if these constructs are operationalized such that they provide meaningful methodologies and empirical tests to validate their utility.

As the chapters in this volume document, many efforts are addressing problems with operationalization and measurement, and the theories are becoming more sophisticated, further illustrating the increasing maturity of the field. To use our final metaphor, we can then ask at what stage of *development* is the field of team cognition. Metaphorically, it is probably safe to characterize the final decade of the 20th century as something similar to early and middle childhood for the team cognition construct. We mean not to be disparaging, rather we wish to illustrate that much like in the early years of childhood, we have seen not only rapid growth but also a building of vocabulary (i.e., terminology) and a building of competencies (i.e., methodologies).

As for the current state of the field, it is more akin to adolescence as the vocabulary and competencies are beginning to coalesce and we are more confident in testing ourselves. For example, only in the last few years has the field shifted from being primarily theoretically based to now also being empirically based. Again, this is not meant to be critical commentary, only a characterization of where we are, and how far we need to go. Although the field's level of maturity is still low, it is beginning to express some independence, not only from organizational psychology but also from cognitive psychology. This independence, while still somewhat awkward, does suggest where the field must now go—a real shift from what previously could be characterized as multidisciplinary to what may be truly interdisciplinary. Social and literary critic Roland Barthes noted an important distinction between these ideas: "To do something interdisciplinary it's not enough to choose a 'subject' (a theme) and gather around it two or three sciences. Interdisciplinarity consists in creating a new object that belongs to no one"

(Roland Barthes in *Jeunes Chercheurs*, quoted from Clifford & Marcus, 1986, p. 1). Thus, rather than adapting the vocabulary of other disciplines, for team cognition to reach its next developmental stage, what may be necessary is the creation of a truly independent discipline in which the old disciplines have dissolved for the sake of a new language and a new object (Barthes, 1977).

REFERENCES

Barthes, R. (1977). *Image music text*. London: Harper Collins.

Cannon-Bowers, J. A., & Salas, E. (2001). Reflections on shared cognition. *Journal of Organizational Behavior, 22*, 195–202.

Chi, M. T. H., de Leeuw, N., Chiu, M., & Lavancher, C. (1994). Eliciting self-explanations improves understanding. *Cognitive Science, 18*, 439–477.

Chi, M. T. H., Glaser, R., & Rees, E. (1982). Expertise in problem solving. In R. J. Sternberg (Ed.), *Advances in the psychology of human intelligence* (pp. 7–75). Hillsdale, NJ: Erlbaum.

Clifford, J., & Marcus, G. E. (1986). *Writing culture: The poetics and politics of ethnography*. Berkeley: University of California Press.

Cohen, J. D., & Schooler, J. W. (Eds.). (1997). *Cognitive and neurocognitive approaches to consciousness*. Mahwah, NJ: Erlbaum.

Dunbar, K. (1995). How scientists really reason: Scientific reasoning in real-world laboratories. In R. J. Sternberg & J. E. Davidson (Eds.), *The nature of insight* (pp. 265–396). Cambridge, MA: MIT Press.

Dunbar, K. (1997). Conceptual change in science. In T. B. Ward, S. M. Smith, & J. Vaid (Eds.), *Creative thought: An investigation of conceptual structures and processes* (pp. 461–494). Washington, DC: American Psychological Association.

Entin, E. E., & Serfaty, D. (1999). Adaptive team coordination. *Human Factors, 41*, 312–325.

Ericsson, K. A., & Simon, H. A. (1993). *Protocol analysis: Verbal reports as data*. Cambridge, MA: MIT Press.

Fiore, S. M., Salas, E., & Cannon-Bowers, J. A. (2001). Group dynamics and shared mental model development. In M. London (Ed.), *How people evaluate others in organizations: Person perception and interpersonal judgment in industrial/organizational psychology* (pp. 309–336). Mahwah, NJ: Erlbaum.

Fiore, S. M., Salas, E., Cuevas, H. M., & Bowers, C. A. (2003). Distributed coordination space: Toward a theory of distributed team process and performance. *Theoretical Issues in Ergonomic Science, 4*, 340–363.

Foltz, P. W., Kintsch, W., & Landauer, T. K. (1998). The measurement of textual coherence with latent semantic analysis. *Discourse Processes, 25*, 285–307.

Fussell, S., & Krauss, R. (1989). The effects of intended audience on message production and comprehension: Reference in a common ground framework. *Journal of Experimental Social Psychology, 25*, 203–219.

Glaser, R. (1958). Descriptive variables for the study of task-oriented groups. In R. A. Patton (Ed.), *Current trends in the description and analysis of behavior* (pp. 1–21). Pittsburgh, PA: University of Pittsburgh Press.

Hackman, J. R. (1998). Why teams don't work. In R. S. Tindale (Ed.), *Theory and research on small groups: Vol. 4. Social psychological applications to social issues* (pp. 245–267). New York: Plenum.

Hastie, R. (1986). Review essay: Experimental evidence on group accuracy. In G. Owen & B. Grofman (Eds.), *Information pooling and group decision making* (pp. 129–157). Westport, CT: JAI.

Hinsz, V. B., Tindale, R. S., & Vollrath, D. A. (1997). The emerging conceptualization of groups as information processors. *Psychological Bulletin, 121,* 43–64.

Janis, I. L. (1972). *Victims of groupthink: A psychological study of foreign-policy decisions and fiascoes.* Boston: Houghton Mifflin.

Klein, K. J., Cannella, A., & Tosi, H. (1999). Multilevel theory: Challenges and contributions. *Academy of Management Review, 24,* 243–248.

Klein, K. J., & Kozlowski, S. W. J., (Eds.). (2000). *Multilevel theory, research, and methods in organizations: Foundations, extensions, and new directions.* Society for Industrial and Organizational Psychology Frontiers Series. San Francisco: Jossey-Bass.

Larson, J. R., & Christensen, C. (1993). Groups as problem-solving units: Toward a new meaning of social cognition. *British Journal of Social Psychology, 32,* 5–30.

Liang, D. W., Moreland, R. L., & Argote, L. (1995). Group versus individual training and group performance: The mediating role of transactive memory. *Personality and Social Psychology Bulletin, 21,* 384–393.

McGrath, J. E. (1984). *Groups: Interaction and performance.* Englewood Cliffs, NJ: Prentice-Hall.

McNeese, M., Salas, E., & Endsley, M. (Eds.). (2001). *New trends in collaborative activities: Understanding system dynamics in complex environments.* Santa Monica, CA: Human Factors and Ergonomics Society.

Moreland, R. L., & Argote, L. (2003). Transactive memory in dynamic organizations. In R. Peterson & E. Mannix (Eds.), *Understanding the dynamic organization* (pp. 135–162). Mahwah, NJ: Erlbaum.

Moreland, R. L., & Myaskovsky, L. (2000). Explaining the performance benefits of group training: Transactive memory or improved communication? *Organizational Behavior and Human Decision Processes, 82,* 117–133.

Newell, A., & Simon, H. A. (1972). *Human problem solving.* Englewood Cliffs, NJ: Prentice Hall.

Reitman, W. (1965). *Cognition and thought: An information processing approach.* New York: Wiley.

Salas, E., Cannon-Bowers, J. A., Fiore, S. M., & Stout, R. J. (2001). Cue-recognition training to enhance team situation awareness. In M. McNeese, E. Salas, & M. Endsley, (Eds.), *New trends in collaborative activities: Understanding system dynamics in complex environments* (pp. 169–190). Santa Monica, CA: Human Factors and Ergonomics Society.

Schooler, J. W., Fallshore, M., & Fiore, S. M. (1995). Putting insight into perspective. In R. J. Sternberg & J. E. Davidson (Eds.), *The nature of insight* (pp. 559–587). Cambridge, MA: MIT Press.

Schooler, J. W., & Fiore, S. M. (1997). Consciousness and the limits of language: You can't always say what you think or think what you say. In J. D. Cohen & J. W. Schooler (Eds.), *Cognitive and neurocognitive approaches to consciousness* (pp. 241–257). Mahwah, NJ: Erlbaum.

Schooler, J. W., Fiore, S. M., & Brandimonte, M. A. (1997). At a loss *from* words: Verbal overshadowing of perceptual memories. In D. Medin (Ed.), *The psychology of learning and motivation* (Vol. 37, pp. 291–340). New York: Academic Press.

Simon, H. A. (1997). Scientific approaches to the question of consciousness. In J. D. Cohen & J. W. Schooler (Eds.), *Cognitive and neurocognitive approaches to consciousness* (pp. 513–520). Mahwah, NJ: Erlbaum.

Simon, H. A. (1973). The structure of ill-structured problems. *Artificial Intelligence, 4,* 181–201.

Smythies, J. (1999). Consciousness: Some basic issues—A neurophilosophical perspective. *Consciousness and Cognition, 8,* 164–172.

Steiner, I. D. (1972). *Group processes and productivity.* New York: Academic Press.

Stroebe, W., & Diehl, M. (1994). Why groups are less effective than their members: On productivity losses in idea-generating groups. In W. Stroebe & M. Hewstone (Eds.), *European Review of Social Psychology, 5,* 271–303.

Thordsen, M. L., & Klein, G. A. (1989). Cognitive processes of the team mind *IEEE International Conference on Systems, Man, and Cybernetics Proceedings, 1,* 46–49.

Treisman, A. (1996). The binding problem. *Current Opinion in Neurobiology, 6,* 171–178.

von der Malsburg, C. (1995). Binding in models of perception and brain function. *Current Opinion in Neurobiology, 5,* 520–526.

Voss, J. F., & Post, T. A. (1988). On the solving of ill-structured problems. In M. Chi, R. Glaser, & M. Farr (Eds.), *The nature of expertise* (pp. 261–285). Hillsdale, NJ: Erlbaum.

Weick, K. E., & Roberts, K. H. (1993). Collective mind in organizations: Heedful interrelating on flight decks. *Administrative Science Quarterly, 38,* 357–381.

AUTHOR INDEX

Numbers in italics refer to listings in the references.

249

Carley, K. M., 108, 112, 114, 122, 125, *126*, *129*, 143, *148*, 156, *171*

Castellan, Jr., N. J., 8, *28*, *55*, *79*, *103*, *126*, *147*, *198*

Chaiken, S., 40, *55*

Chase, W. G., 85, *104*

Chemers, M. M., 146, *148*

Chen, L., 210, *229*

Chi, M. T. H., 85, *104*, *105*, 135, *148*, 241, 242, *246*, *248*

Chiu, M., 241, *246*

Choi, H. S., 42, 56, 156, *173*

Christensen, C., 4, 8, 34, 56, 136, 138, 144, *149*, 235, *247*

Christie, B., 183, *200*

Clark, H. H., 87, *104*, *106*, 177, 181, 183, 185, 186, 196, *198*

Clark, N. K., 36, 50, 55, *58*

Clifford, J., 246, *246*

Cockburn, A., 192, *199*

Code, S., 56, 89, *106*

Cohen, J. D., 238, 239, *246*, *248*

Cohen, P. R., 208, *229*

Cohen, S. G., 33, *55*

Collins, A., 185, *200*

Combs, V., *229*

Converse, S. A., 4, 8, 11, *28*, 42, 52, *55*, 57, 63, *79*, 87, 88, *103*, *106*, 112, *126*, 134, 135, *147*, *151*, 154, *175*, *179*, *198*

Cooke, N. J., 64, 80, 85, 87, 89, 90, 94, 95–96, 96, 97, 98, 99, 100, 101, 102, *104*, *105*, 124, 125, *126*

Cooke, N. M., *106*

Cooper, C. L., *29*

Cooper, J. T., *58*

Cosier, R. A., 19, *29*

Cowan, D. A., 136, *148*

Cramton, C. D., 113, *126*

Crandall, B., 136, *149*

Cronbach, L. J., 20, *29*

Cross, K. F., 146, *151*

Crowston, K., 109, 110, 111, 113, 116, 122, *126*, *127*, *128*

Crutchfield, J., *104*

Cuevas, H. M., 205, *229*, 239, *246*

Cummings, L. L., *171*

Cunningham, R. J., *199*

Curtis, B., 118, *126*

Davidson, J. E., 35, *55*, *151*, *246*, *248*

Davis, J. H., 36, 38, *54*, *55*, *58*, 89, 93, *104*, *150*, *174*

Decker, K., 203, 205, 206, *229*, *230*

Deckert, J. C., 64, *79*

De Dreu, K. W., *28*

Deighton, J., *31*

Delbecq, L. A., 110, *128*

de Leeuw, N., 241, *246*

DeMaio, J. C., *106*

de Meuse, K. P., 134, *151*

DeSanctis, G., 122, *126*

Deuser, R., 35, *55*

Devadas, R., 156, 159, *171*

Diamond, W. D., *172*

Dickinson, T. L., 52, *57*, 88, *106*, 135, *151*, 154, *175*

Diehl, M., 243, *248*

Dix, A., 184, *199*

Dourish, P., 178, 184–185, *199*

Drenan, S., *172*

Driskell, J. E., 160, *174*

Duffy, L. T., 145, *151*

Duguid, P., 185, *200*

Dumais, S. T., *104*

Dumville, B. C., 13, *30*, 124, *128*, 138, 145, *150*, 158, *174*

Dunbar, K., 136, 145, *149*, 245, *246*

Duncomb, J., *229*

Dunnette, M. D., 29, *105*

Durso, F. T., 89, 94, *104*, *106*

Dwyer, D. J., 64, *79*

Dykema-Engblade, A. A., 158, *175*

Dyson, R., *229*

Dzindolet, M. T., 146, *150*

Eagly, A. H., 40, *55*

Edens, E., 154, *175*, 203, *230*

Edwards, J., *172*, *174*, *175*

Egido, C., *127*, *200*

Elliott, L., 69, *81*, 144, *150*

Ellis, A., 80, *81*

Ellis, C., 178, *199*

Endsley, 65, *79*

Endsley, M. R., 35, 42, *55*, 80, 89, 94, *104*, *105*, 113, *126*, 181, *199*, *200*, 203, *230*, 244, *247*

Entin, E., 142, 144, *150*, *151*, 203

Entin, E. B., 64, *79*

Entin, E. E., 63, 64, 67, 69, *79*, 80, *81*, 112, *126*, 144, *148*, 208, *229*, 239, *246*

Epple, D., 156, *171*

Erber, R., 36, *58*

Ericsson, K. A., 241, *246*

Espinosa, J. A., 108, 114, 117, 121, 122, 125, 126

Everitt, B. S., 93, *105*

Fahlen, L., 188, *198*

Fallshore, M., 136, *151*, 237, *248*

Fan, E. T., 155, *172*

Faraj, S., 113, 122, *127*

Farr, M. J., *105*, *248*

Fay, A. L., 136, *149*

Fiedler, F. E., 146, *148*

Filkins, J., 42, *58*

Finholt, T., 123, *127*

Finlay, J., 184, *199*

Fiore, S. M., 19, *29*, 63, 80, 136, 138, *148*, *151*, 158, 159, 162, *171*, 205, 208, 229, 237, 239, 240, 244, *246*, *247*, *248*

Fischer, U., 63, *81*

Fishbein, M., 41, *55*, *56*

Fisher, C., 64, *81*

Fiske, S. T., 40, *55*, *56*, *173*

Flach, J., 58, *200*

Flanagan, D. L., 133, *147*

Flavell, J. H., 36, *55*

Fleishman, E. A., 135, *148*

Fleiss, J. L., 43, *58*

Fletcher, J. D., 8

Foltz, P. W., 64, 80, 95–96, 96, *105*, *106*, 241, *246*

Ford, J. K., 20, *29*

Foster, G., 185, *201*

Foushee, H. C., 80, 208, *229*

Fowlkes, J. E., 64, 79, 80

Fracker, M. L., 89, *105*

Franz, T., 64, 80

Fraser, M., 189, *199*

Freeman, J., 80

Fuller, R., *150*

Fussell, S. R., 108, 113, *126*, *127*, 162, *173*, 240, *246*

Futrell, D., 134, *151*

Gaafar, L. K., 141, *147*

Galegher, J., *127*, *200*

Garland, D. J., *106*

Gaver, W., 184, 185, 191, *199*

Gentner, D., 34, 40, *55*, *57*

George, J. M., 19, *29*

Gersick, C. J., 141, 146, *148*, 169, *171*

Giampapa, J., 205, 228, *229*, *230*

Gibbs, S., 178, *199*

Gibson, C. R., 159, *172*

Gigone, D., 141, *148*

Gilbert, D. T., 56, *173*

Gilmore, R., *172*,

Gilson, R. D., *106*, 181, *199*

Glaser, R., 85, *105*, 135, 138, *148*, 156, *172*, 236, 242, *246*, *247*, *248*

Gleser, G. C., 20, *29*

Goethals, G. R., 58, *106*

Goldsmith, T. E., *106*

Gomez, L. M., 185, *198*

Goodchilds, J. D., 155, *176*

Goodman, P. S., 155, *172*

Goodwin, G. F., 11, *30*, 42, 56, 113, *128*, 134, *150*, 158, *174*

Gorman, J., 96, *105*

Greenberg, S., 179, 182, 186, 188, 192, 194, 195, 197, *199*, *200*

Greenhalgh, C., 188, *198*

Gregg, L., *151*

Gregory, W. J., 146, *148*

Grinter, R. E., 117, 122, 123, *127*

Gronlund, S. D., 89, *104*

Grosz, B., 205, 208, *229*

Gruenfeld, D. H., 155, 170, *172*

Gurtner, A., 163n, *175*

Gutwin, C., 179, 182, 188, 190, 192, 194, 195, 197, *199*

Guzzo, R. A., 33, *55*, *57*, 84, *104*, *105*, 133, *148*, 154, *171*, *172*

Hackman, J. R., 4, 8, 19, *29*, 133, 135, 141, 142, 146, *148*, 153, 154, 169, *171*, *172*, 243, *247*

Hackman, R. A., 84, *105*

Hackworth, C. A., *104*

Hains, S. C., 33, *57*

Hall, R. J., 11, 12, 14, 15n, *30*, 42, 51, *57*

Hallmark, B. W., 155, *172*

Hancock, P., 58, *200*

Harris, D., 80, *105*

Harris, T. C., 54, *55*

Hart, 68

Hastie, R., 141, *148*, 243, *247*

Heath, C., 183, 185, 189, *199*, *200*

Heath, L., *152*, *172*, *174*, *175*

Hedlund, J., *172*

Heffner, T. S., 11, *30*, 42, 56, 113, *128*, 134, 145, *150*, *151*, 158, *174*

Helm, E., 97, 98, 99, 100, 101, *104*

Helmreich, R. L., *57*, *81*

Henderson, C. M., *31*

SUBJECT INDEX

Accuracy
of metacognition, 36–38
of metamemory (study on), 45–47, 49–50
schema, 13, 15, 24, 27–28
target, 22–23, 26
taskwork knowledge, 99
of team member schema, 25
See also Meta-accuracy
Acquisition curve, 91
Action indicators, 191
Adaptive Architecture for Command and Control (A2C2) program, 65, 66
Aegis command and control tasks, TANDEM simulation of, 214–215
Agent technology, 7, 203. *See also* Intelligent agents
Aggregation
of team data, 92–94
methods, need for improving, 89
Airlift mission, in experiment, 62, 69–76, 77
Air surveillance task, in experimental study of membership change, 159–169
Air Warfare Team Observation (ATOM) model, 206–207, 227
Analogies, 236, 237, 241
to consciousness, 239, 243
Animations, 191
Anticipation ratio, communication, 64
in experiment, 68, 75, 76–77
Anticipatory/proactive information delivery, 211
Artifacts, in workspace awareness, 184
Artificial intelligence, 7, 203. *See also* Intelligent agents
Assimilation, 20–21
Assumed reciprocity, 22, 24
Assumed similarity, 22, 24
Asynchronous and geographically dispersed environments, 108, 113, 115, 122–123. *See also* Real-time distributed systems
ATOM (Air Warfare Team Observation) model, 206–207, 227
Automated measures, 97
need for, 90–91

Automated text processing technology, 64
latent semantic analysis (LSA), 64, 96–97, 241
Avatars, 188–189
Awareness, 177, 181
as basic theme, 239
and consciousness 239
and mental model, 240
and phenomenology of consciousness, 238
team cognition as, 240
See also Workspace awareness

Barthes, Roland, 245
Belief assessment, 41
Belief association matrix, 6, 41, 51
and sharedness of metamemory, 52
in study, 43, 46
Binding problem, 237–238
Bodies, in workspace awareness, 183–184

CAMPS (military asset deployment agent), 210, 213
Card sorting, 13
Carnegie Mellon University's Management Game course, 108, 111
Changing environments, and shared mental models, 42
ClearBoard System, 189
Clustering Hypothesized Underlying Models in Sequence (CHUMS), 96
Cognition
distributed, 87
emergent, 143
as interpersonal, 158
as puzzle, 238–239
shared, 137–138, 157–158, 235–236
and communication, 158–159, 160, 166–168
increased attention to, 34
measurement of, 124
and membership change, 160, 166–168, 170
See also Metacognition; Team cognition
Cognition in teams. *See* Team cognition
Cognitive congruence, 14

Holistic knowledge, 86, 87–88, 241
  measurement of, 6, 85–87, 87–88, 91–92
Homogeneous measurement, 88–89

Information
  common vs. unique, 143
  and intelligent agents, 219–220
  perceptual (workspace awareness), 197
  in workspace awareness, 182–183
    gathering of, 183–184
  See also Knowledge
Information processing
  groups as units for, 138
  inter- and intraindividual outcomes in, 4
  metacognitive perspective for, 34
Information sharing, 143
Infosphere, 219–220, 228
Intelligent agents, 7, 203–204, 226–228, 242
  functions of, 204–205
  information amenable to, 219–220
  and models of teamwork, 206–209
  in MokSAF teamwork experiment, 220–226
  NEO demonstration of, 209–213
  RETSINA, 205–206, 207, 209–210, 211, 212, 213–214
  in TANDEM target identification experiment, 214–219, 227
Interdisciplinarity, 245–246
Interpersonal perception approach, to team member schema similarity, 16–17
  and components of interpersonal schemas, 17–19
  and person perception, 20–23
  and social relations model, 19–20
Interpersonal schemas, components of, 17–19
Interpositional knowledge, 139

Joint Battlespace Infosphere, 227
Joint intentions theory, 208
Joint Task Force Command Team, in experiment, 62, 66–69, 76
  and airlift team, 71

Knowledge
  dynamic fleeting vs. long-term static, 89
  holistic, 86, 87–88, 241
    measurement of, 6, 85–87, 87–88, 91–92

interpositional, 139
need for broader focus on different types of, 90
as process or product, 4
shared, 89
strategic, procedural and declarative, 90
taskwork vs. teamwork, 90, 94 (*see also* Taskwork knowledge; Teamwork knowledge)
team, 85
  and coordination, 124
  measuring broader varieties of, 94–95
See also Information
Knowledge elicitation methods, need for broader application of, 90

Latent semantic analysis (LSA), 64, 96–97, 102, 241
Leader emerges strategy, 94

Majority rules strategy, 94
Measurement
  See Communication Measurement
  heterogeneous vs. homogeneous, 88–89
  holistic vs. collective, 6, 85–87, 87–88, 91-92
  of shared cognition, 124
  of team cognition, 84
    aspects of and issues in, 87–91
    experimental findings on, 98–102
    and holistic metrics, 85–87, 87–88
    new approaches to, 91–97
    validation of, 97–98
  and theories, 62
Membership change in teams, 7, 154–157, 170, 242
  and exiting of members, 170
  experimental study of, 159–169
  and newcomers, 170
  and preprocess coordination, 169
Memory
  group recognition, 38–39
  in groups, 37–38
  transactive, 87, 113, 123
  See also Metamemory
Mental model(s), 34, 40, 240
  accuracy vs. sharedness of, 145
  construct, 138, 245
  of groups, 40
  and preplanning, 75
  shared, 42–43, 63, 138–139, 179, 244

communication efficiency from, 65, 75

and coordination, 119–120

focus on, 90

literature on, 134

and perspectives on task, 99

pitfalls in, 52

and process mapping, 134, 140, 141–144

and shared cognition, 157–158

from strategy discussions stimulated by newcomer entry, 169

in studies, 47–49, 51–52, 54, 77

and task coordination, 114

of task vs. of team, 122–123

and team performance, 137–140

utility of, 140

in study, 50–51

Mental (mental model) representations

and metacognition in groups, 39–41

in study, 52–53

of metamemory in groups, 39–41

Meta-accuracy, 23, 25–26

Metacognition, 34, 239

accuracy of, 36–38

in groups, 34–36, 39–41, 53–54

study on, 43–54

and metamemory, 36

and phenomenology of consciousness, 238

Metamemory, 6, 34, 35, 36, 49

accuracy of (study), 45–47, 49–50

assessment of, 36–37

in groups

and belief association matrix, 41, 50

and group recognition memory performance, 38–39

mental model representation of, 39–41

study on, 43–54

and metacognition, 36

sharedness of, 42–43

in study, 48–49

Metaperception, 20

Metaphors, 236, 238

Middle agents, 206

Mission planning, with electronic collaborative tools, 72, 74, 75

Mobile Communications Among Heterogeneous Agents (Mocha), 227

Modular Semi-Automated Forces (ModSAF) simulation environment, 209, 220

MokSAF simulation, 220–226

Motivational communication, in membership-change experiment, 166–169

Multidimensional scaling analysis, 13

Multilevel theoretical approach, 244

Mutual organizational awareness, 64–65, 79

in experiment, 68, 76–77, 78

Naval Postgraduate School, Monterey, 67

Network analysis, 13

Network-Based Air Traffic Control (Net ATC), 160–162

Newcomers, 170

Noncombatant Evacuation Operations (NEO), 209, 209–213

Office of Naval Research, 65

Openness behaviors, 18–19

Operationalization of constructs, 238, 239, 245

Organizational factors, as input variables, 122

Organizational structures, divisional and functional, 70–72, 73–74, 75, 76

Over-the-shoulder views, for workspace awareness, 193

Overview, as awareness interface, 194–196

Pathfinder

analysis, 13

network scaling, 95

network scaling algorithm, 99

Perceiver accuracy, 23

Perception

of characteristics related to teamwork, 18

of other team members' schemas, 16

See also Person perception

Perceptual information, in workspace awareness, 197

Personnel turnover. See Membership change in teams

Person perception, 6

components in, 20–23, 24

and schemas, 19

and social relations model, 24, 27

Perspective on task

and high performance, 100, 103

and shared mental models, 99

Planning medium, in coordination experiment, 72, 74, 75

Plan recognition, 208

ABOUT THE EDITORS

Eduardo Salas, PhD, is trustee chair and professor of psychology at the University of Central Florida, where he is also program director for the Human Systems Integration Research Department at the Institute for Simulation and Training and director of the Applied Experimental and Human Factors PhD Program. Previously, he was a senior research psychologist and head of the Training Technology Development Branch of the Naval Air Warfare Center Training Systems Division for 15 years. During this period, Dr. Salas served as a principal investigator for numerous research and development programs focusing on teamwork, team training, decision making under stress, and performance assessment. Dr. Salas has coauthored over 200 journal articles and book chapters and has coedited 11 books. He has been on the editorial boards of the *Journal of Applied Psychology*, *Personnel Psychology*, *Military Psychology*, the *Interamerican Journal of Psychology*, *Applied Psychology: An International Journal*, *International Journal of Aviation Psychology*, *Group Dynamics*, and the *Journal of Organizational Behavior*. He is the current editor of *Human Factors*. Dr. Salas is a fellow of the American Psychological Association (Division 14, Society for Industrial and Organizational Psychology; Division 21, Applied Experimental and Engineering Psychology). In 1984, he received his PhD in industrial and organizational psychology from Old Dominion University.

Stephen M. Fiore, PhD, is director of the Consortium for Research in Adaptive Distributed Learning Environments at the University of Central Florida, Institute for Simulation and Training and Team Performance Laboratory. In 2000, he earned his PhD in cognitive psychology from the University of Pittsburgh, Learning Research and Development Center. He maintains a multidisciplinary research interest that incorporates aspects of cognitive, social, and organizational psychology in the investigation of learning and performance in individuals and groups. Dr. Fiore has published in the areas of learning, memory, and problem solving at the individual and the group level. He has also served as an ad hoc reviewer for scientific journals such as *Applied Cognitive Psychology*, *Human Factors*, the *International Journal of Human Computer Studies*, *Group Processes and Intergroup Relations*, and the *Journal of Organizational Behavior*. As principal investigator or coprincipal investigator, he has been involved in a number of research efforts federally funded by the National Science Foundation; the Office of Naval Research; the Air Force Office of Scientific Research; the Transportation Security Administration; and the United States Army Simulation, Training, and Instrumentation Command.